GRANBLUE FANTASY
グランブルーファンタジー

volume.

03

Original story: Cygames   Art: cocho   Layouts: Makoto Fugetsu volume. 03

CONTENTS

GRANBLUE FANTASY

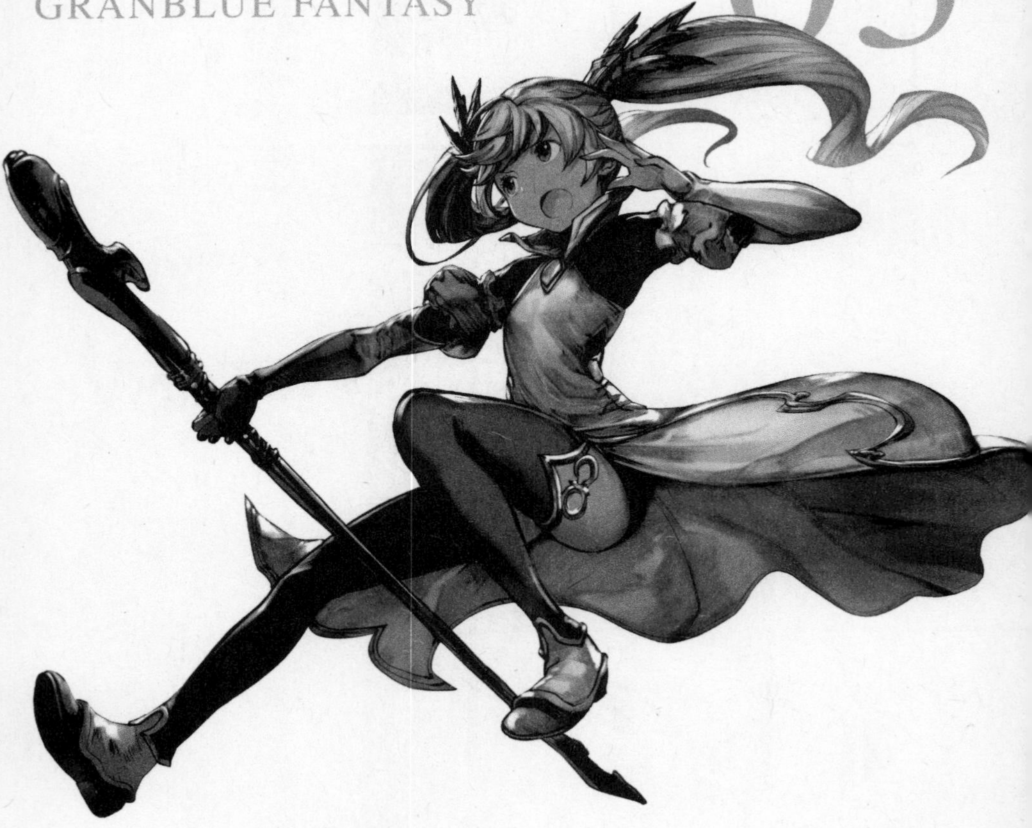

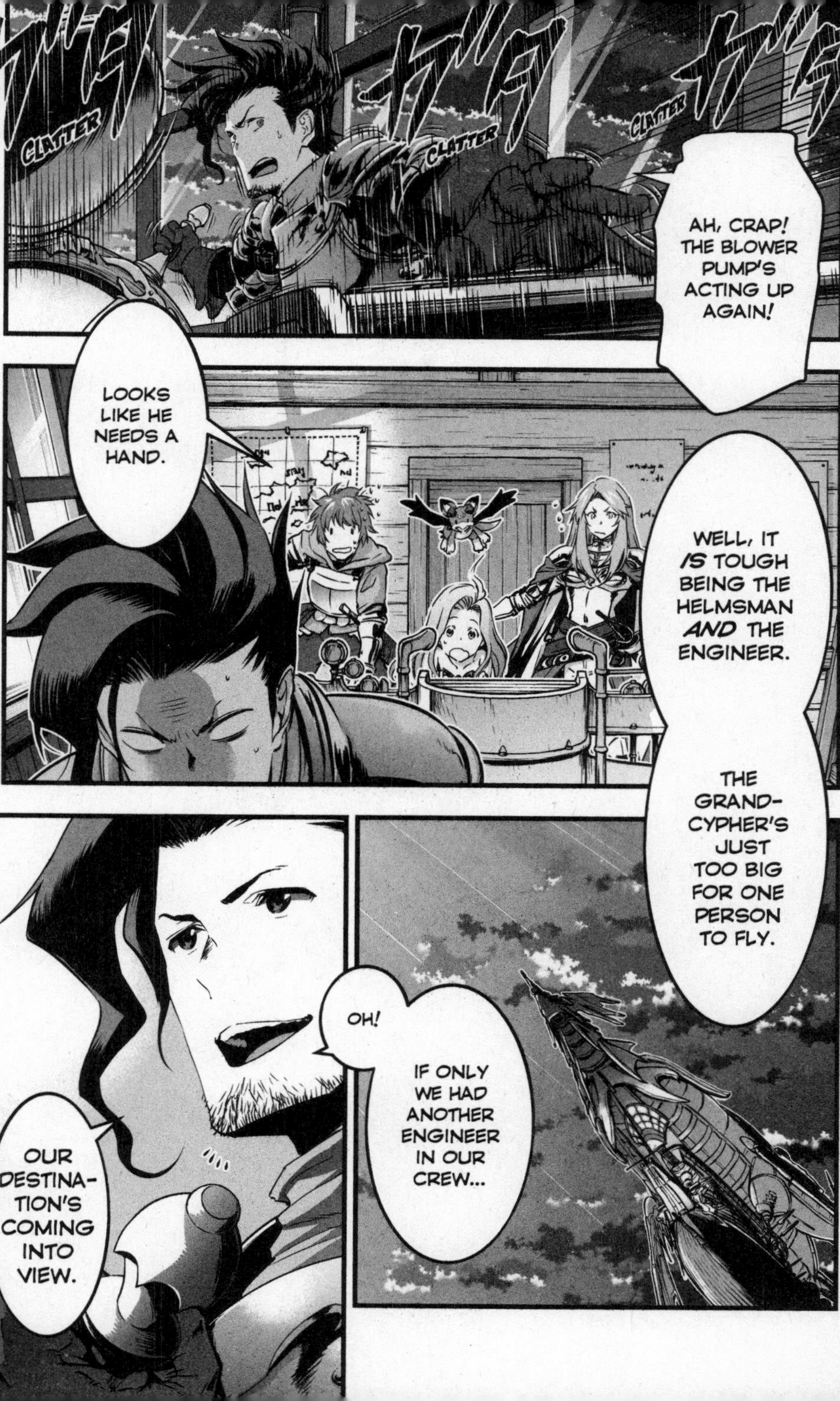
CLATTER
CLATTER
CLATTER
AH, CRAP! THE BLOWER PUMP'S ACTING UP AGAIN!
LOOKS LIKE HE NEEDS A HAND.
WELL, IT *IS* TOUGH BEING THE HELMSMAN *AND* THE ENGINEER.
THE GRAND-CYPHER'S JUST TOO BIG FOR ONE PERSON TO FLY.
IF ONLY WE HAD ANOTHER ENGINEER IN OUR CREW...
OH!
OUR DESTINA-TION'S COMING INTO VIEW.

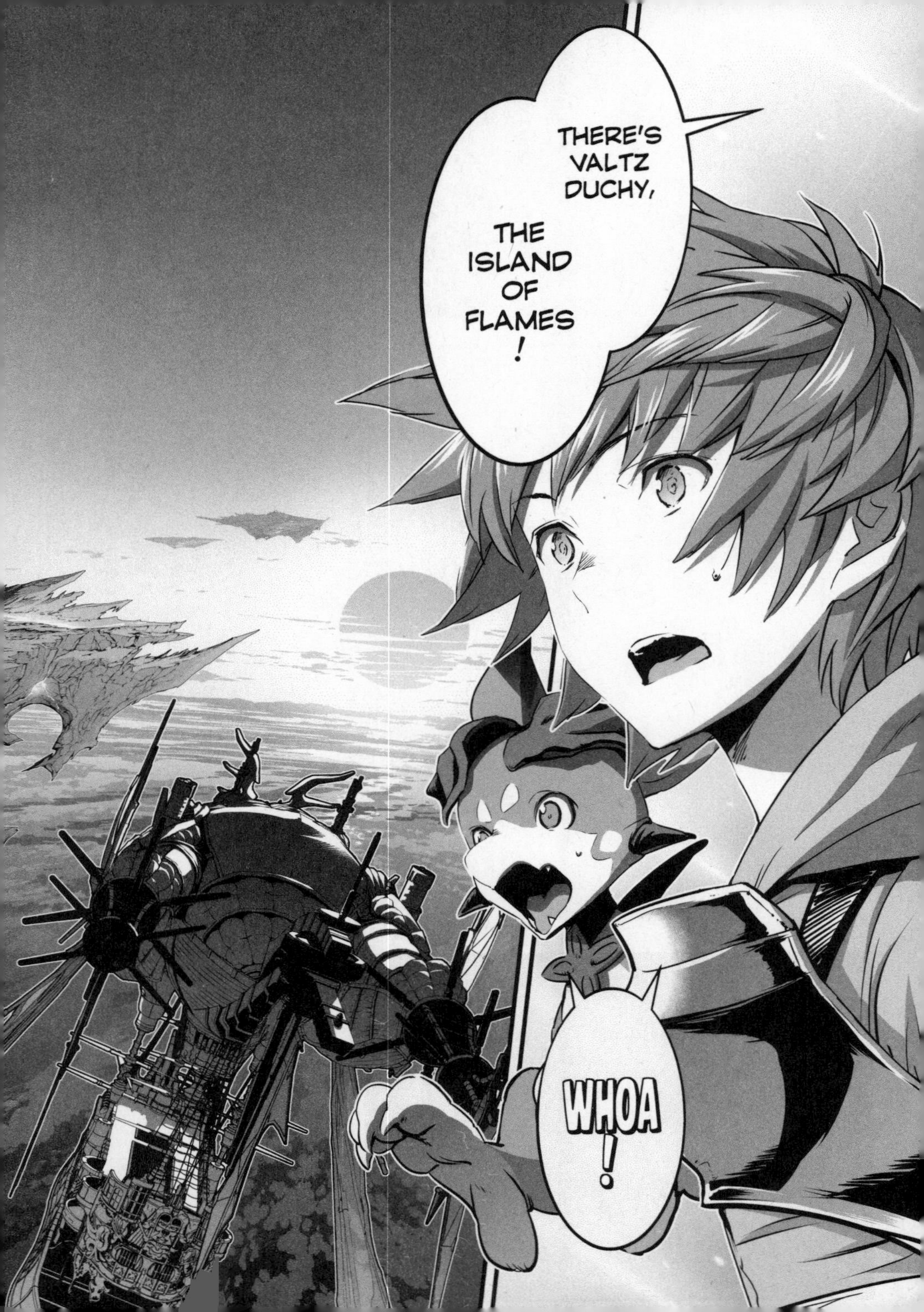
THERE'S VALTZ DUCHY,
THE ISLAND OF FLAMES!
WHOA!

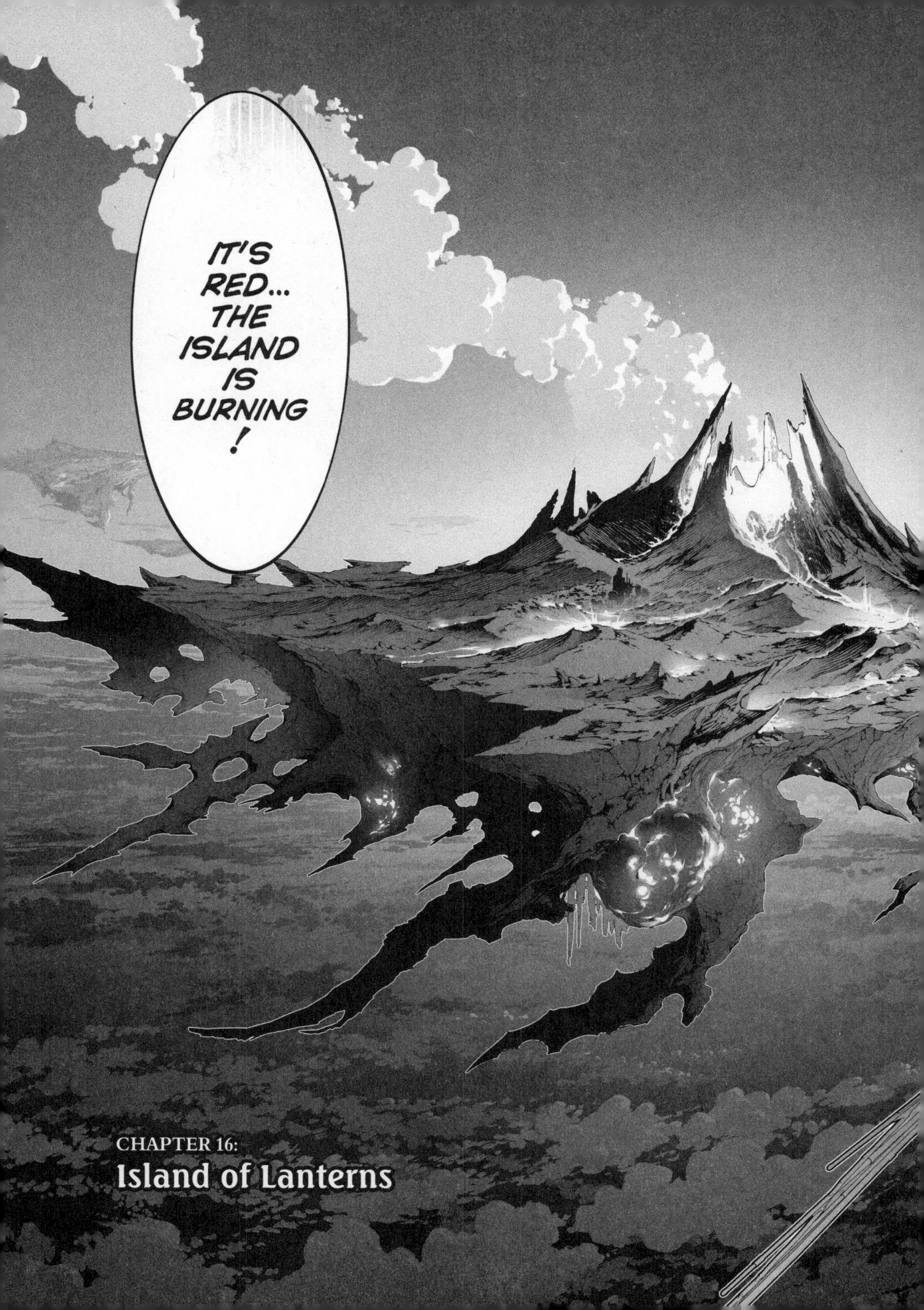
IT'S RED... THE ISLAND IS BURNING!

CHAPTER 16:

Island of Lanterns

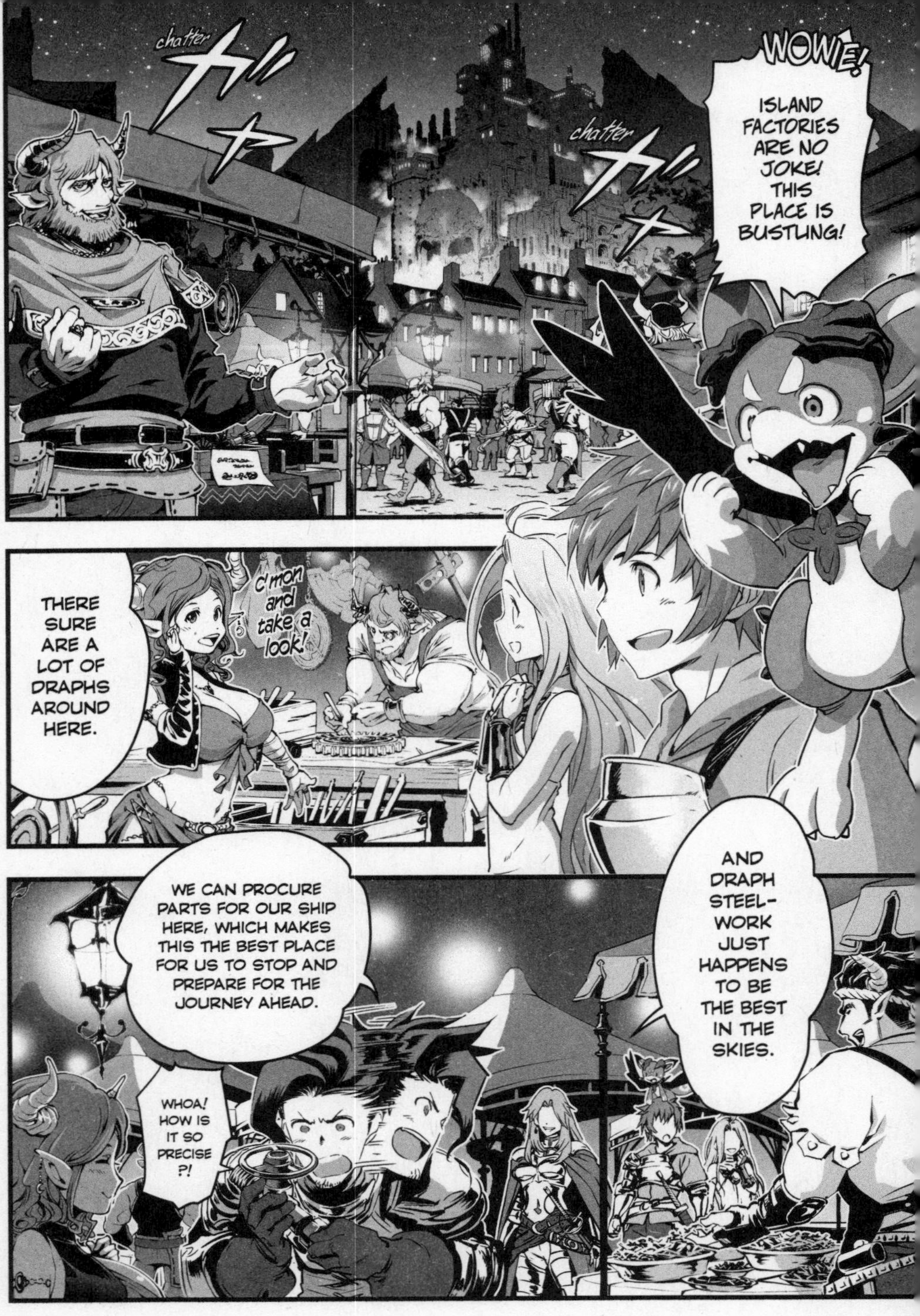
WOWIE!
ISLAND FACTORIES ARE NO JOKE! THIS PLACE IS BUSTLING!
chatter
chatter
c'mon and take a look!
THERE SURE ARE A LOT OF DRAPHS AROUND HERE.
AND DRAPH STEEL-WORK JUST HAPPENS TO BE THE BEST IN THE SKIES.
WE CAN PROCURE PARTS FOR OUR SHIP HERE, WHICH MAKES THIS THE BEST PLACE FOR US TO STOP AND PREPARE FOR THE JOURNEY AHEAD.
WHOA! HOW IS IT SO PRECISE ?!

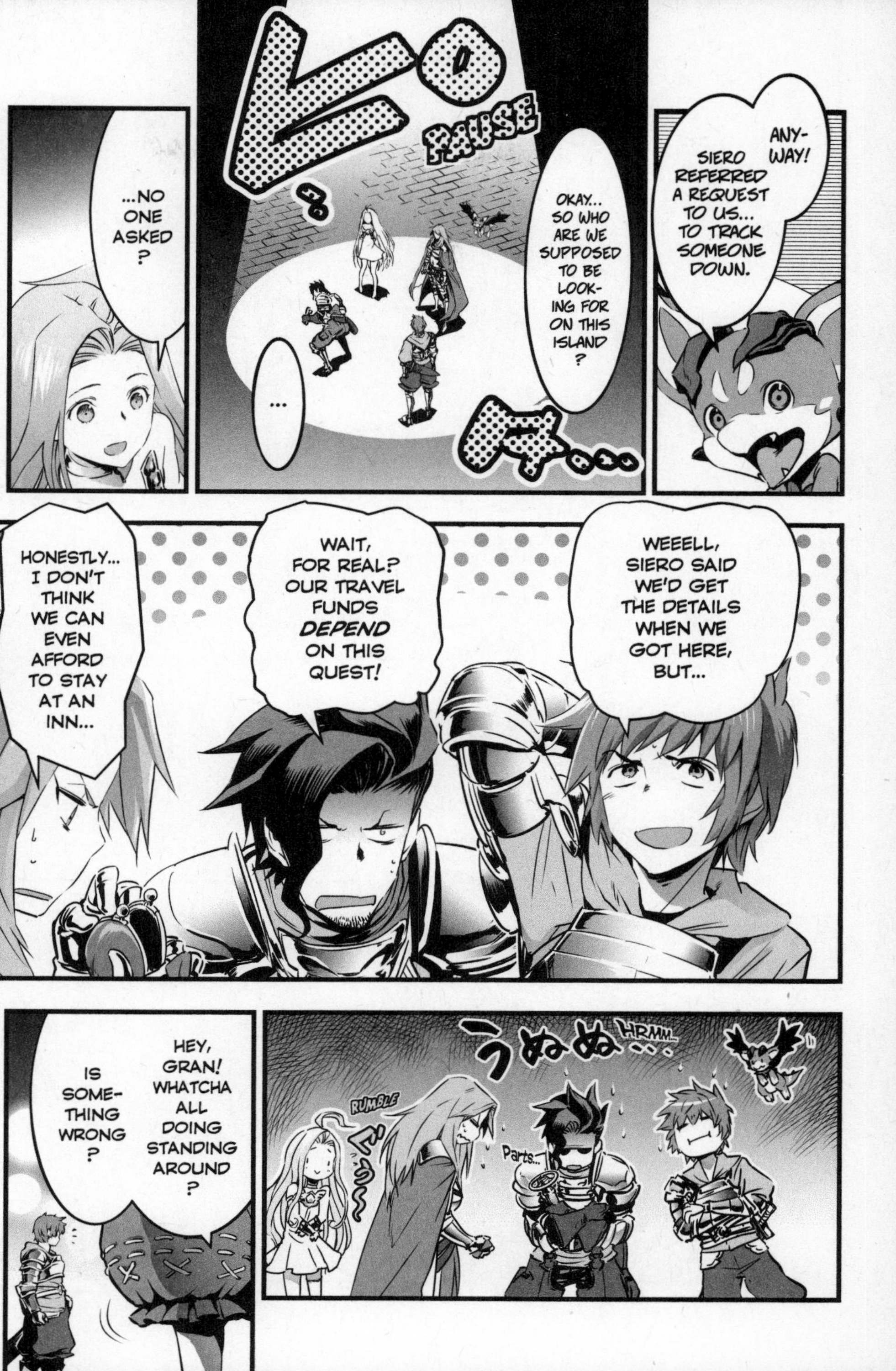
ANY-WAY!
SIERO REFERRED A REQUEST TO US... TO TRACK SOMEONE DOWN.
PAUSE
OKAY... SO WHO ARE WE SUPPOSED TO BE LOOKING FOR ON THIS ISLAND?
...
...NO ONE ASKED?
WEEELL, SIERO SAID WE'D GET THE DETAILS WHEN WE GOT HERE, BUT...
WAIT, FOR REAL? OUR TRAVEL FUNDS DEPEND ON THIS QUEST!
HONESTLY... I DON'T THINK WE CAN EVEN AFFORD TO STAY AT AN INN...
うぬぬ
HRMM...
RUMBLE
Parts...
HEY, GRAN! WHATCHA ALL DOING STANDING AROUND?
IS SOME-THING WRONG?

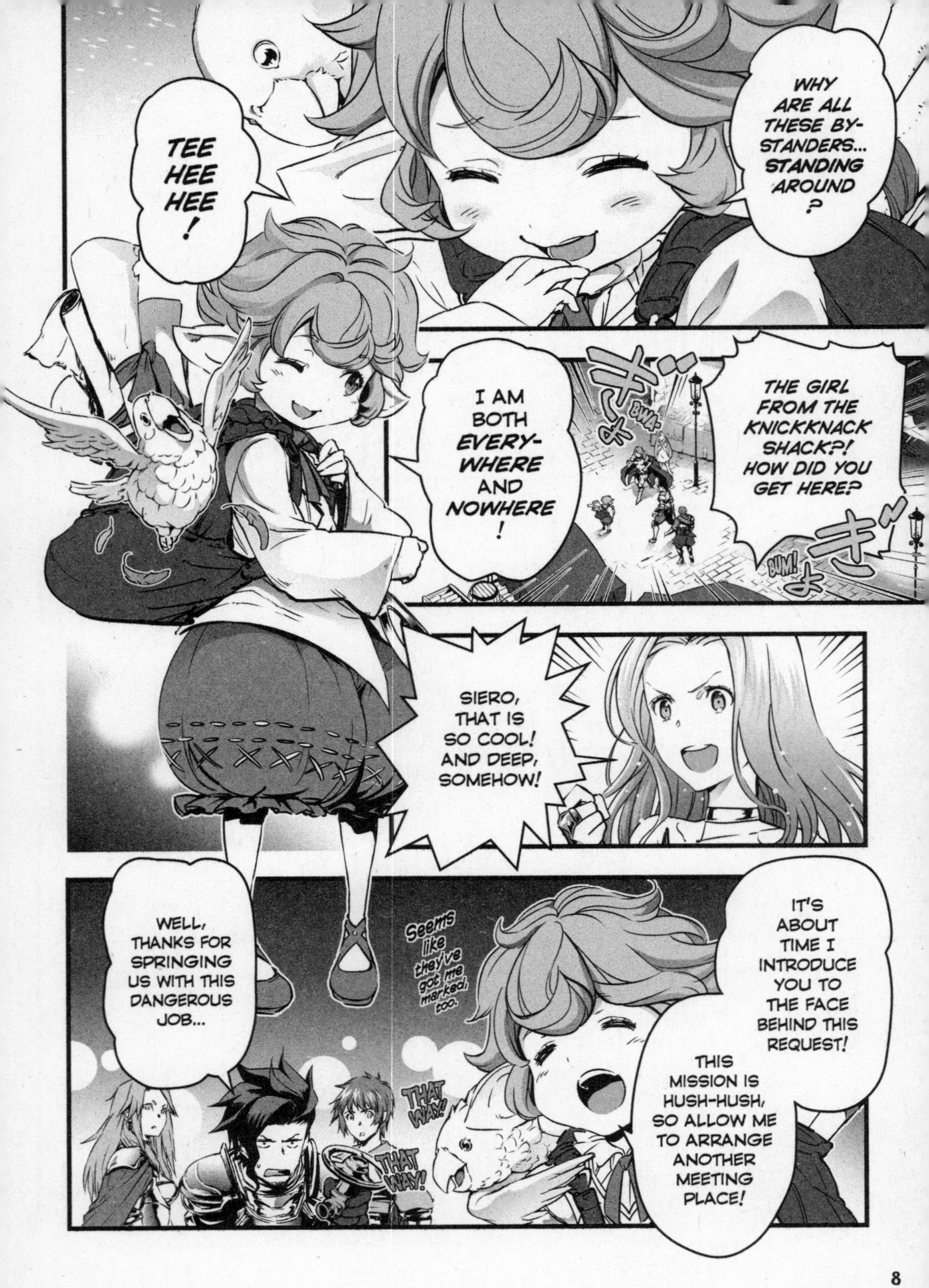
WHY ARE ALL THESE BY-STANDERS... STANDING AROUND?
TEE HEE HEE!
THE GIRL FROM THE KNICKKNACK SHACK?! HOW DID YOU GET HERE?
BWA
BUM!
I AM BOTH *EVERYWHERE* AND *NOWHERE*!
SIERO, THAT IS SO COOL! AND DEEP, SOMEHOW!
IT'S ABOUT TIME I INTRODUCE YOU TO THE FACE BEHIND THIS REQUEST!
THIS MISSION IS HUSH-HUSH, SO ALLOW ME TO ARRANGE ANOTHER MEETING PLACE!
THAT WAY!
THAT WAY!
Seems like they've got me marked, too.
WELL, THANKS FOR SPRINGING US WITH THIS DANGEROUS JOB...

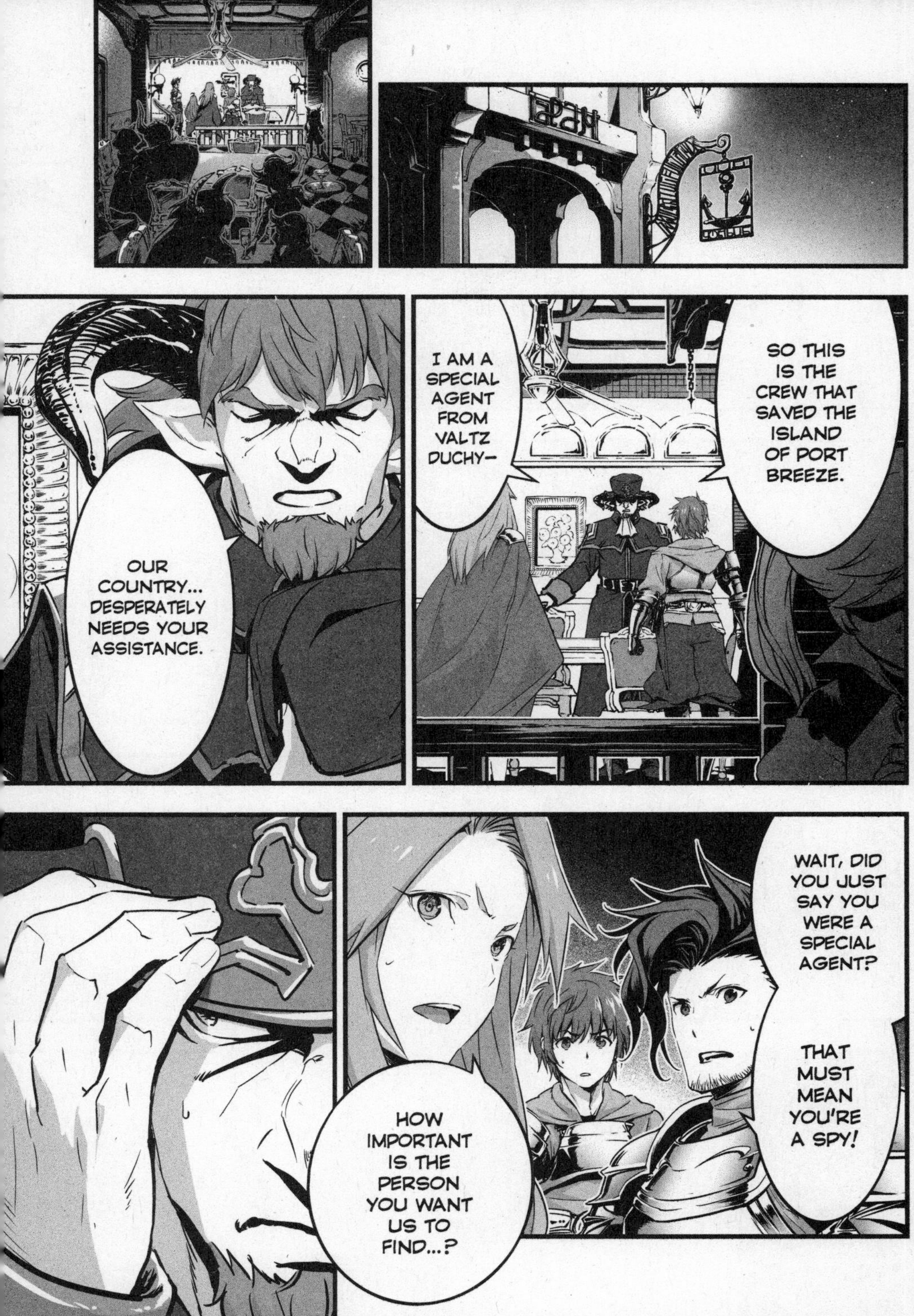
SO THIS IS THE CREW THAT SAVED THE ISLAND OF PORT BREEZE.
I AM A SPECIAL AGENT FROM VALTZ DUCHY—
OUR COUNTRY... DESPERATELY NEEDS YOUR ASSISTANCE.
WAIT, DID YOU JUST SAY YOU WERE A SPECIAL AGENT?
THAT MUST MEAN YOU'RE A SPY!
HOW IMPORTANT IS THE PERSON YOU WANT US TO FIND...?

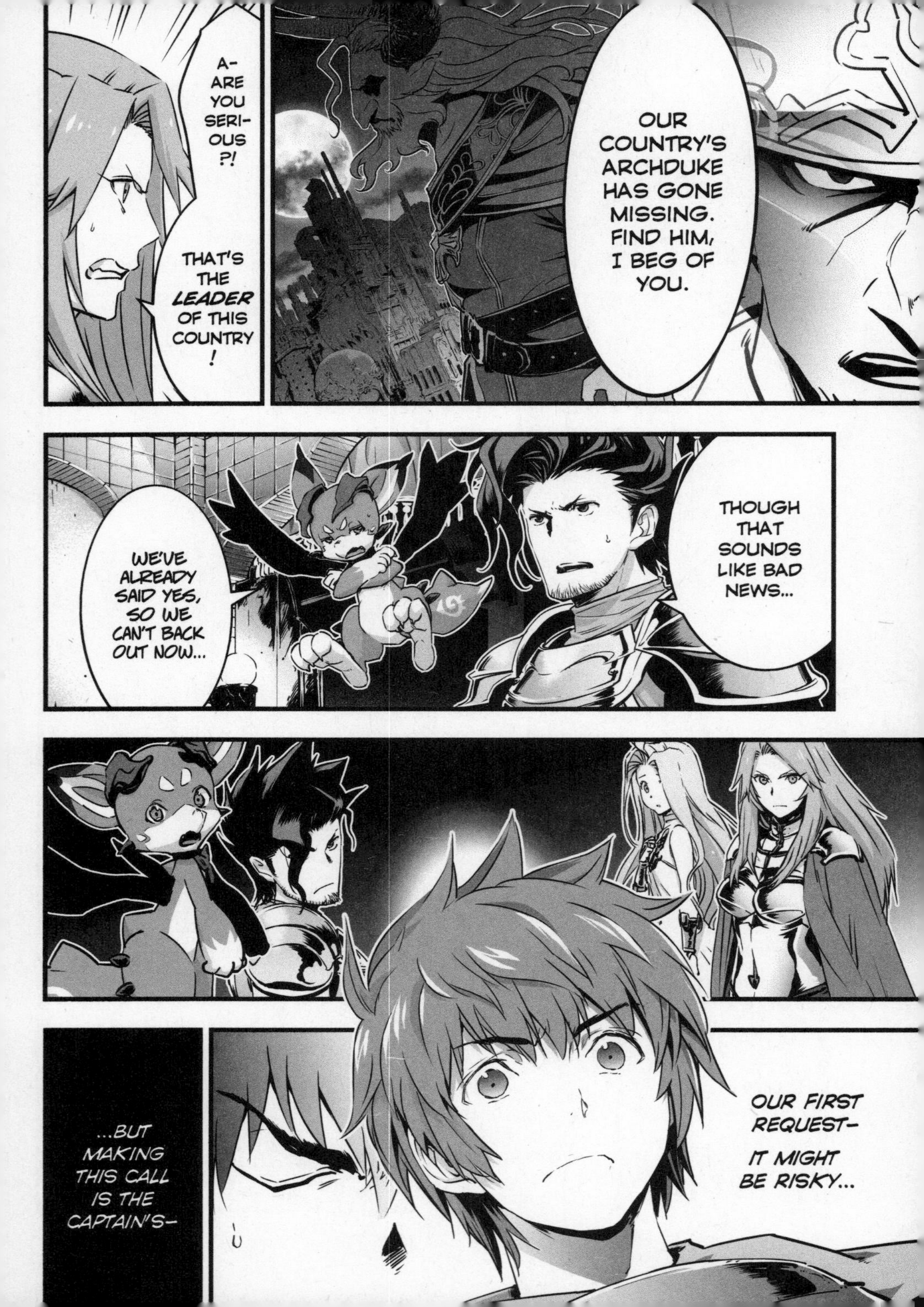
OUR COUNTRY'S ARCHDUKE HAS GONE MISSING. FIND HIM, I BEG OF YOU.
A-ARE YOU SERIOUS?!
THAT'S THE *LEADER* OF THIS COUNTRY!
THOUGH THAT SOUNDS LIKE BAD NEWS...
WE'VE ALREADY SAID YES, SO WE CAN'T BACK OUT NOW...
OUR FIRST REQUEST—
IT MIGHT BE RISKY...
...BUT MAKING THIS CALL IS THE CAPTAIN'S—

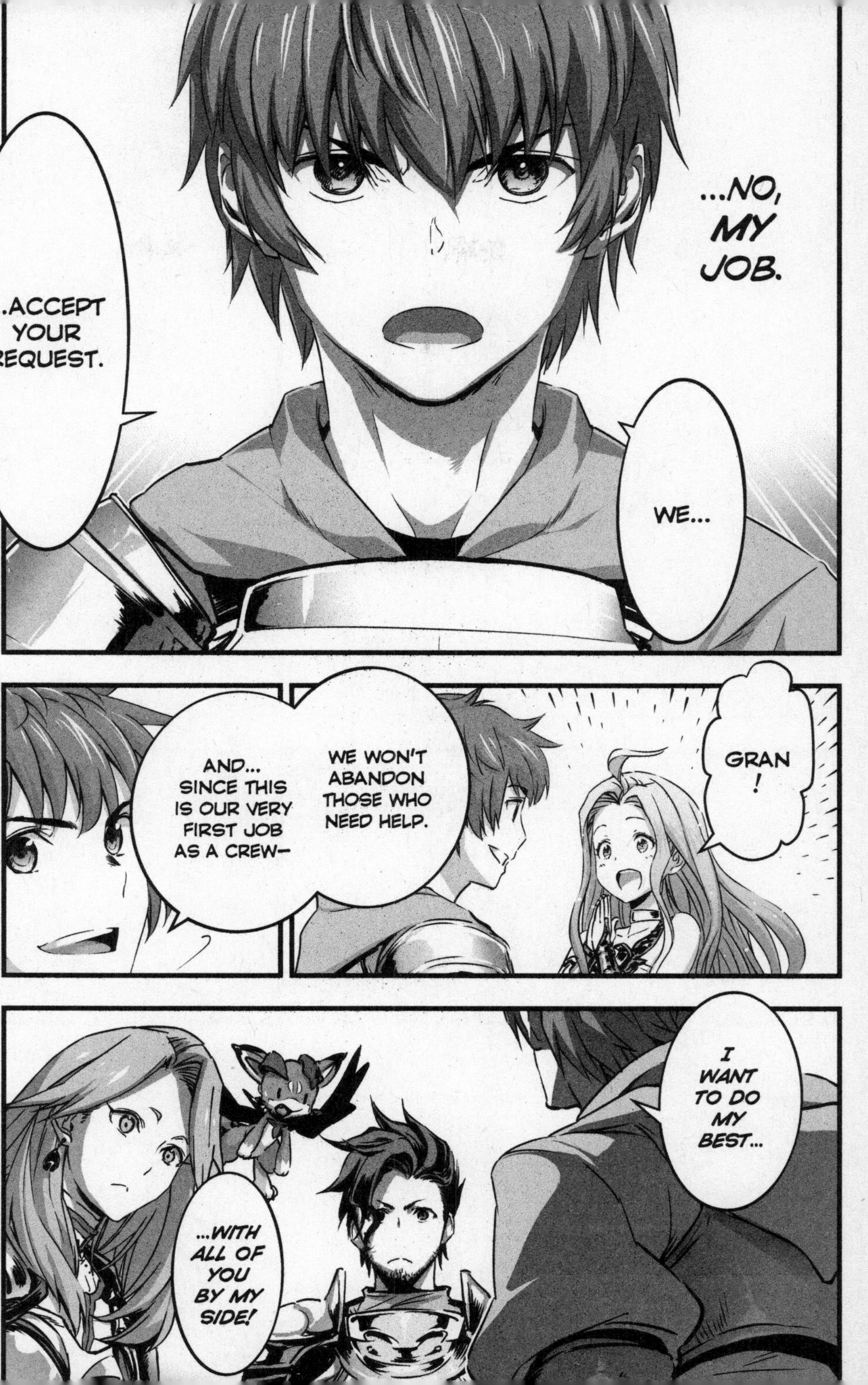
...NO, MY JOB.
WE...
...ACCEPT YOUR REQUEST.
GRAN!
WE WON'T ABANDON THOSE WHO NEED HELP.
AND... SINCE THIS IS OUR VERY FIRST JOB AS A CREW—
I WANT TO DO MY BEST...
...WITH ALL OF YOU BY MY SIDE!

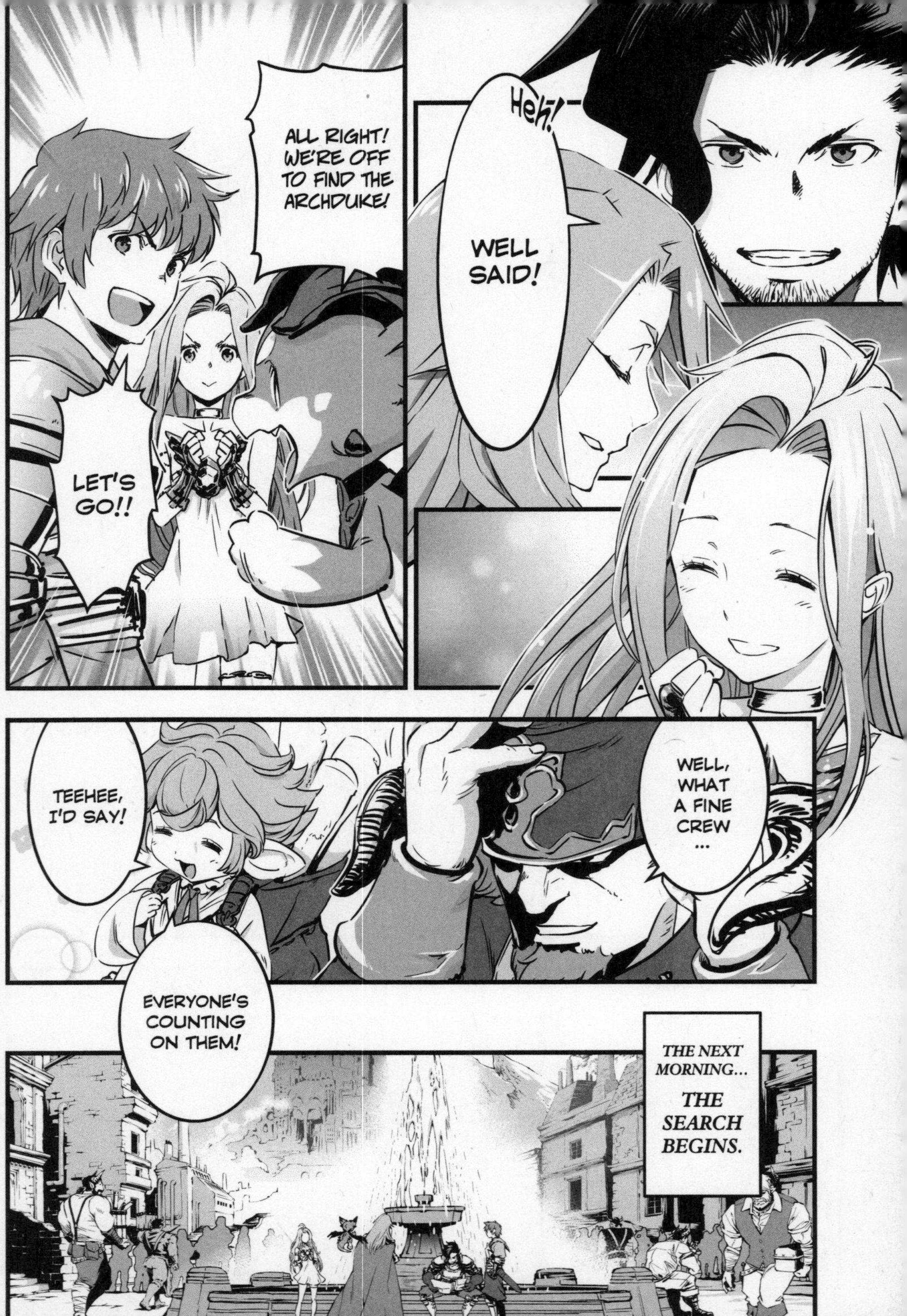
Heh!
WELL SAID!
ALL RIGHT! WE'RE OFF TO FIND THE ARCHDUKE!
LET'S GO!!
WELL, WHAT A FINE CREW ...
TEEHEE, I'D SAY!
EVERYONE'S COUNTING ON THEM!
THE NEXT MORNING…
THE SEARCH BEGINS.

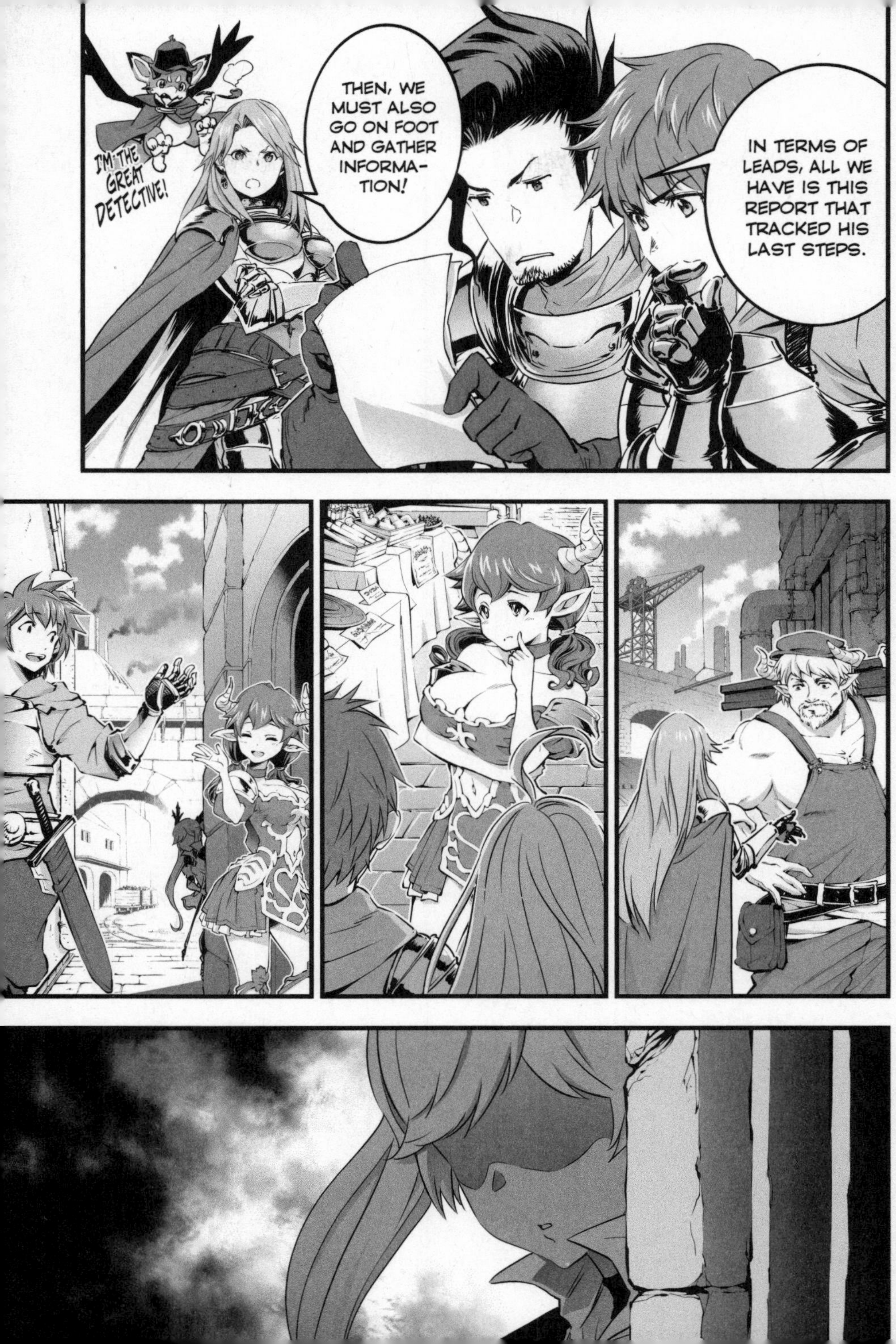
IN TERMS OF LEADS, ALL WE HAVE IS THIS REPORT THAT TRACKED HIS LAST STEPS.
THEN, WE MUST ALSO GO ON FOOT AND GATHER INFORMATION!
I'M THE GREAT DETECTIVE!

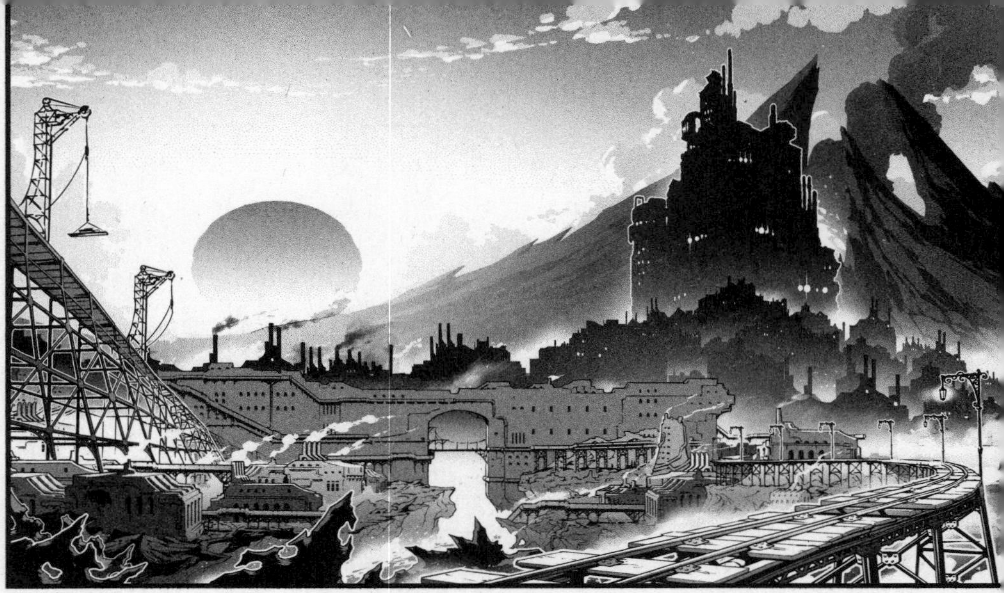

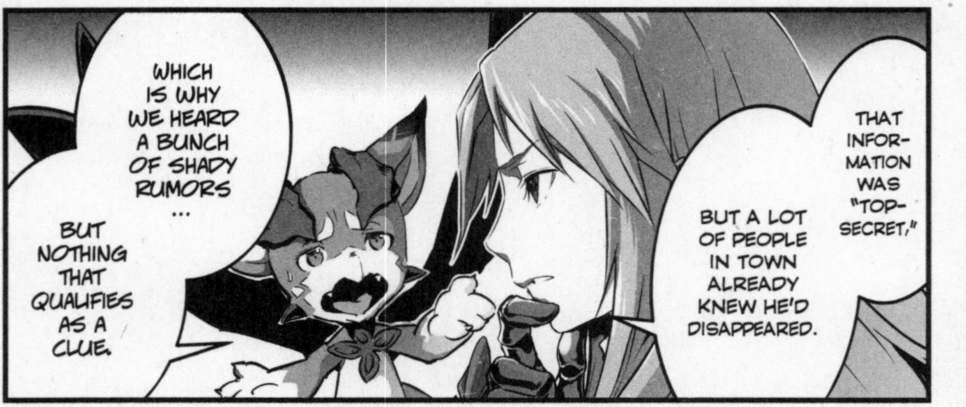
THAT INFORMATION WAS "TOP-SECRET,"
BUT A LOT OF PEOPLE IN TOWN ALREADY KNEW HE'D DISAPPEARED.
WHICH IS WHY WE HEARD A BUNCH OF SHADY RUMORS...
BUT NOTHING THAT QUALIFIES AS A CLUE.

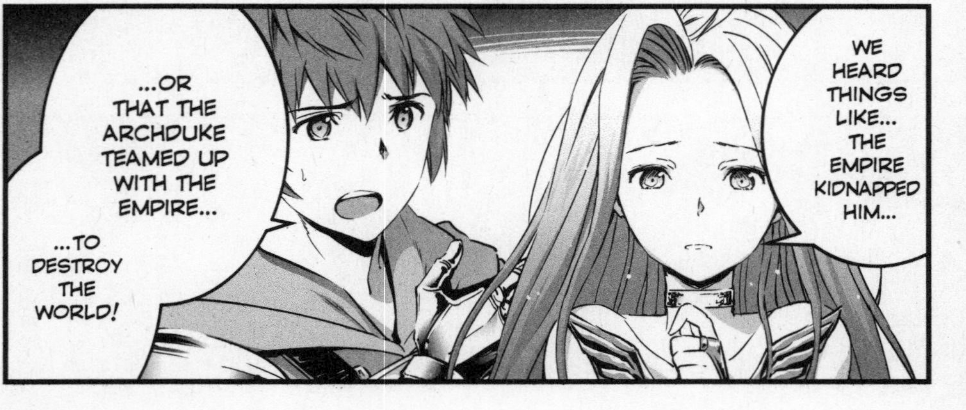
WE HEARD THINGS LIKE... THE EMPIRE KIDNAPPED HIM...
...OR THAT THE ARCHDUKE TEAMED UP WITH THE EMPIRE...
...TO DESTROY THE WORLD!

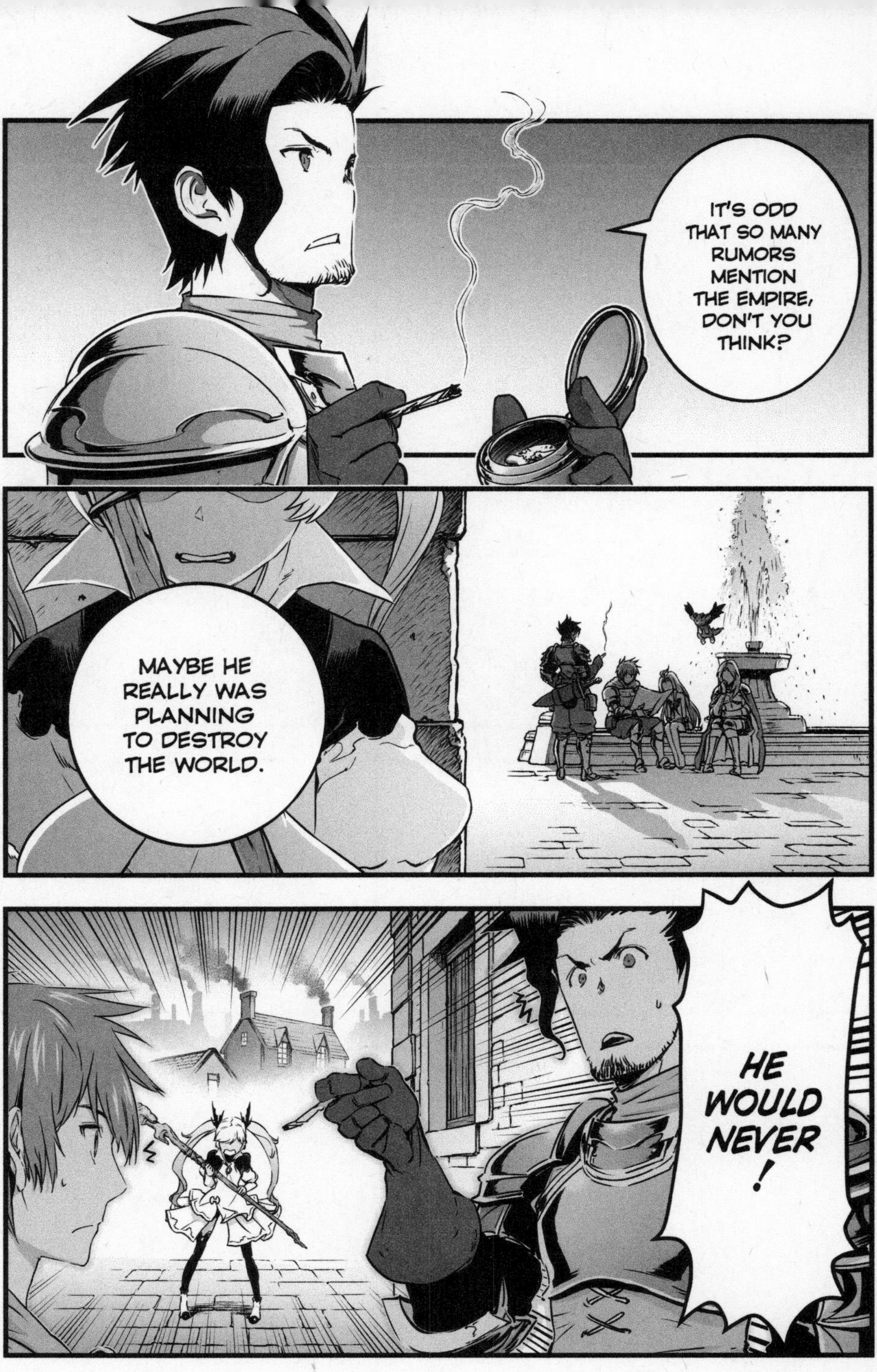
IT'S ODD THAT SO MANY RUMORS MENTION THE EMPIRE, DON'T YOU THINK?
MAYBE HE REALLY WAS PLANNING TO DESTROY THE WORLD.
HE WOULD NEVER!

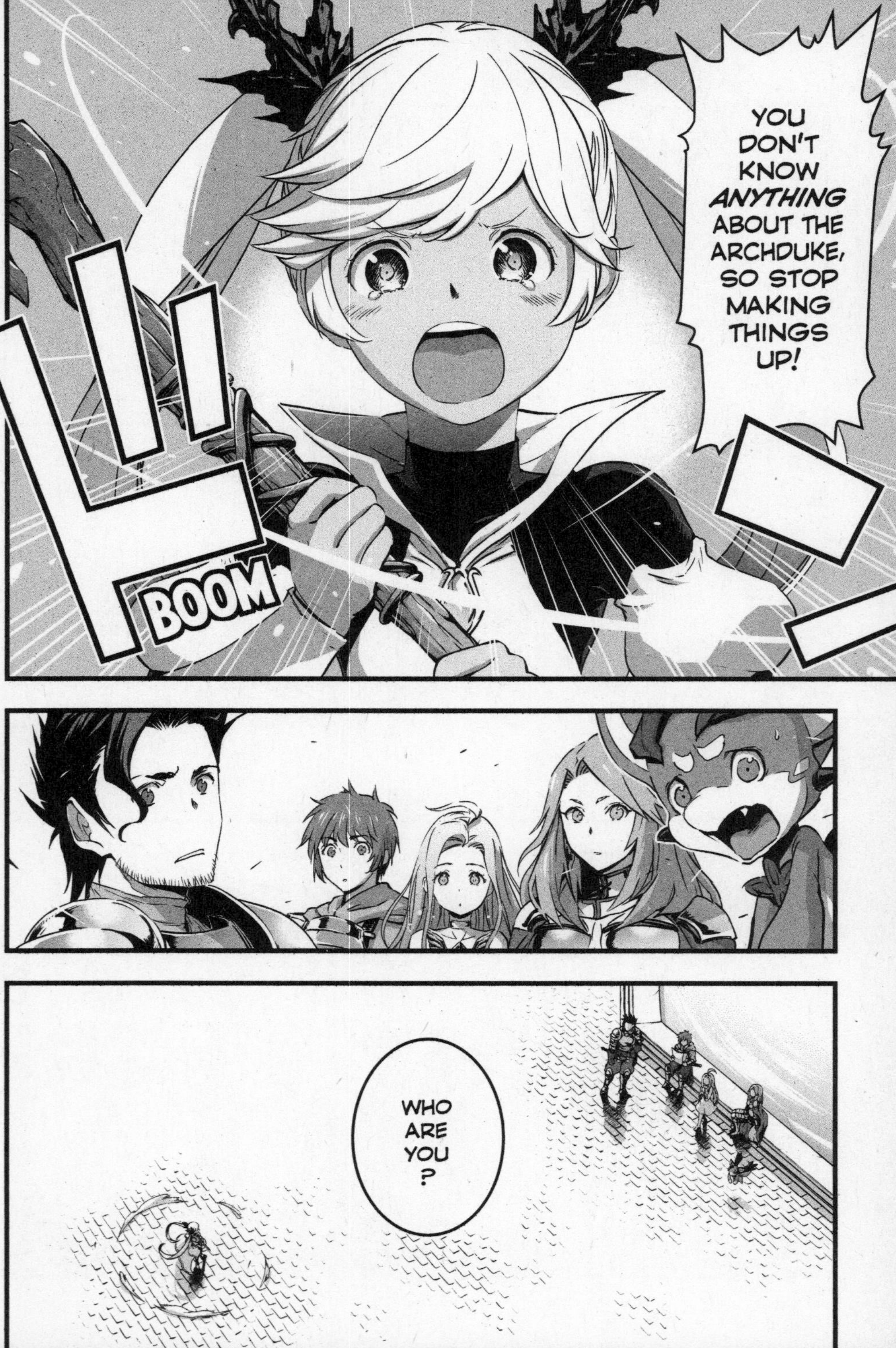
YOU DON'T KNOW *ANYTHING* ABOUT THE ARCHDUKE, SO STOP MAKING THINGS UP!
BOOM
WHO ARE YOU ?

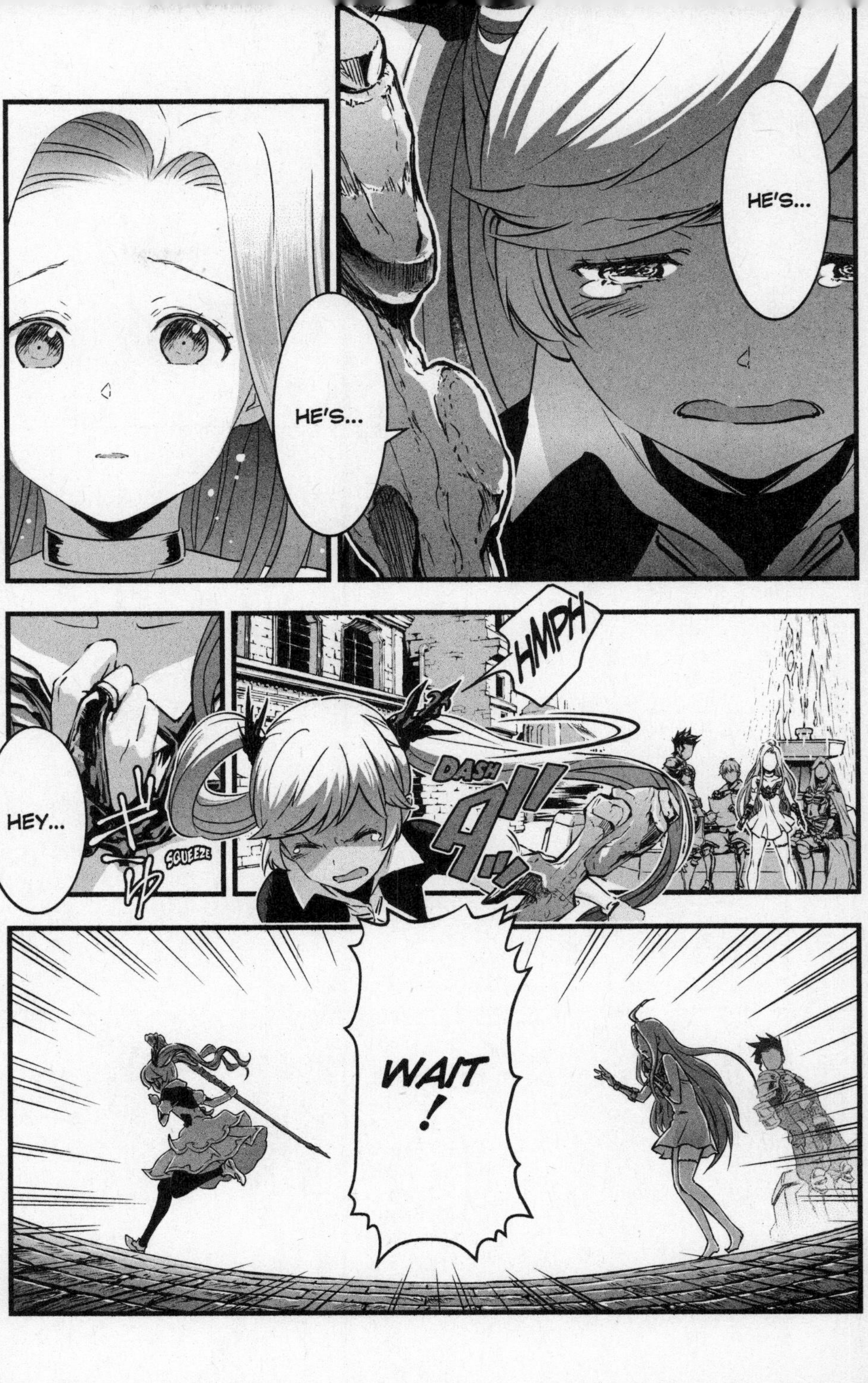
HE'S...
HE'S...
HMPH
DASH
HEY...
SQUEEZE
WAIT!

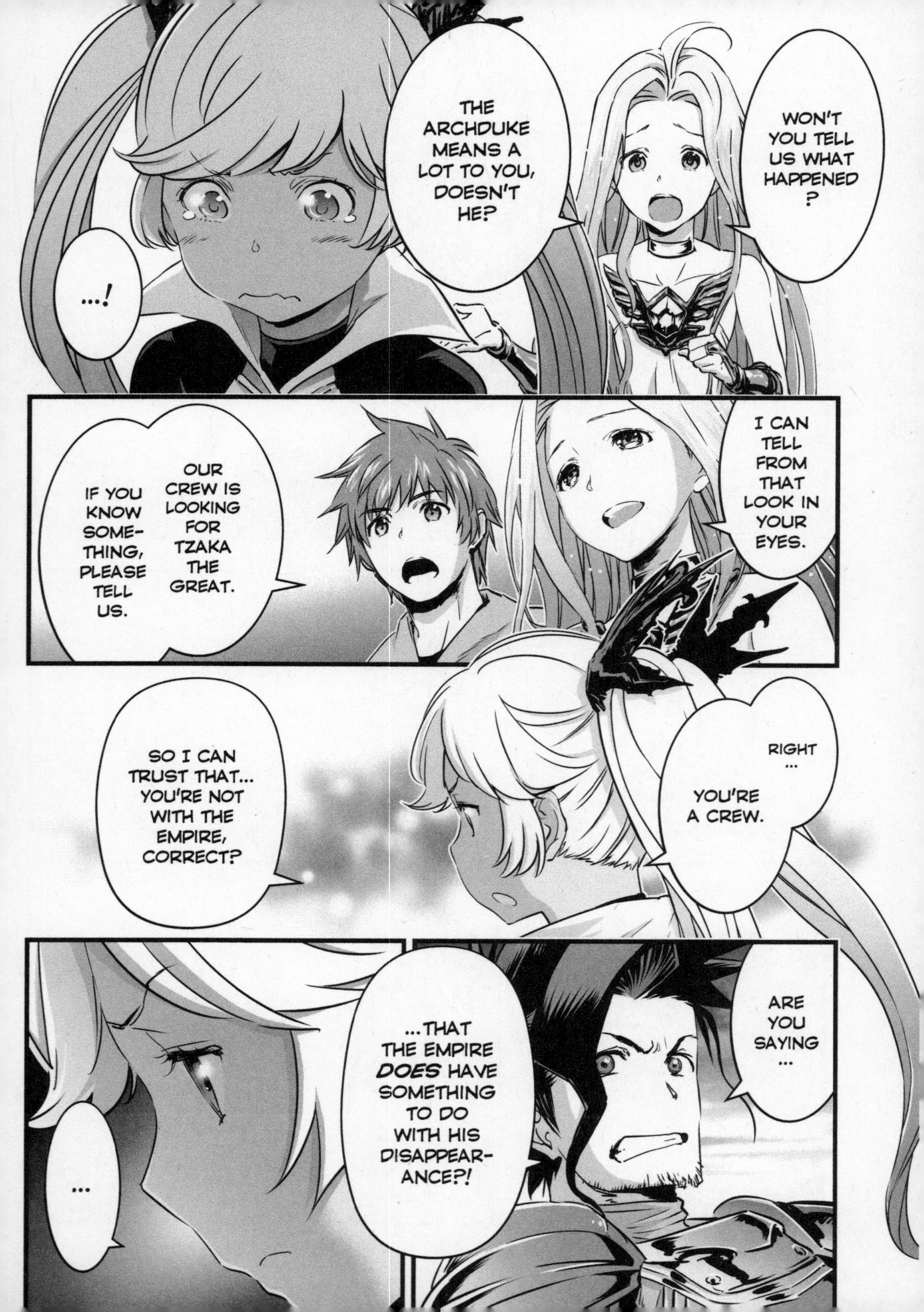
WON'T YOU TELL US WHAT HAPPENED?
THE ARCHDUKE MEANS A LOT TO YOU, DOESN'T HE?
...!
I CAN TELL FROM THAT LOOK IN YOUR EYES.
OUR CREW IS LOOKING FOR TZAKA THE GREAT.
IF YOU KNOW SOMETHING, PLEASE TELL US.
RIGHT... YOU'RE A CREW.
SO I CAN TRUST THAT... YOU'RE NOT WITH THE EMPIRE, CORRECT?
ARE YOU SAYING...
...THAT THE EMPIRE *DOES* HAVE SOMETHING TO DO WITH HIS DISAPPEARANCE?!
...

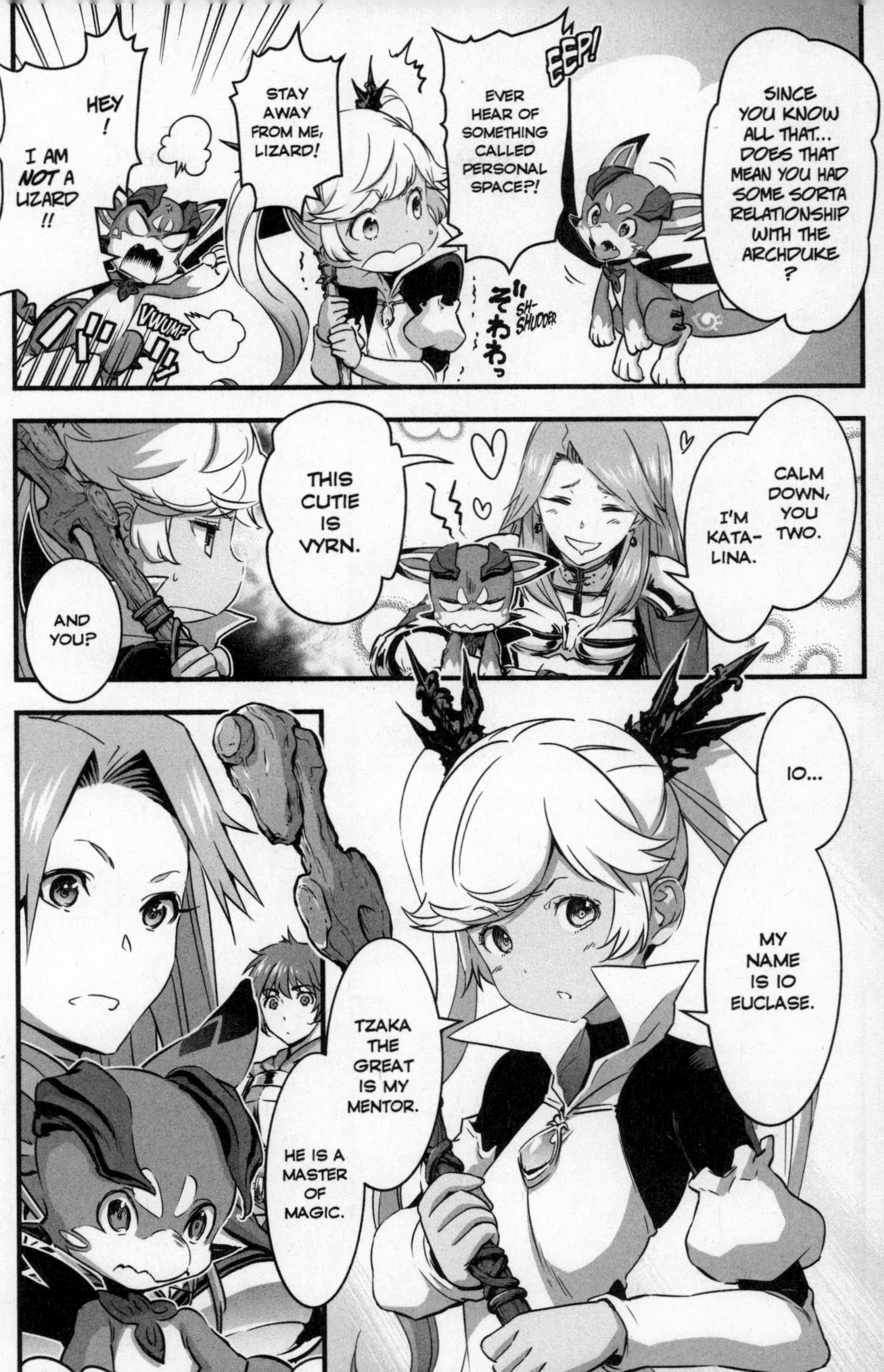
SINCE YOU KNOW ALL THAT... DOES THAT MEAN YOU HAD SOME SORTA RELATIONSHIP WITH THE ARCHDUKE?
EEP!
EVER HEAR OF SOMETHING CALLED PERSONAL SPACE?!
そわわっ
SH-SHUDDER
STAY AWAY FROM ME, LIZARD!
HEY!
I AM NOT A LIZARD!!
VWUMF
CALM DOWN, YOU TWO.
I'M KATA-LINA.
THIS CUTIE IS VYRN.
AND YOU?
IO...
MY NAME IS IO EUCLASE.
TZAKA THE GREAT IS MY MENTOR.
HE IS A MASTER OF MAGIC.

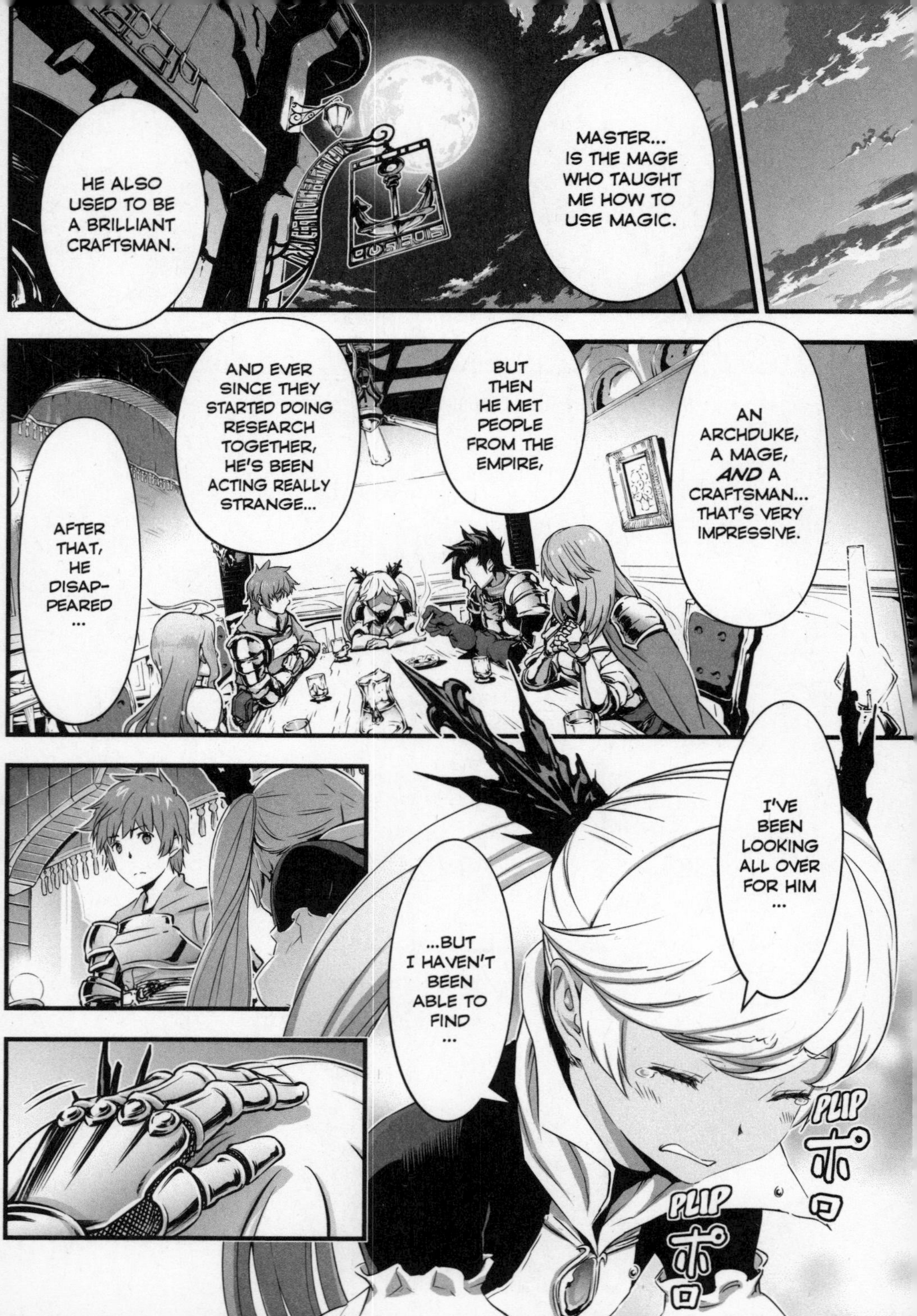
MASTER... IS THE MAGE WHO TAUGHT ME HOW TO USE MAGIC.
HE ALSO USED TO BE A BRILLIANT CRAFTSMAN.
AN ARCHDUKE, A MAGE, *AND* A CRAFTSMAN... THAT'S VERY IMPRESSIVE.
BUT THEN HE MET PEOPLE FROM THE EMPIRE,
AND EVER SINCE THEY STARTED DOING RESEARCH TOGETHER, HE'S BEEN ACTING REALLY STRANGE...
AFTER THAT, HE DISAPPEARED...
I'VE BEEN LOOKING ALL OVER FOR HIM...
...BUT I HAVEN'T BEEN ABLE TO FIND...
PLIP
ポロ
PLIP
ポロ

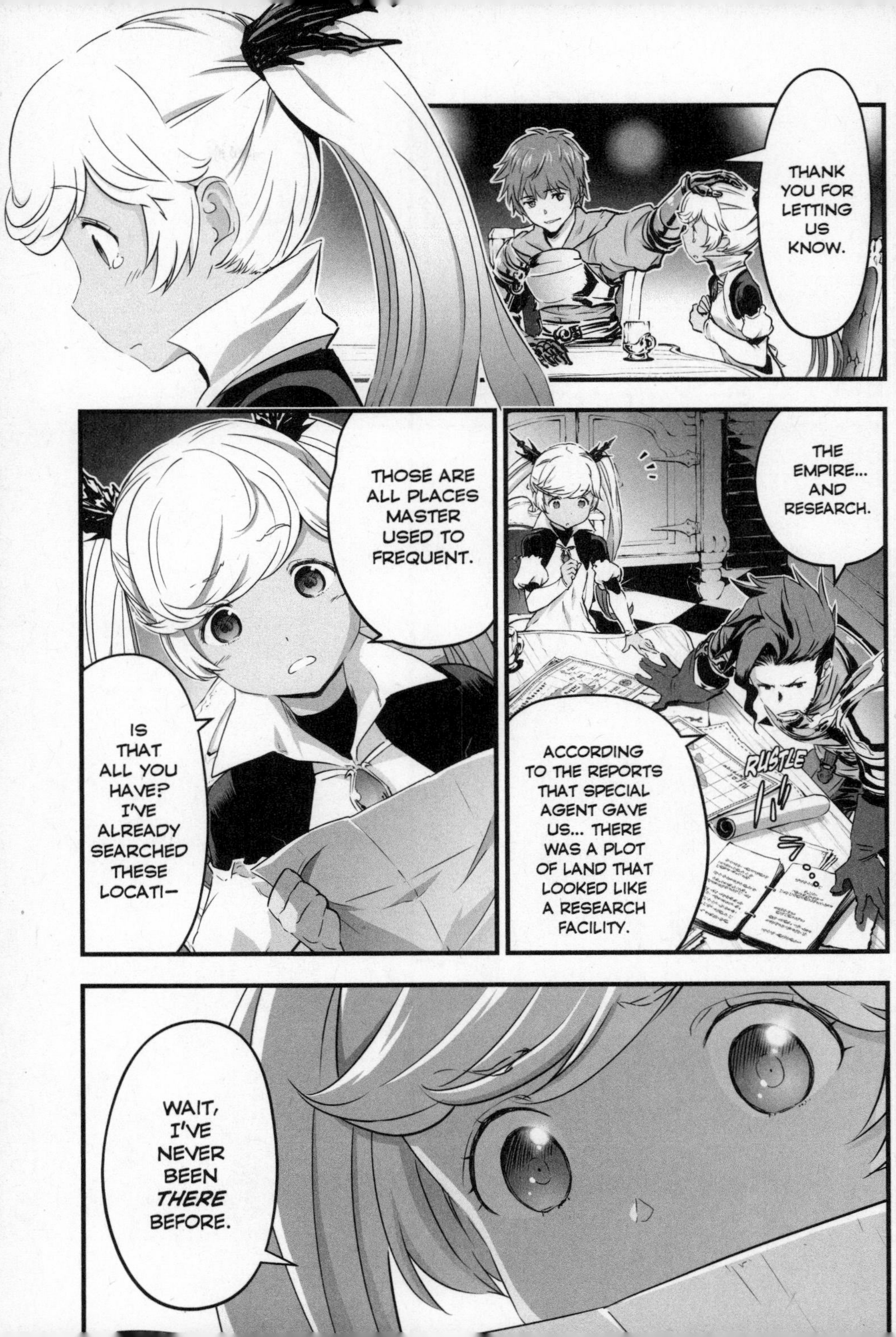
THANK YOU FOR LETTING US KNOW.
THE EMPIRE... AND RESEARCH.
RUSTLE
ACCORDING TO THE REPORTS THAT SPECIAL AGENT GAVE US... THERE WAS A PLOT OF LAND THAT LOOKED LIKE A RESEARCH FACILITY.
THOSE ARE ALL PLACES MASTER USED TO FREQUENT.
IS THAT ALL YOU HAVE? I'VE ALREADY SEARCHED THESE LOCATI—
WAIT, I'VE NEVER BEEN *THERE* BEFORE.

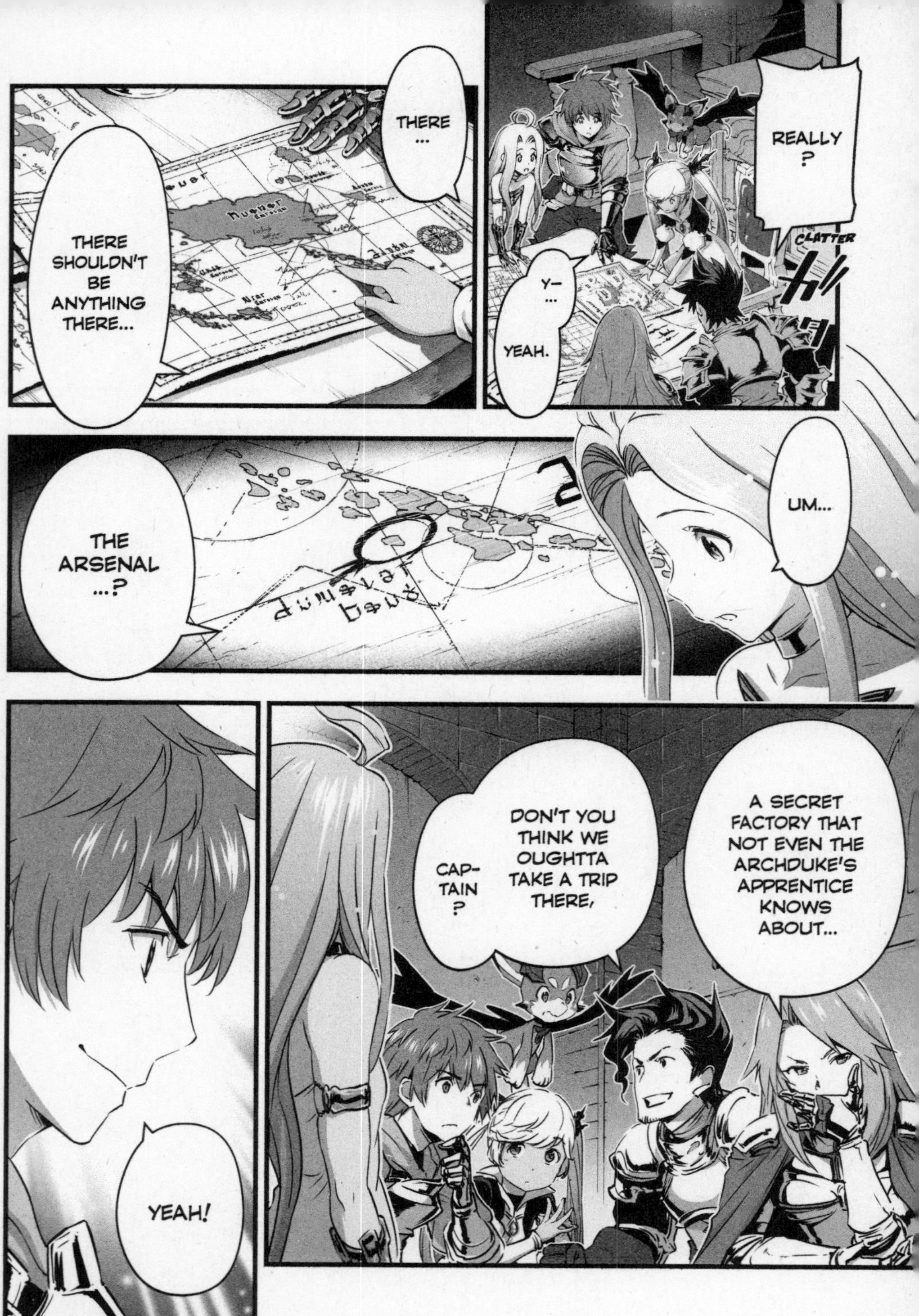
REALLY ?
CLATTER
Y— ...
YEAH.
THERE ...
THERE SHOULDN'T BE ANYTHING THERE...
UM...
THE ARSENAL ...?
A SECRET FACTORY THAT NOT EVEN THE ARCHDUKE'S APPRENTICE KNOWS ABOUT...
DON'T YOU THINK WE OUGHTTA TAKE A TRIP THERE,
CAP-TAIN ?
YEAH!

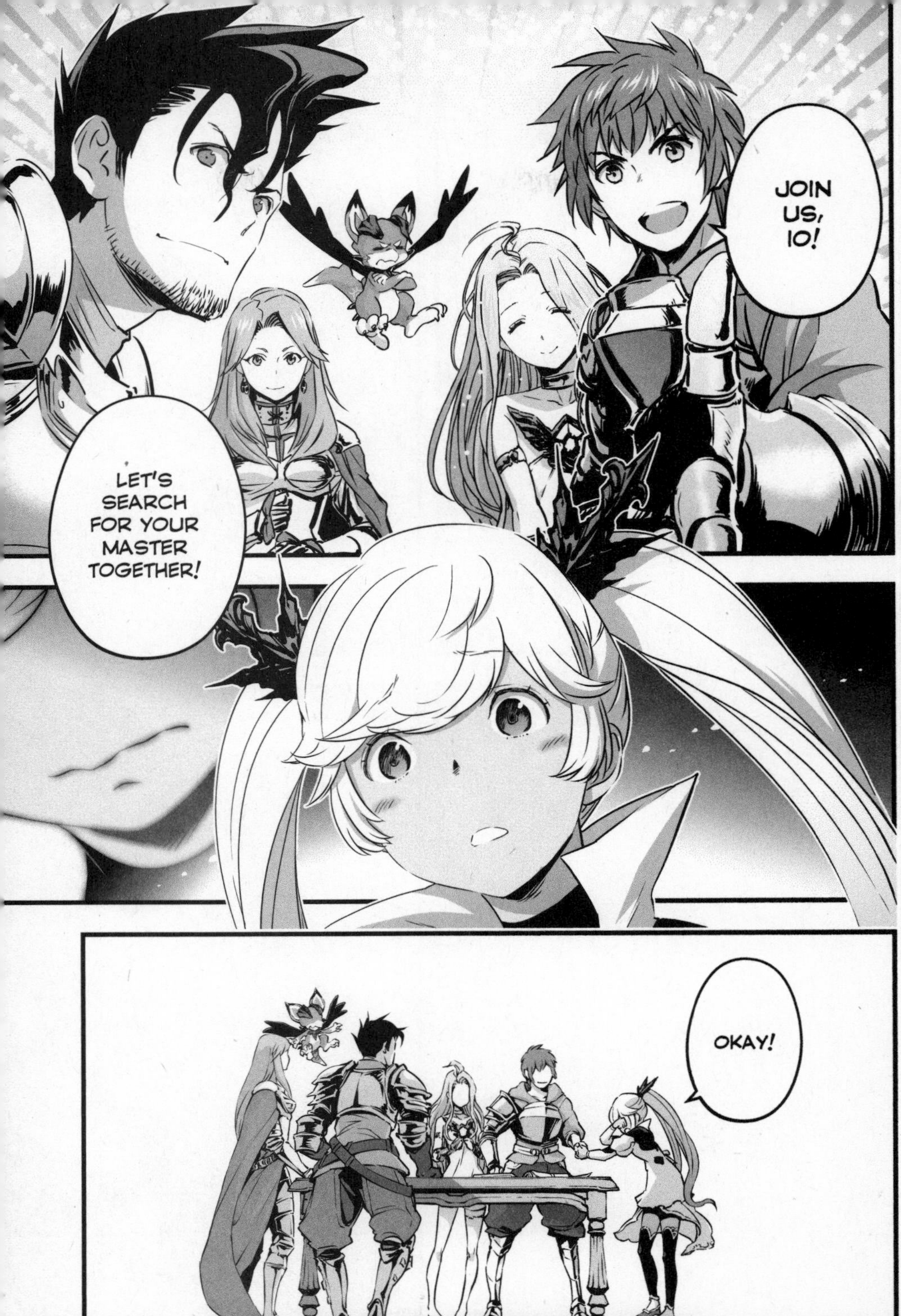
JOIN US, IO!
LET'S SEARCH FOR YOUR MASTER TOGETHER!
OKAY!

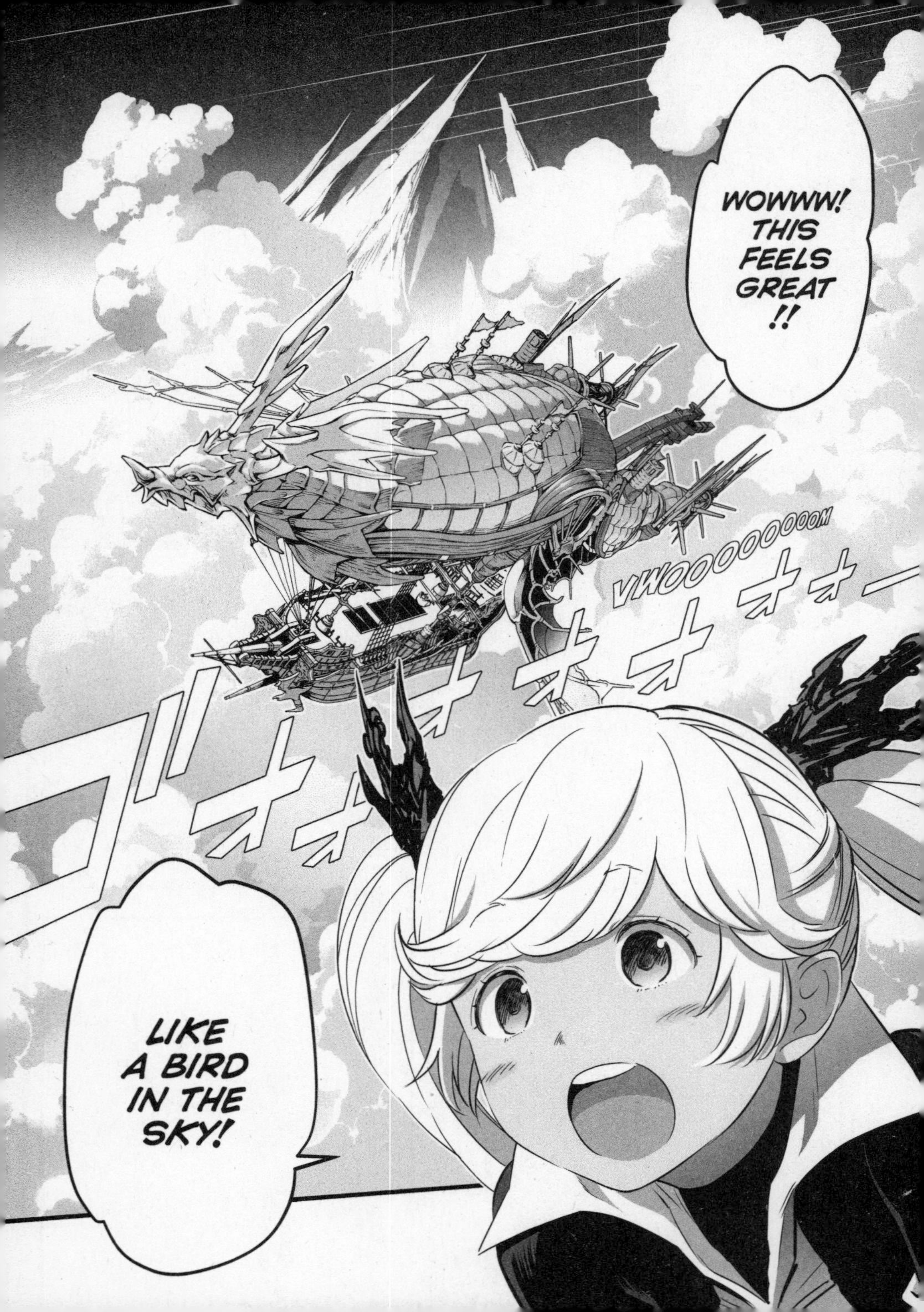
WOWWW! THIS FEELS GREAT!!
VWOOOOOOOOOM
ゴオォォォォォォー
LIKE A BIRD IN THE SKY!

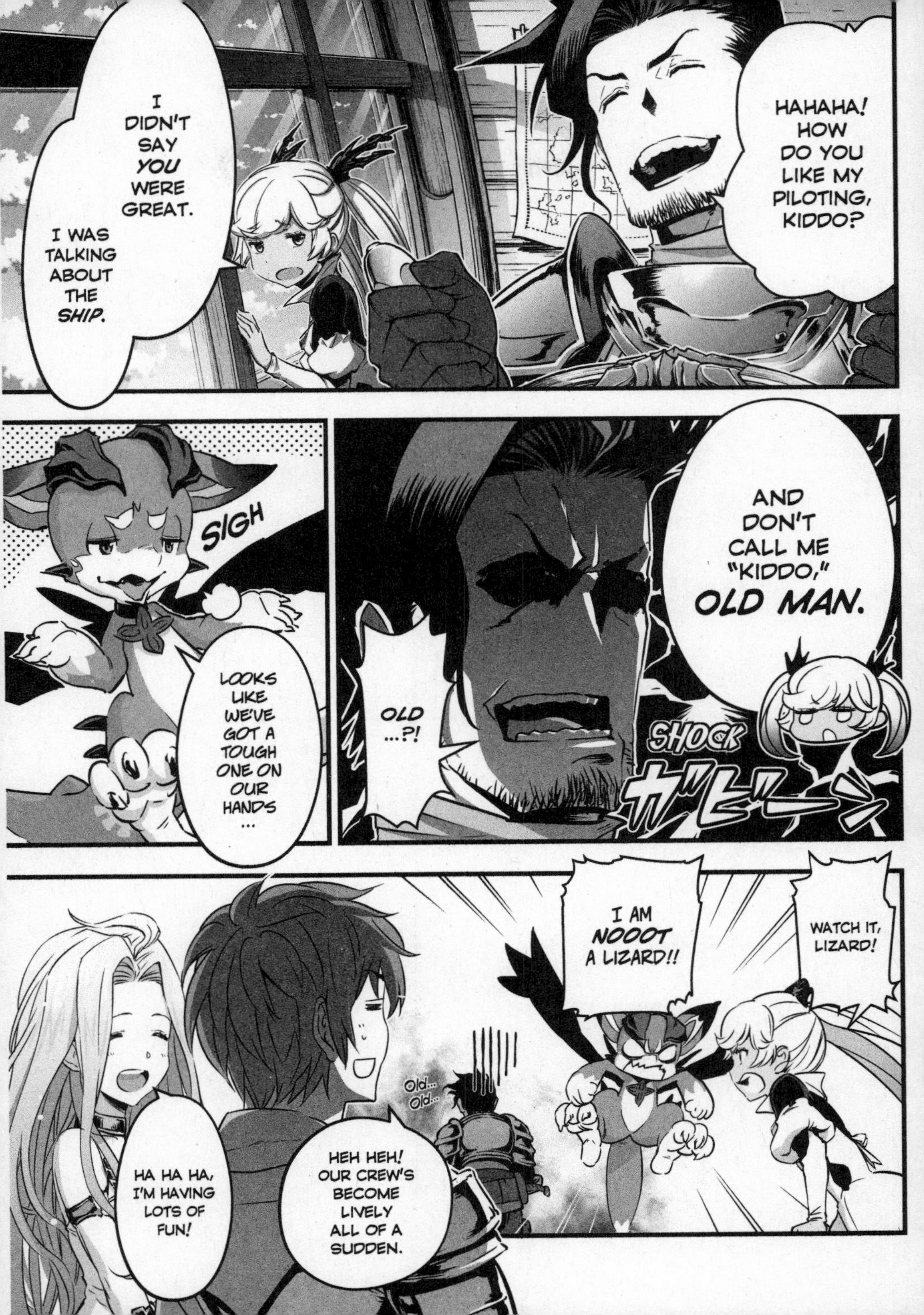
HAHAHA! HOW DO YOU LIKE MY PILOTING, KIDDO?
I DIDN'T SAY *YOU* WERE GREAT.
I WAS TALKING ABOUT THE *SHIP*.
AND DON'T CALL ME "KIDDO," **OLD MAN.**
SHOCK
OLD ...?!
SIGH
LOOKS LIKE WE'VE GOT A TOUGH ONE ON OUR HANDS ...
WATCH IT, LIZARD!
I AM *NOOOT* A LIZARD!!
Old... Old...
HEH HEH! OUR CREW'S BECOME LIVELY ALL OF A SUDDEN.
HA HA HA, I'M HAVING LOTS OF FUN!

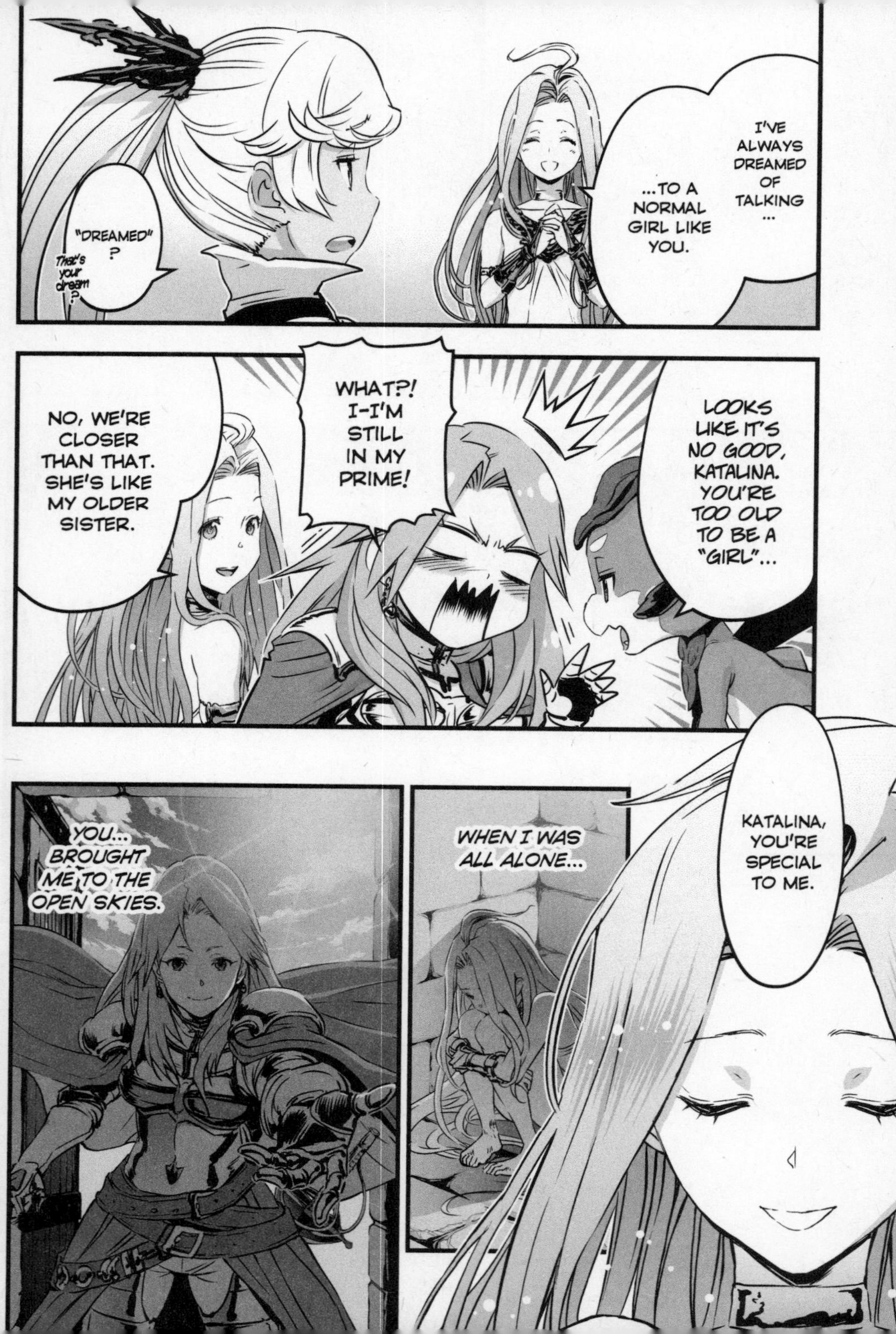
I'VE ALWAYS DREAMED OF TALKING ...
...TO A NORMAL GIRL LIKE YOU.
"DREAMED" ?
That's your dream ?
LOOKS LIKE IT'S NO GOOD, KATALINA. YOU'RE TOO OLD TO BE A "GIRL"...
WHAT?! I-I'M STILL IN MY PRIME!
NO, WE'RE CLOSER THAN THAT. SHE'S LIKE MY OLDER SISTER.
KATALINA, YOU'RE SPECIAL TO ME.
WHEN I WAS ALL ALONE...
YOU... BROUGHT ME TO THE OPEN SKIES.

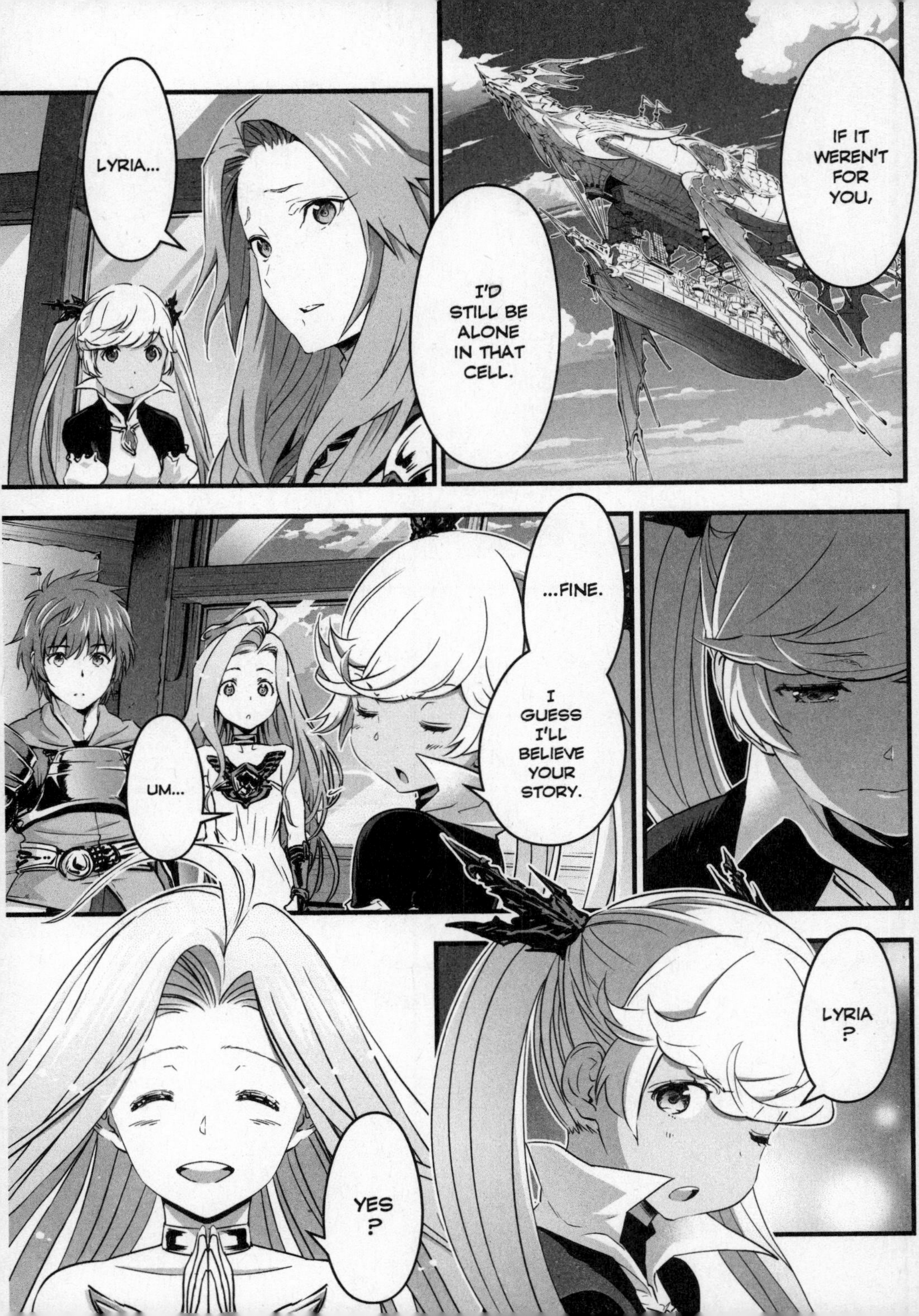
IF IT WEREN'T FOR YOU,
I'D STILL BE ALONE IN THAT CELL.
LYRIA...
...FINE.
I GUESS I'LL BELIEVE YOUR STORY.
UM...
LYRIA?
YES?

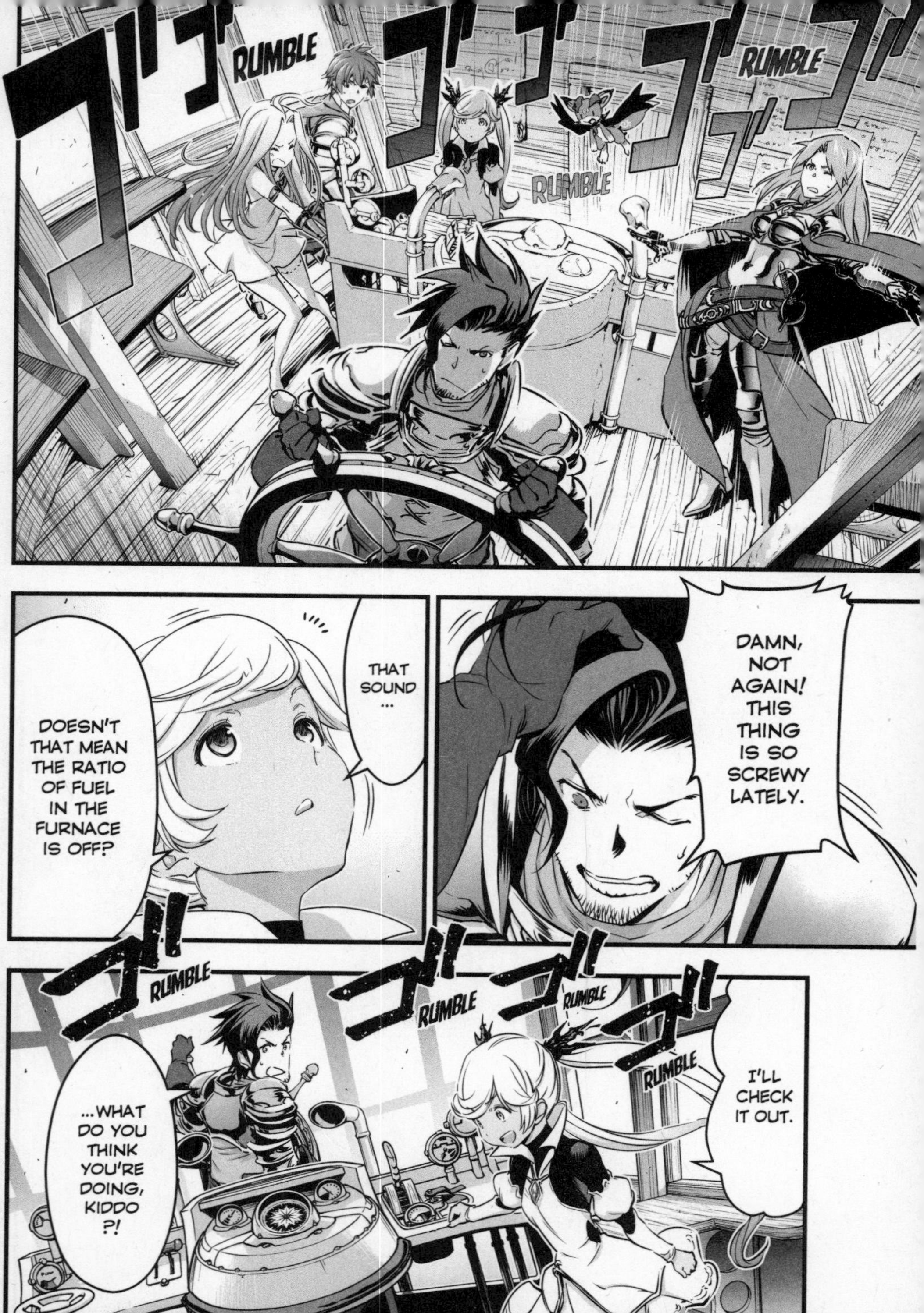
RUMBLE
RUMBLE
RUMBLE
DAMN, NOT AGAIN! THIS THING IS SO SCREWY LATELY.
THAT SOUND ...
DOESN'T THAT MEAN THE RATIO OF FUEL IN THE FURNACE IS OFF?
RUMBLE
RUMBLE
RUMBLE
RUMBLE
I'LL CHECK IT OUT.
...WHAT DO YOU THINK YOU'RE DOING, KIDDO ?!

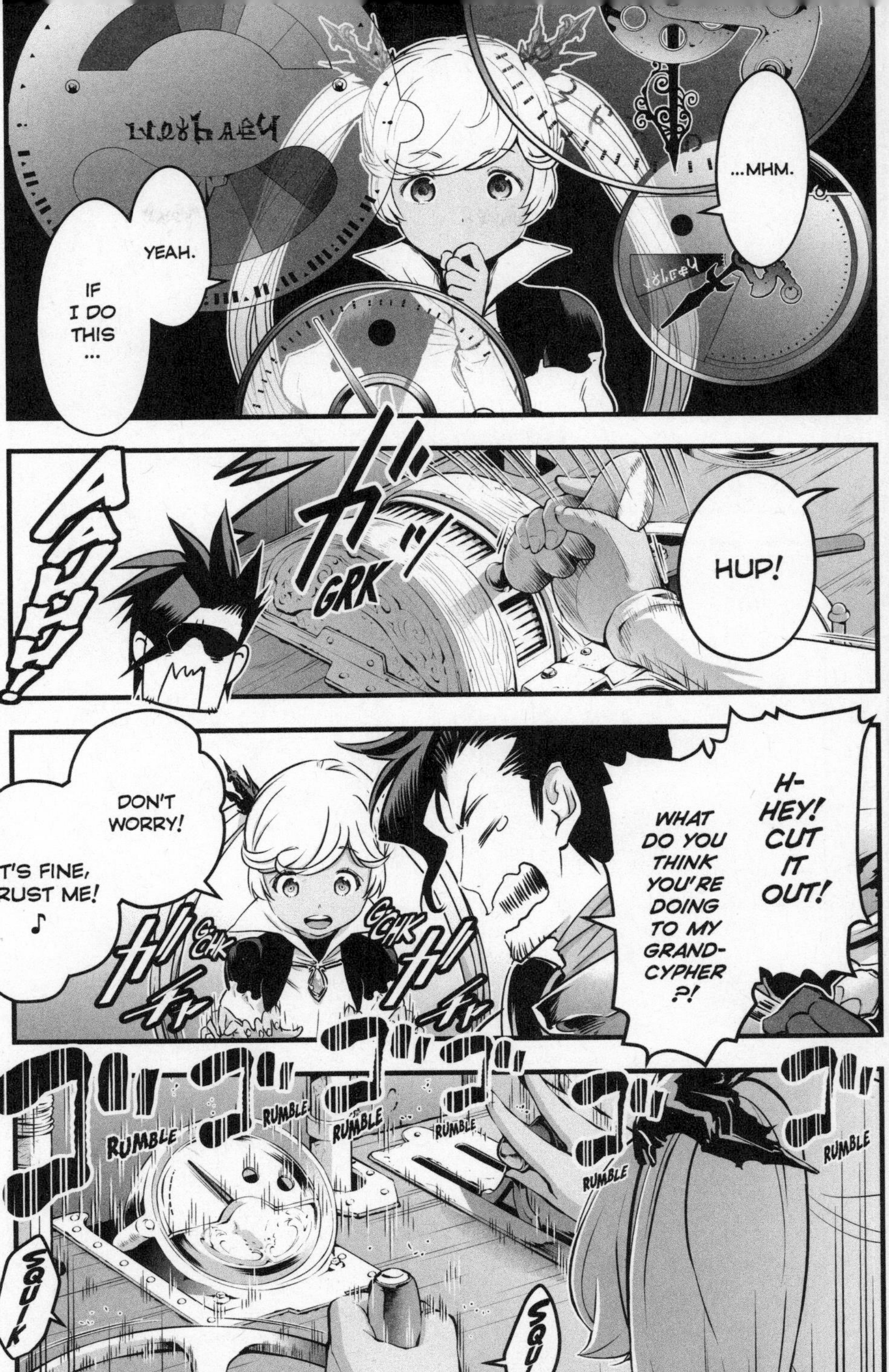
...MHM.
YEAH.
IF I DO THIS ...
HUP!
GRK
AAAHHH!
H- HEY! CUT IT OUT!
WHAT DO YOU THINK YOU'RE DOING TO MY GRAND-CYPHER?!
GCHK
GCHK
DON'T WORRY!
IT'S FINE, TRUST ME! ♪
RUMBLE
RUMBLE
RUMBLE
RUMBLE
RUMBLE
RUMBLE
SQUIK
SQUIK

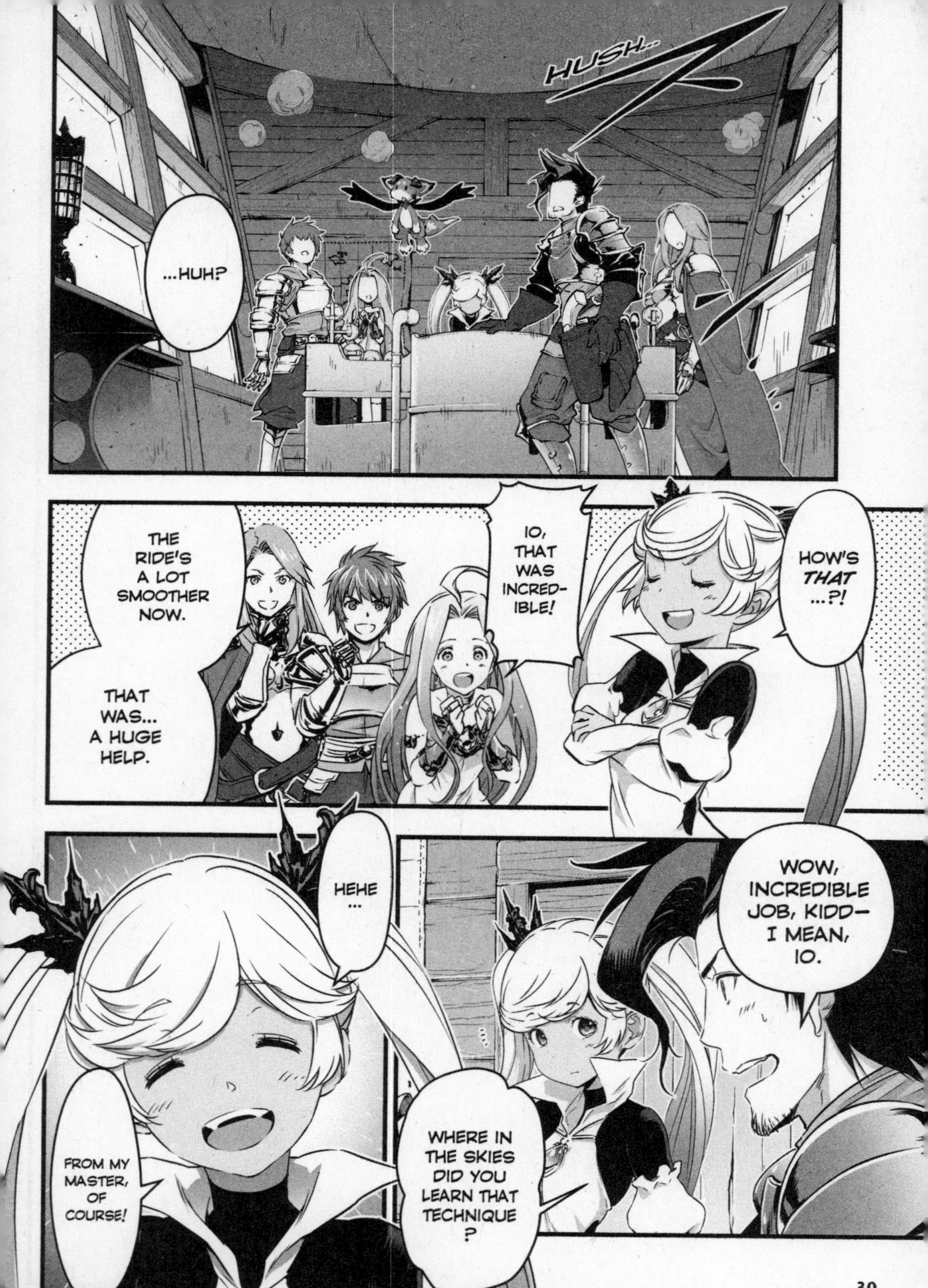
HUSH..
...HUH?
HOW'S *THAT* ...?!
IO, THAT WAS INCREDIBLE!
THE RIDE'S A LOT SMOOTHER NOW.
THAT WAS... A HUGE HELP.
WOW, INCREDIBLE JOB, KIDD— I MEAN, IO.
...
WHERE IN THE SKIES DID YOU LEARN THAT TECHNIQUE?
HEHE ...
FROM MY MASTER, OF COURSE!

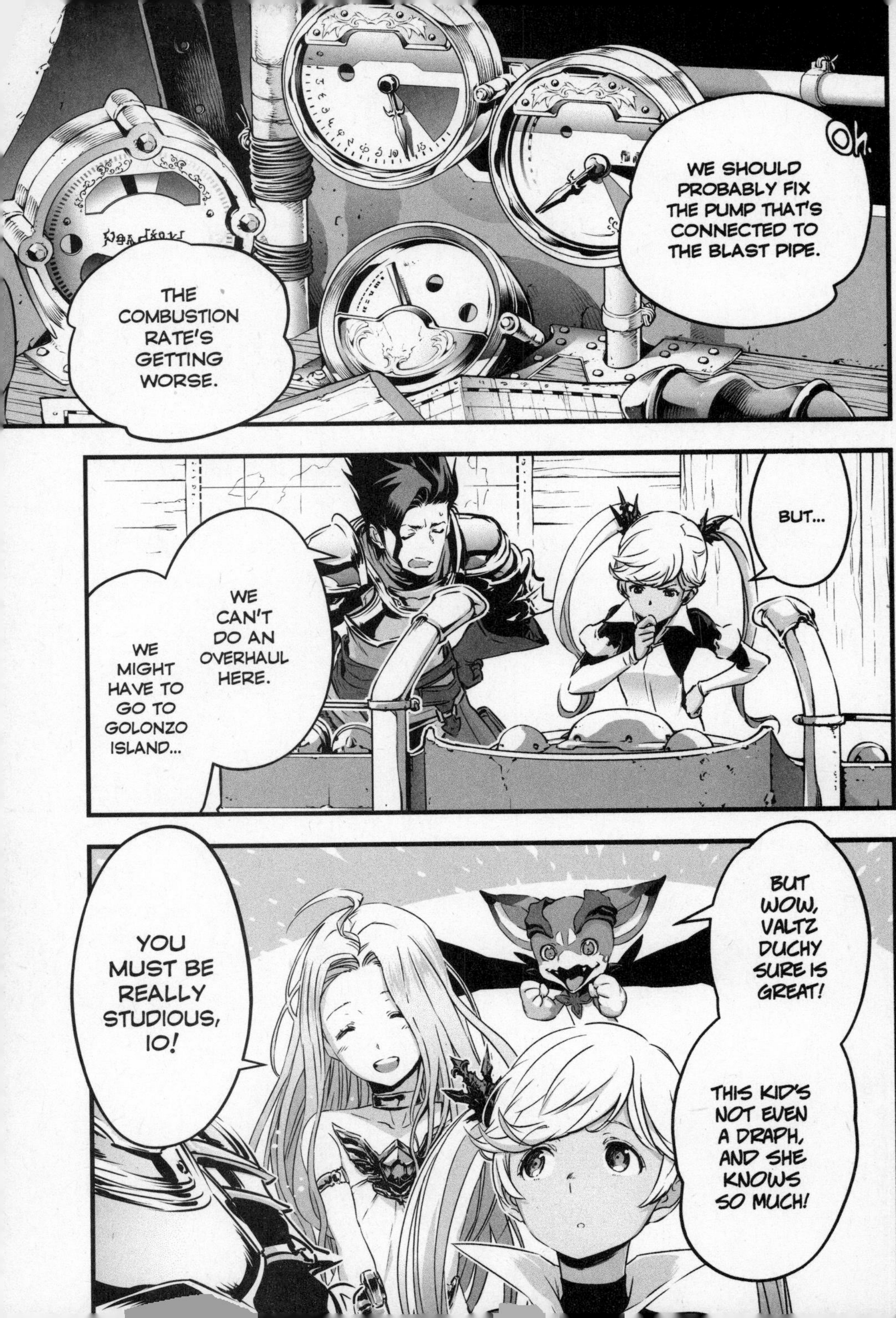
Oh.
WE SHOULD PROBABLY FIX THE PUMP THAT'S CONNECTED TO THE BLAST PIPE.
THE COMBUSTION RATE'S GETTING WORSE.
BUT...
WE CAN'T DO AN OVERHAUL HERE.
WE MIGHT HAVE TO GO TO GOLONZO ISLAND...
BUT WOW, VALTZ DUCHY SURE IS GREAT!
THIS KID'S NOT EVEN A DRAPH, AND SHE KNOWS SO MUCH!
YOU MUST BE REALLY STUDIOUS, IO!

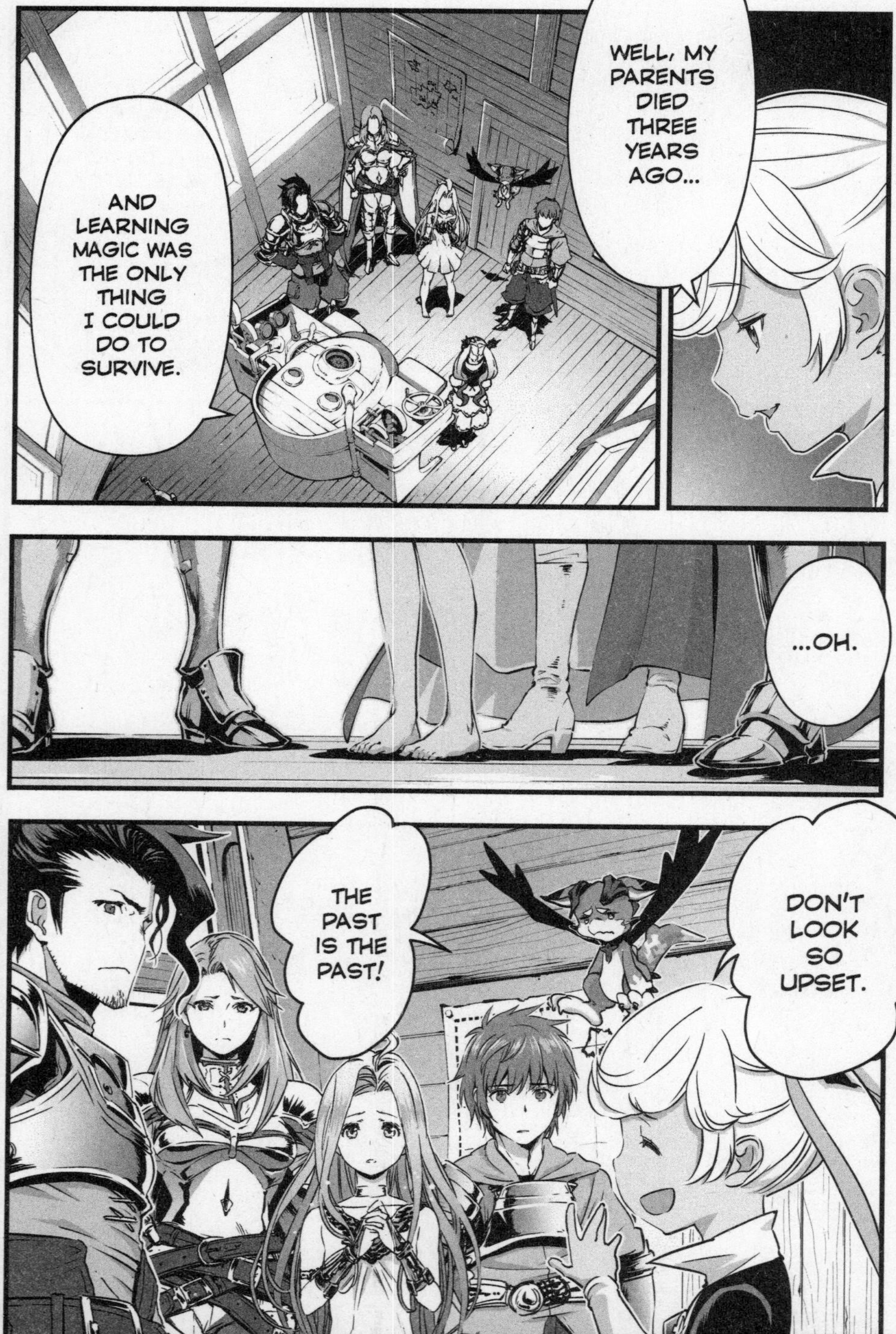
WELL, MY PARENTS DIED THREE YEARS AGO...
AND LEARNING MAGIC WAS THE ONLY THING I COULD DO TO SURVIVE.
...OH.
DON'T LOOK SO UPSET.
THE PAST IS THE PAST!

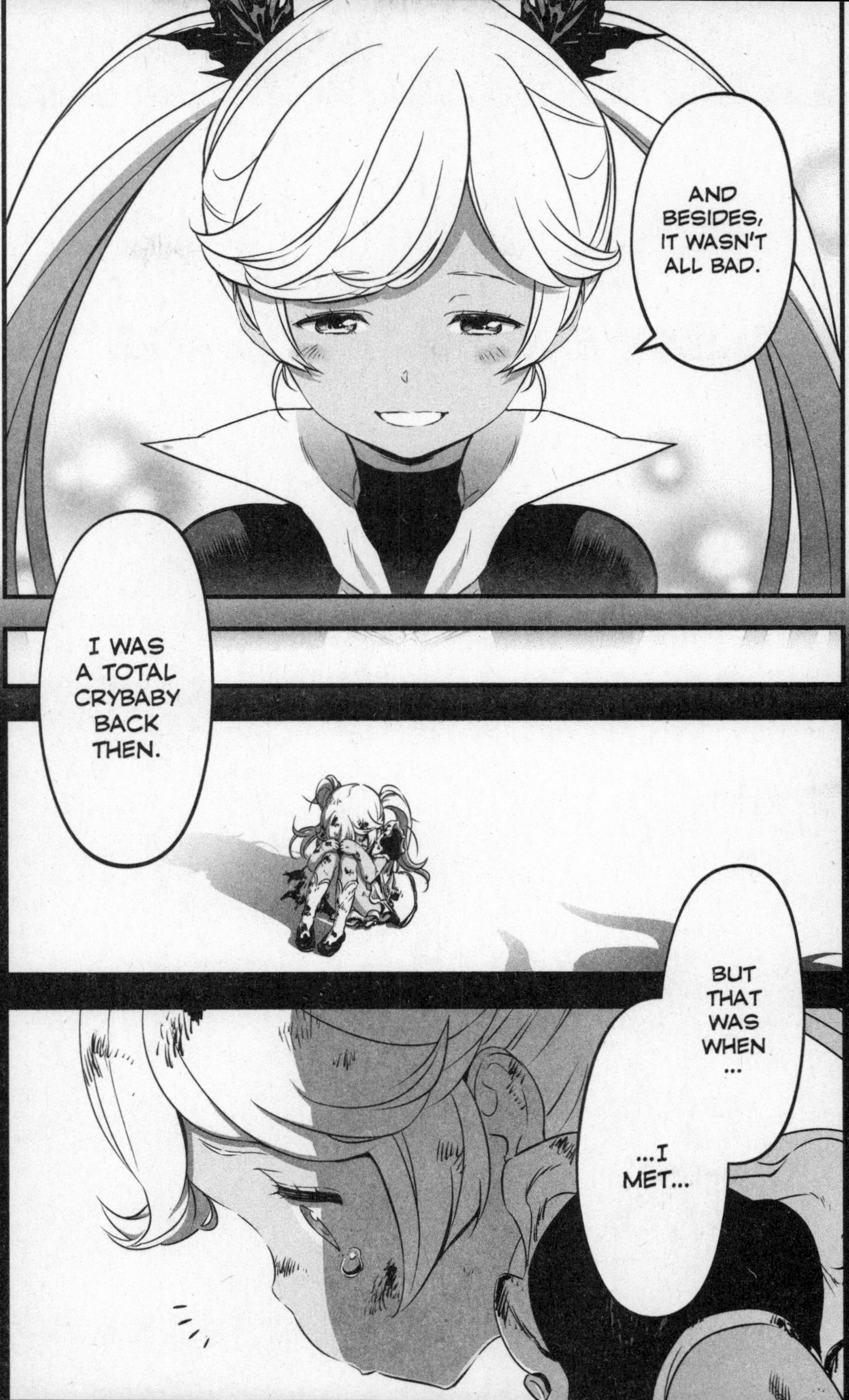
AND BESIDES, IT WASN'T ALL BAD.
I WAS A TOTAL CRYBABY BACK THEN.
BUT THAT WAS WHEN ...
...I MET...

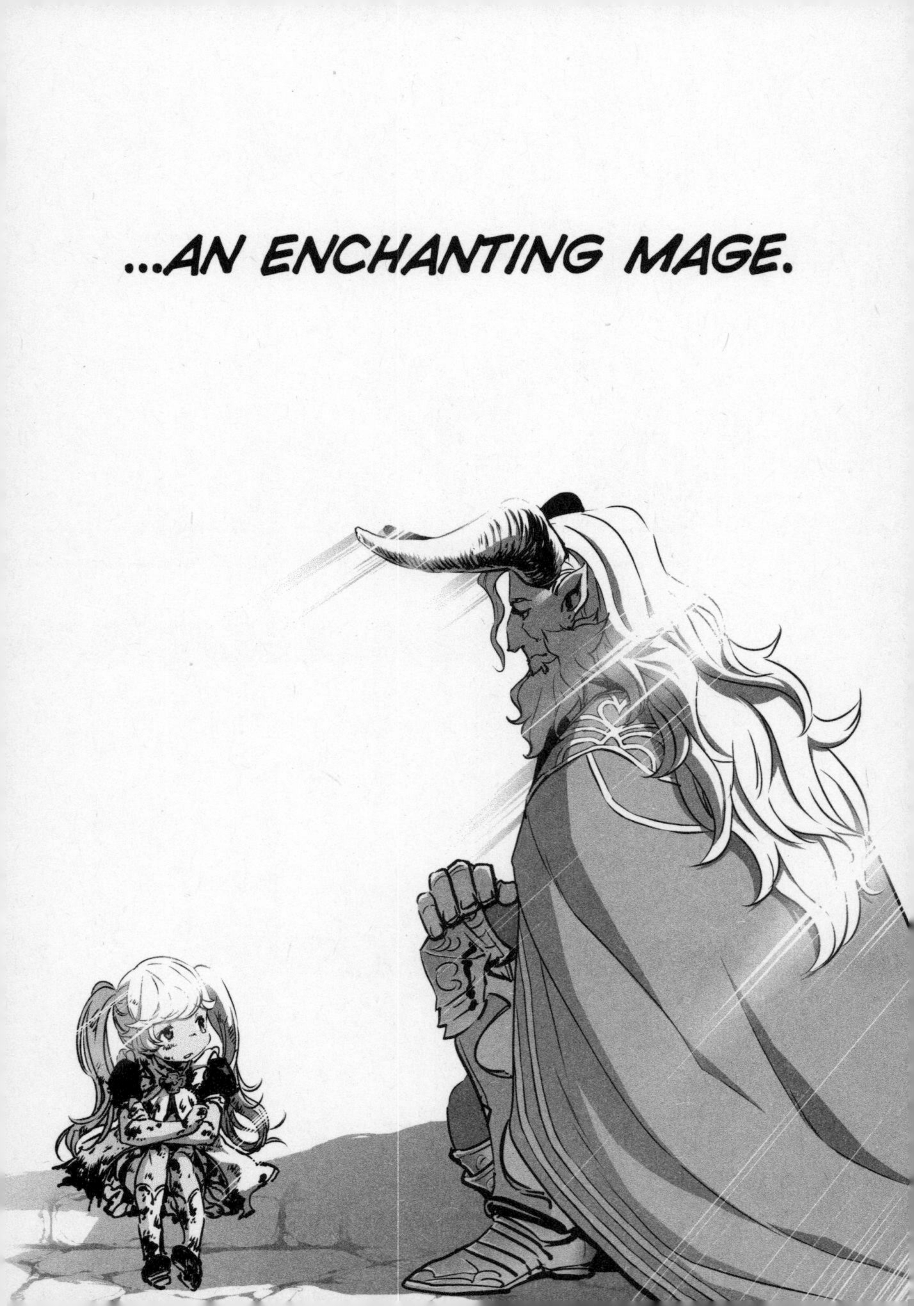
...AN ENCHANTING MAGE.

GRANBLUE FANTASY
グランブルーファンタジー

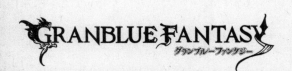

GRANBLUE FANTASY
グランブルーファンタジー

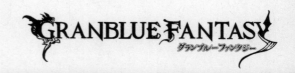

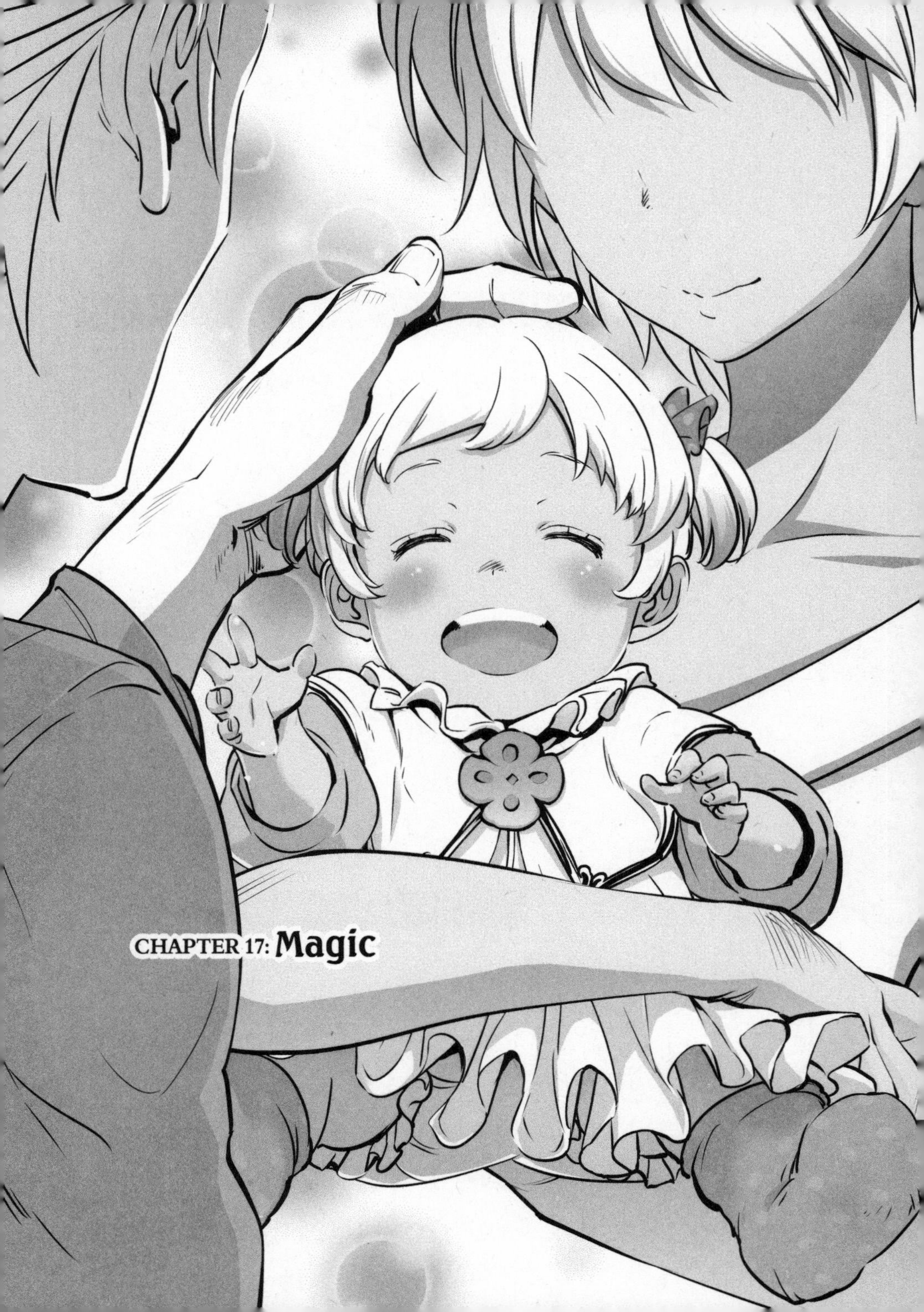

CHAPTER 17: Magic

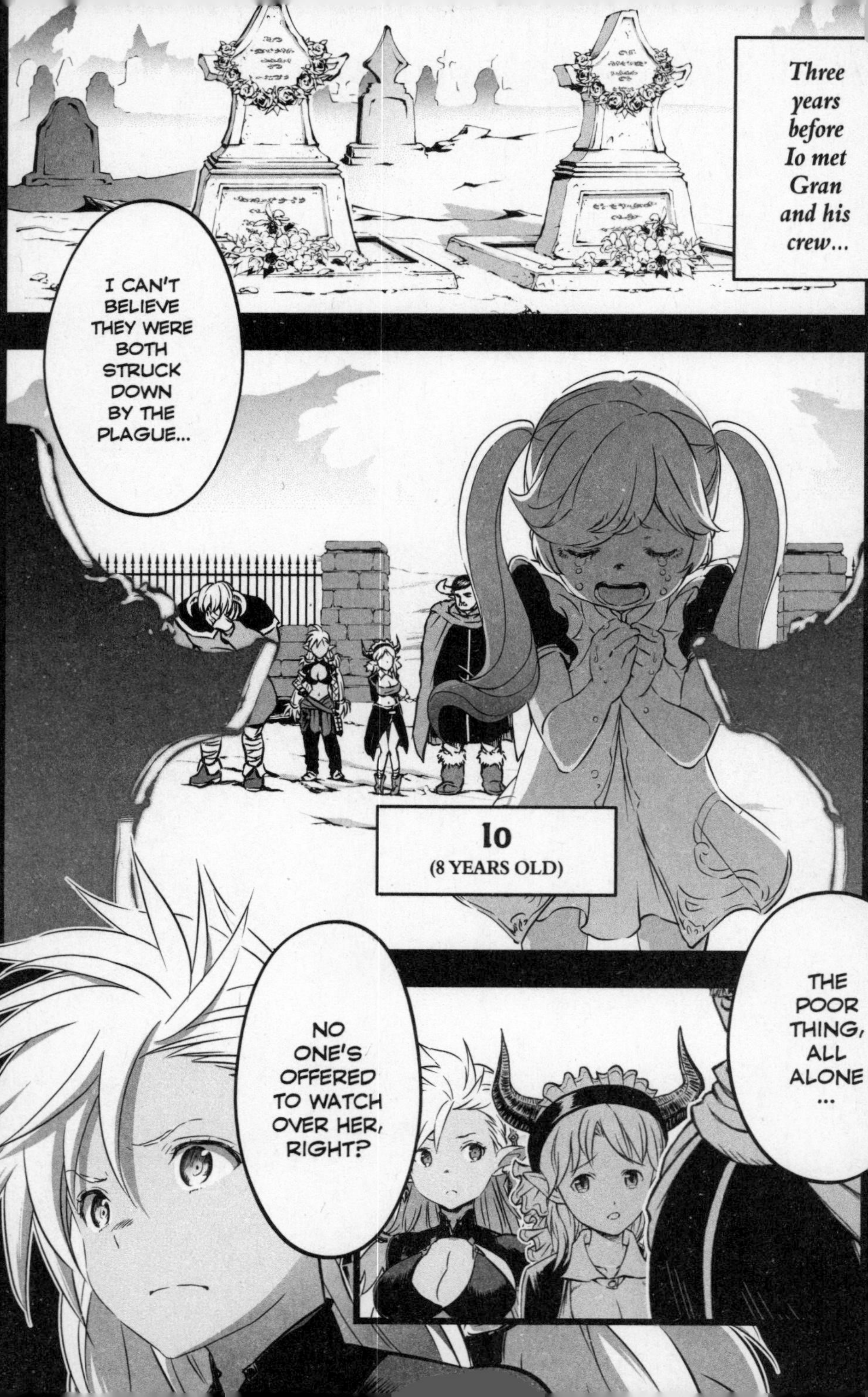
Three years before Io met Gran and his crew...
I CAN'T BELIEVE THEY WERE BOTH STRUCK DOWN BY THE PLAGUE...
Io (8 YEARS OLD)
THE POOR THING, ALL ALONE ...
NO ONE'S OFFERED TO WATCH OVER HER, RIGHT?

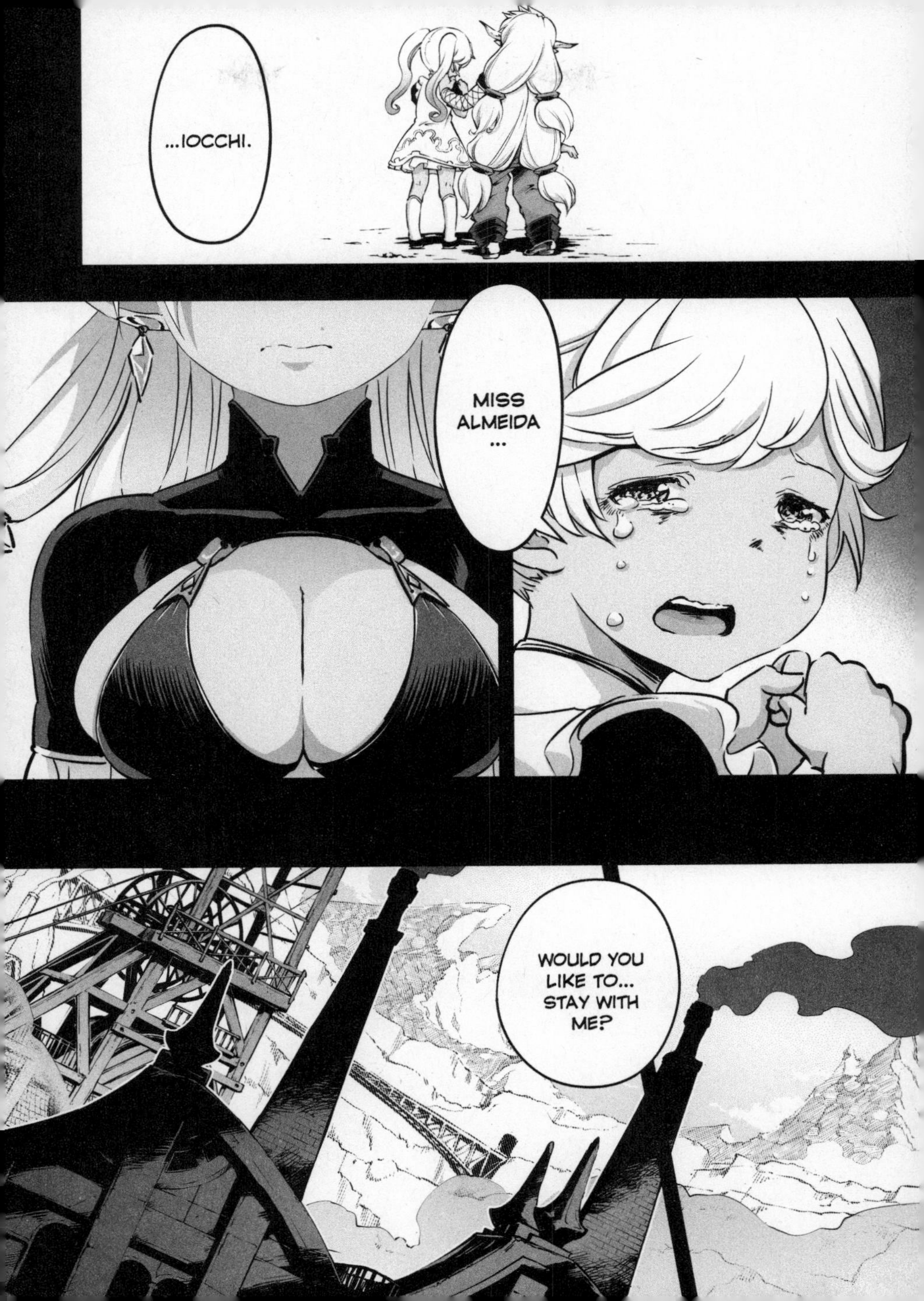
...IOCCHI.
MISS ALMEIDA ...
WOULD YOU LIKE TO... STAY WITH ME?

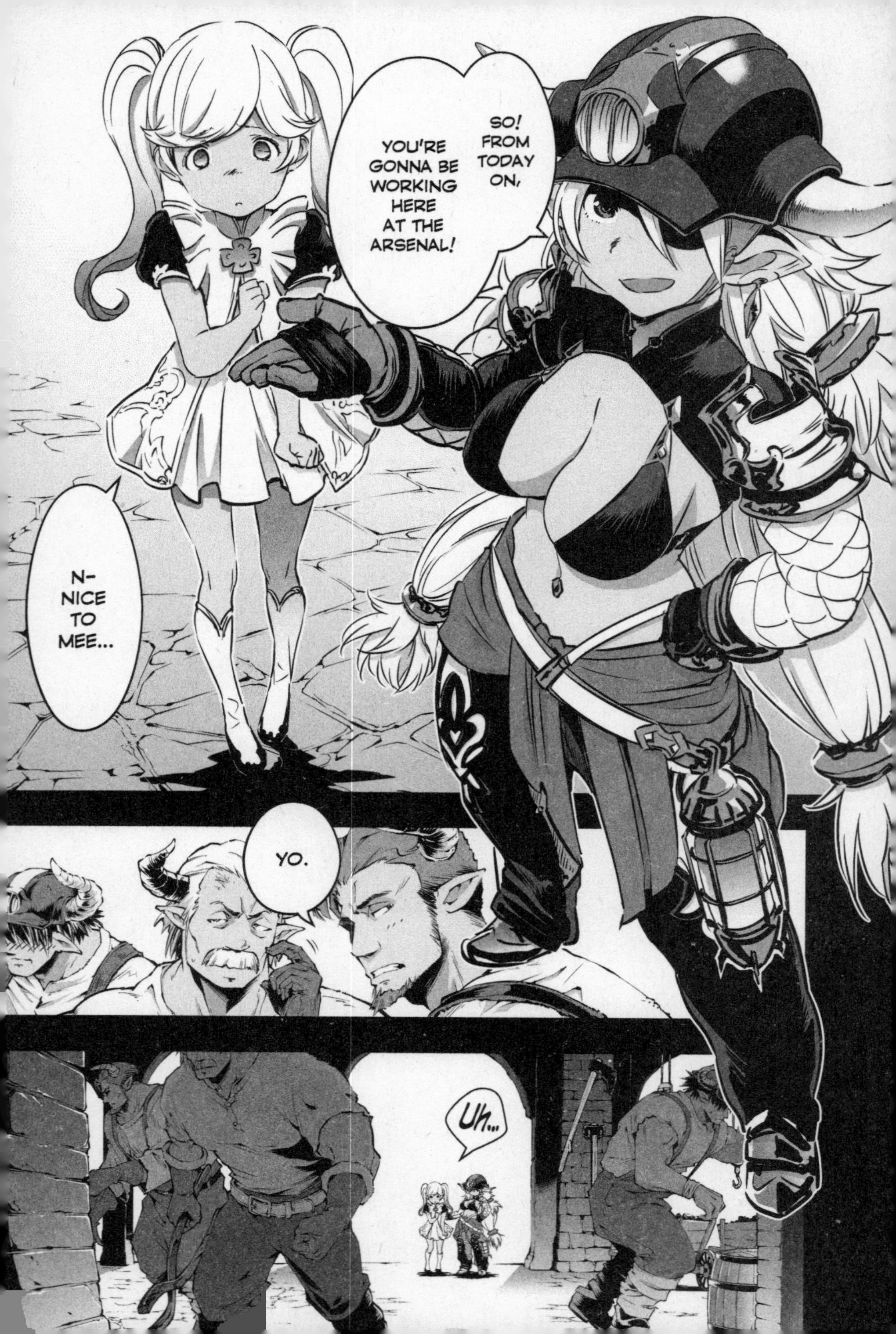
SO! FROM TODAY ON,
YOU'RE GONNA BE WORKING HERE AT THE ARSENAL!
N-NICE TO MEE...
YO.
Uh...

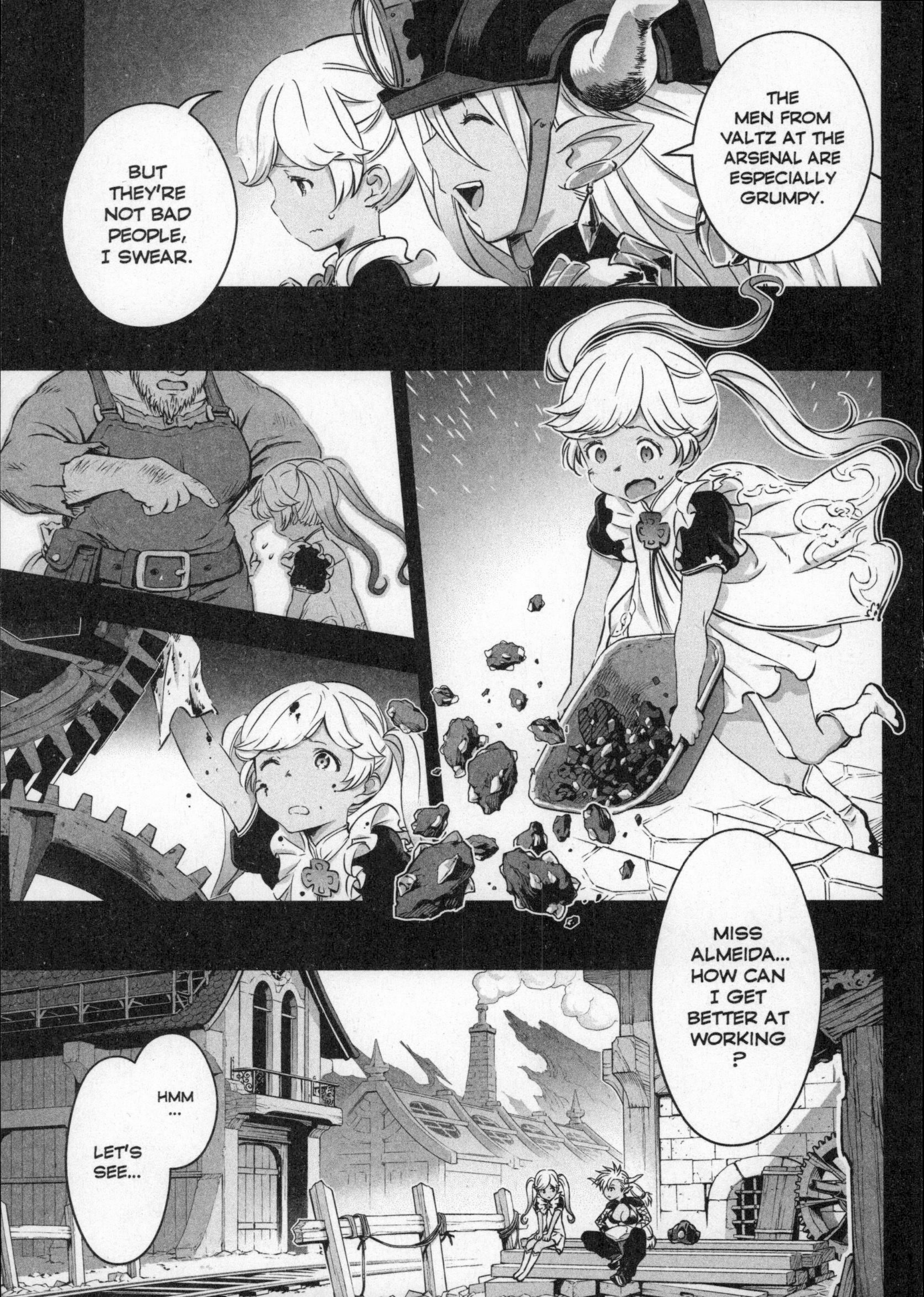
THE MEN FROM VALTZ AT THE ARSENAL ARE ESPECIALLY GRUMPY.
BUT THEY'RE NOT BAD PEOPLE, I SWEAR.
MISS ALMEIDA... HOW CAN I GET BETTER AT WORKING ?
HMM ...
LET'S SEE...

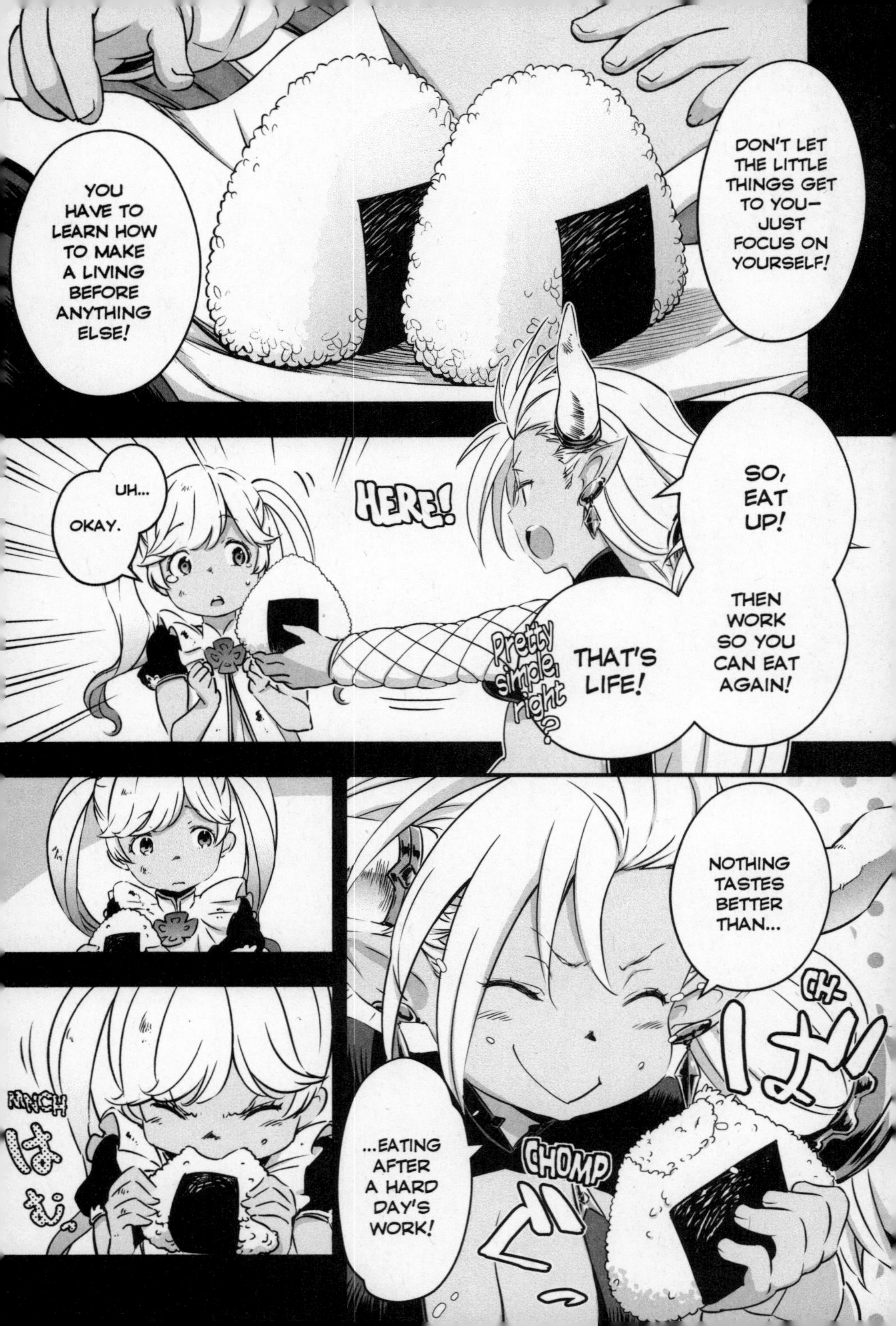
DON'T LET THE LITTLE THINGS GET TO YOU—JUST FOCUS ON YOURSELF!
YOU HAVE TO LEARN HOW TO MAKE A LIVING BEFORE ANYTHING ELSE!
SO, EAT UP!
HERE!
THEN WORK SO YOU CAN EAT AGAIN!
THAT'S LIFE!
Pretty simple, right?
UH... OKAY.
NOTHING TASTES BETTER THAN...
CH
はっ!!
...EATING AFTER A HARD DAY'S WORK!
CHOMP
MNCH
はむ

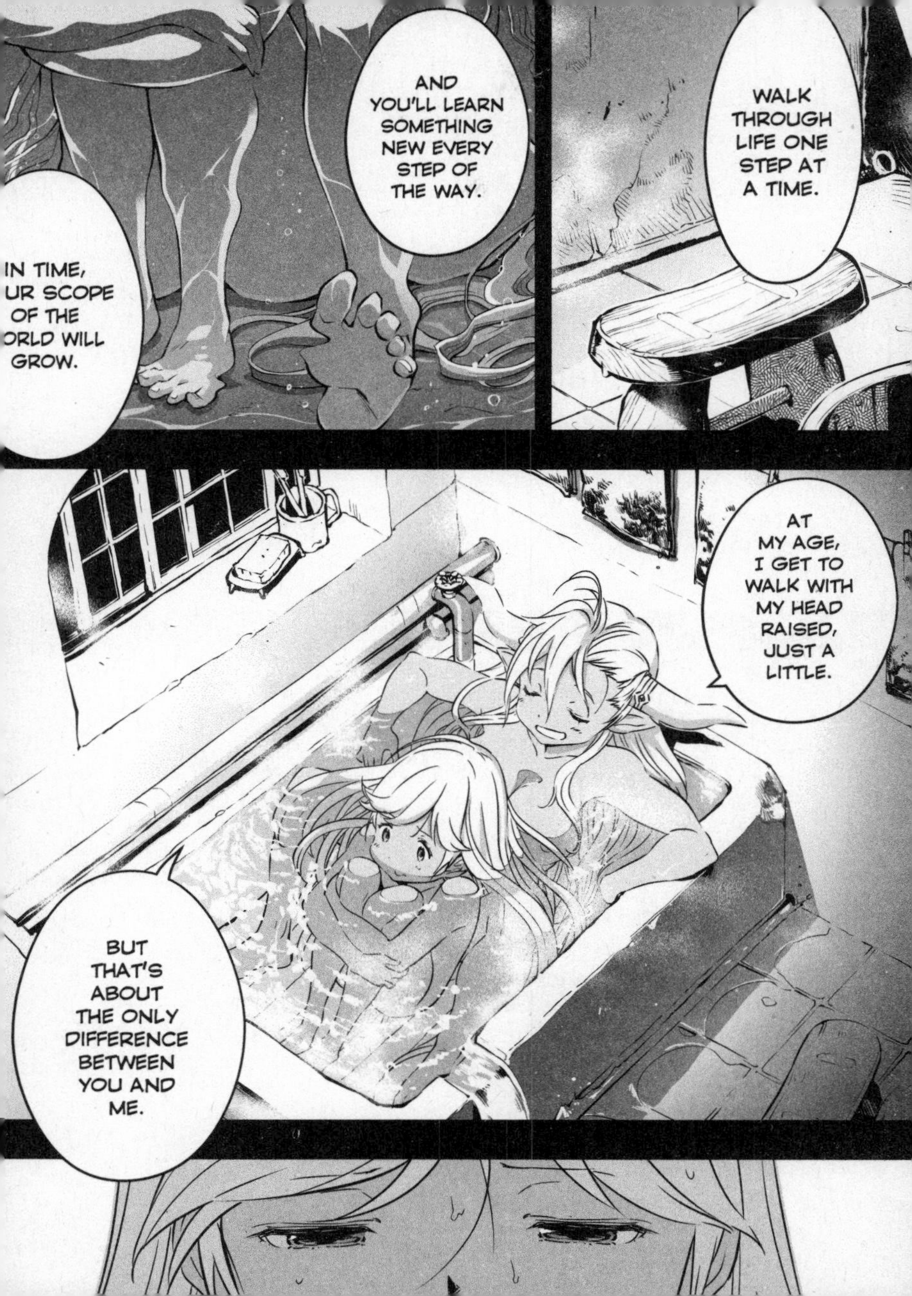
WALK THROUGH LIFE ONE STEP AT A TIME.
AND YOU'LL LEARN SOMETHING NEW EVERY STEP OF THE WAY.
IN TIME, UR SCOPE OF THE ORLD WILL GROW.
AT MY AGE, I GET TO WALK WITH MY HEAD RAISED, JUST A LITTLE.
BUT THAT'S ABOUT THE ONLY DIFFERENCE BETWEEN YOU AND ME.

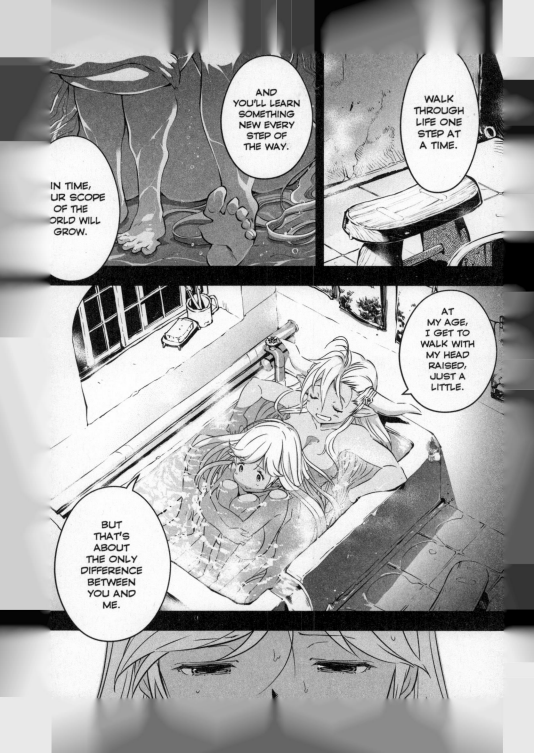

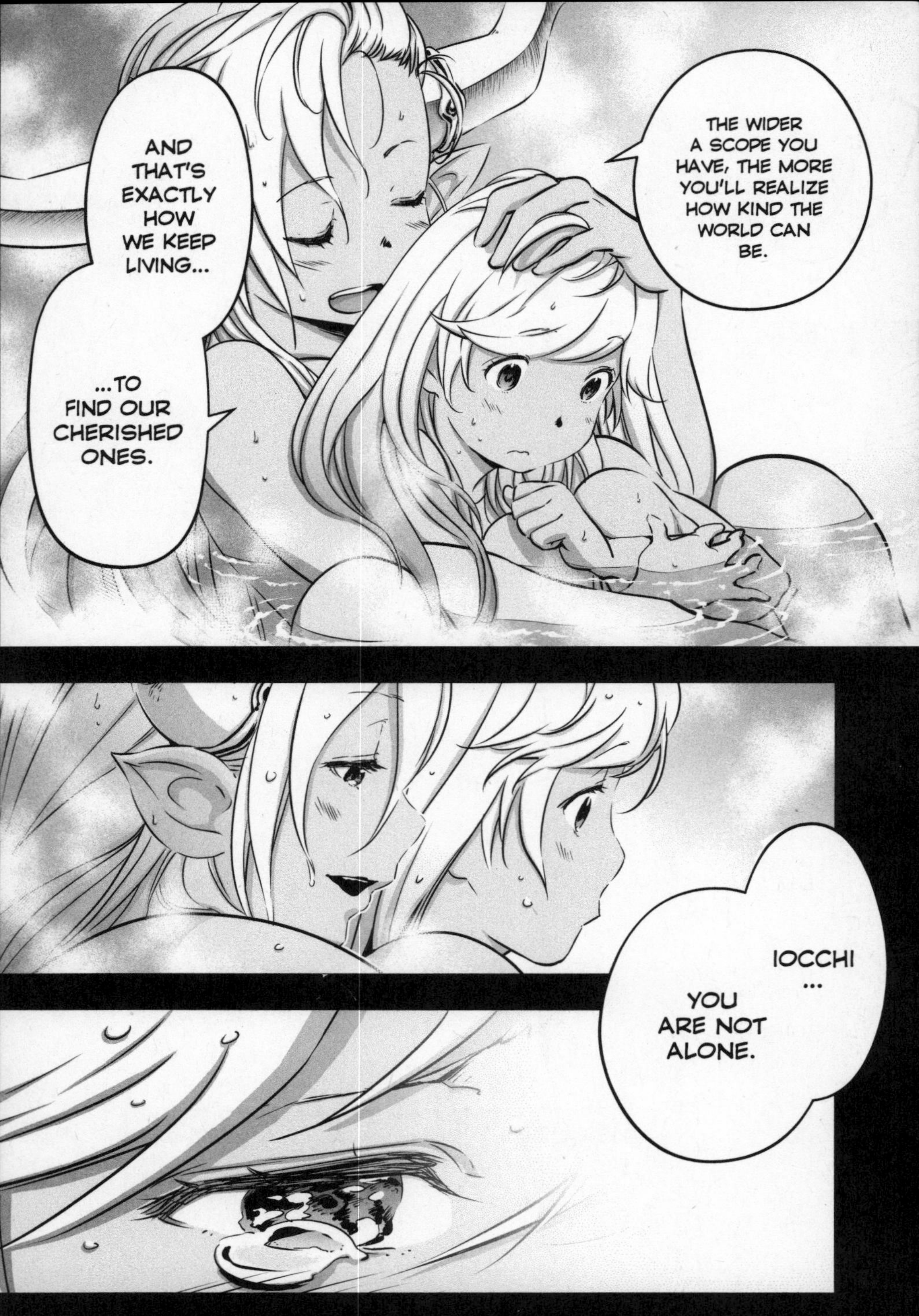
THE WIDER A SCOPE YOU HAVE, THE MORE YOU'LL REALIZE HOW KIND THE WORLD CAN BE.
AND THAT'S EXACTLY HOW WE KEEP LIVING...
...TO FIND OUR CHERISHED ONES.
IOCCHI ...
YOU ARE NOT ALONE.

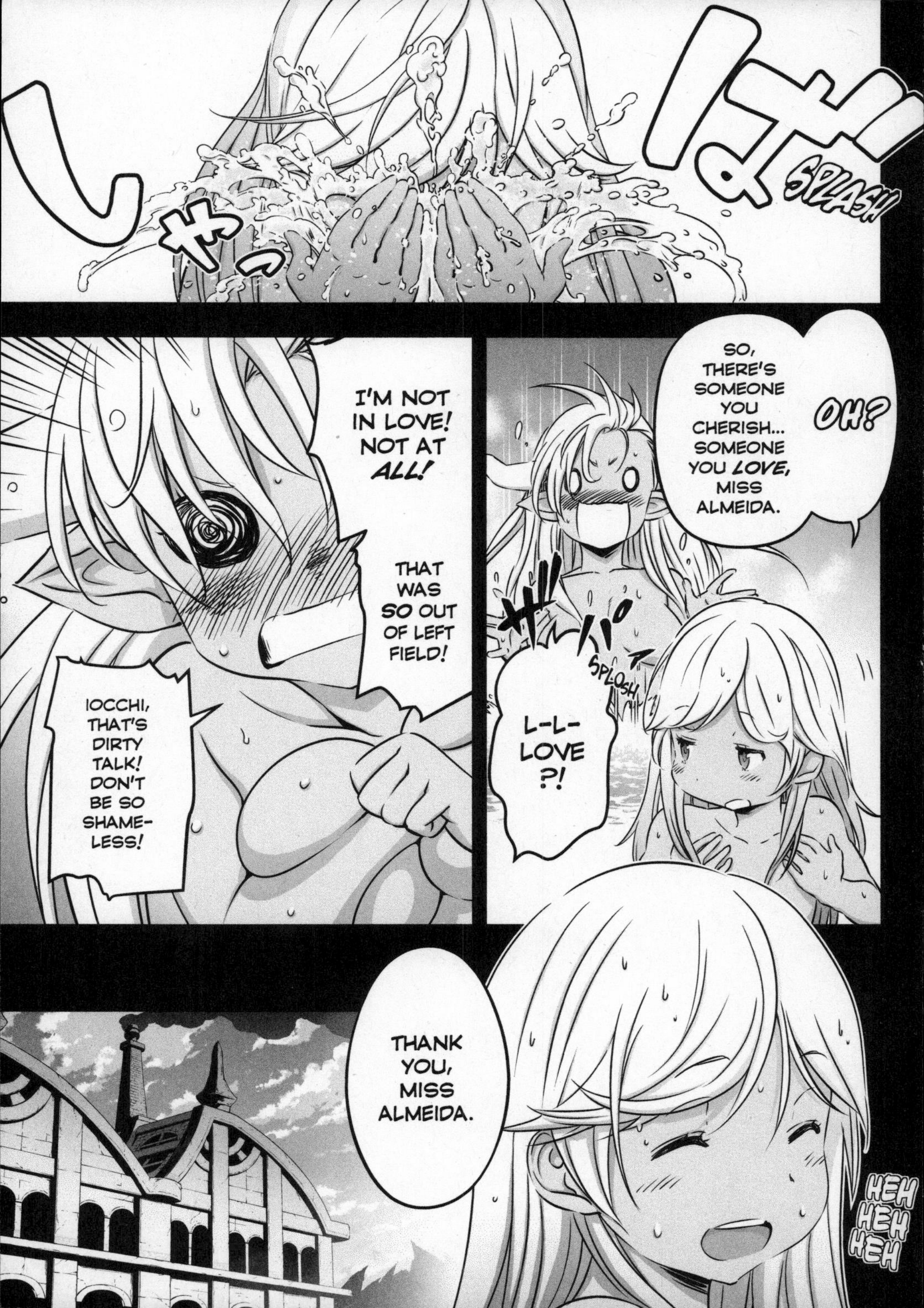
SPLASH
OH?
SO, THERE'S SOMEONE YOU CHERISH... SOMEONE YOU *LOVE*, MISS ALMEIDA.
SPLASH
L-L-LOVE?!
I'M NOT IN LOVE! NOT AT *ALL!*
THAT WAS SO OUT OF LEFT FIELD!
IOCCHI, THAT'S DIRTY TALK! DON'T BE SO SHAME-LESS!
HEH HEH HEH
THANK YOU, MISS ALMEIDA.

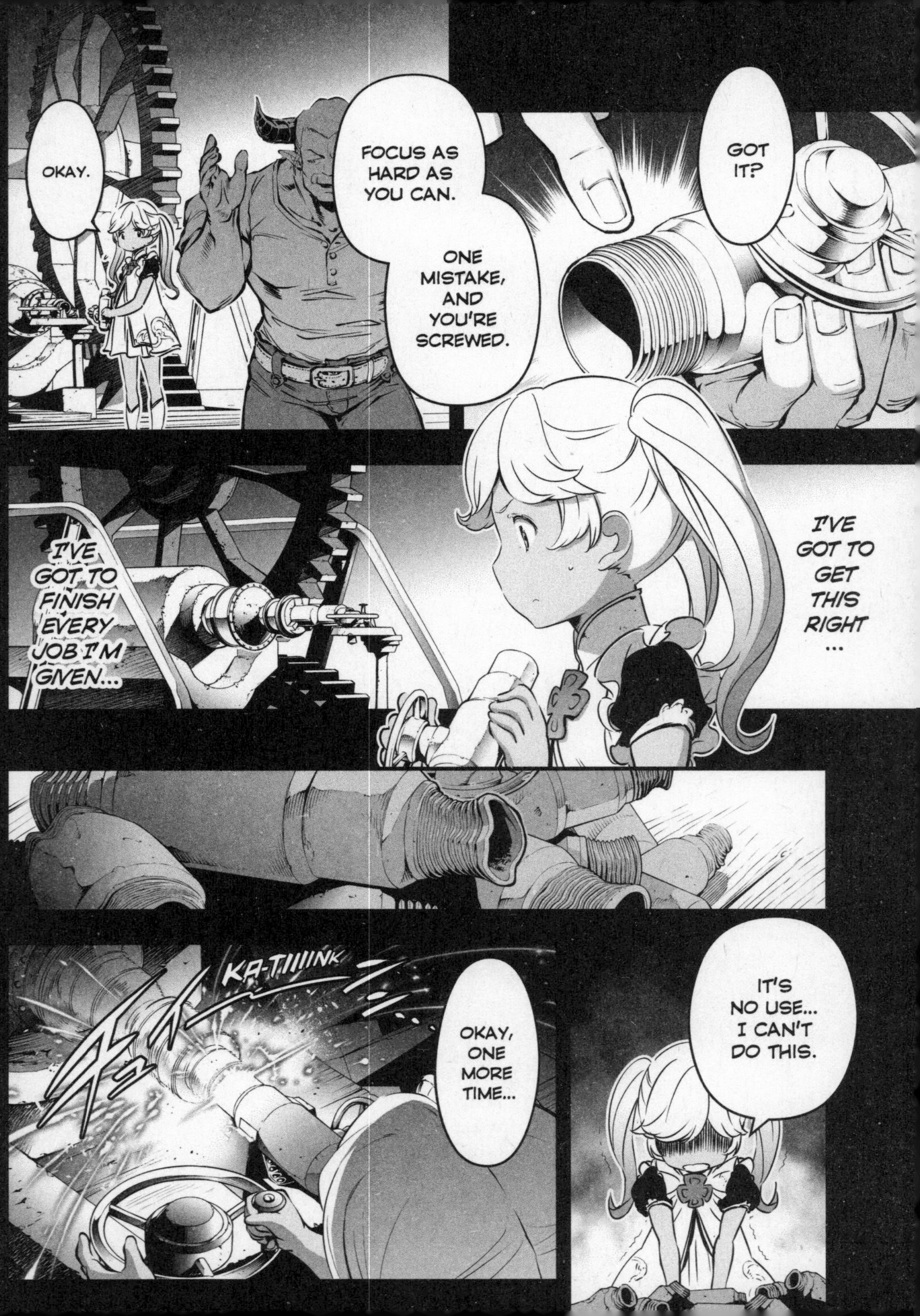
FOCUS AS HARD AS YOU CAN.
ONE MISTAKE, AND YOU'RE SCREWED.
GOT IT?
OKAY.
I'VE GOT TO GET THIS RIGHT...
I'VE GOT TO FINISH EVERY JOB I'M GIVEN...
IT'S NO USE... I CAN'T DO THIS.
OKAY, ONE MORE TIME...
KA-TIIIINK

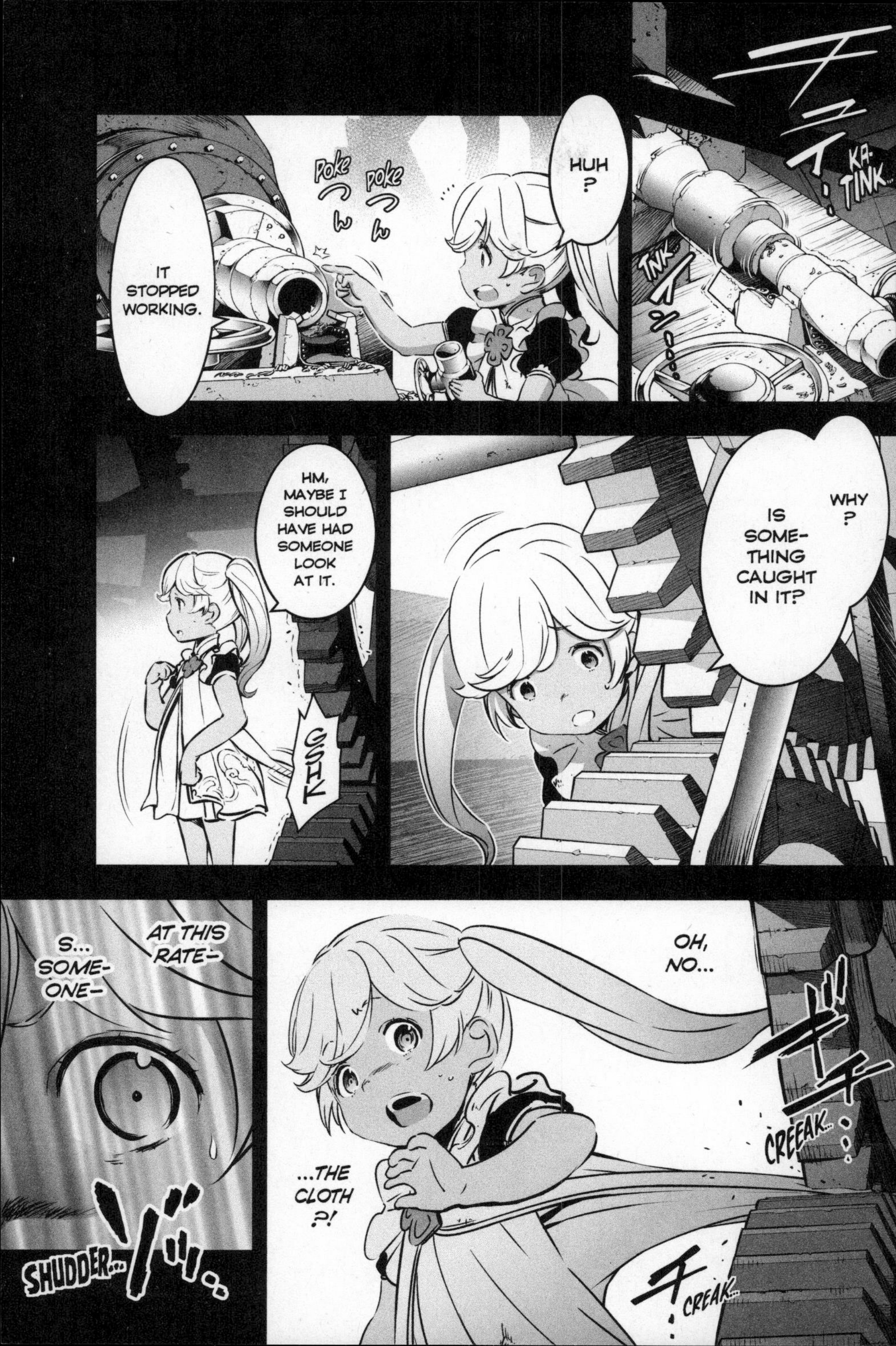
KA-TINK...
TNK
HUH ?
Poke poke
IT STOPPED WORKING.
WHY ?
IS SOME-THING CAUGHT IN IT?
HM, MAYBE I SHOULD HAVE HAD SOMEONE LOOK AT IT.
GSHK
OH, NO...
CREEAK...
...THE CLOTH ?!
CREAK...
AT THIS RATE-
S... SOME-ONE-
SHUDDER...

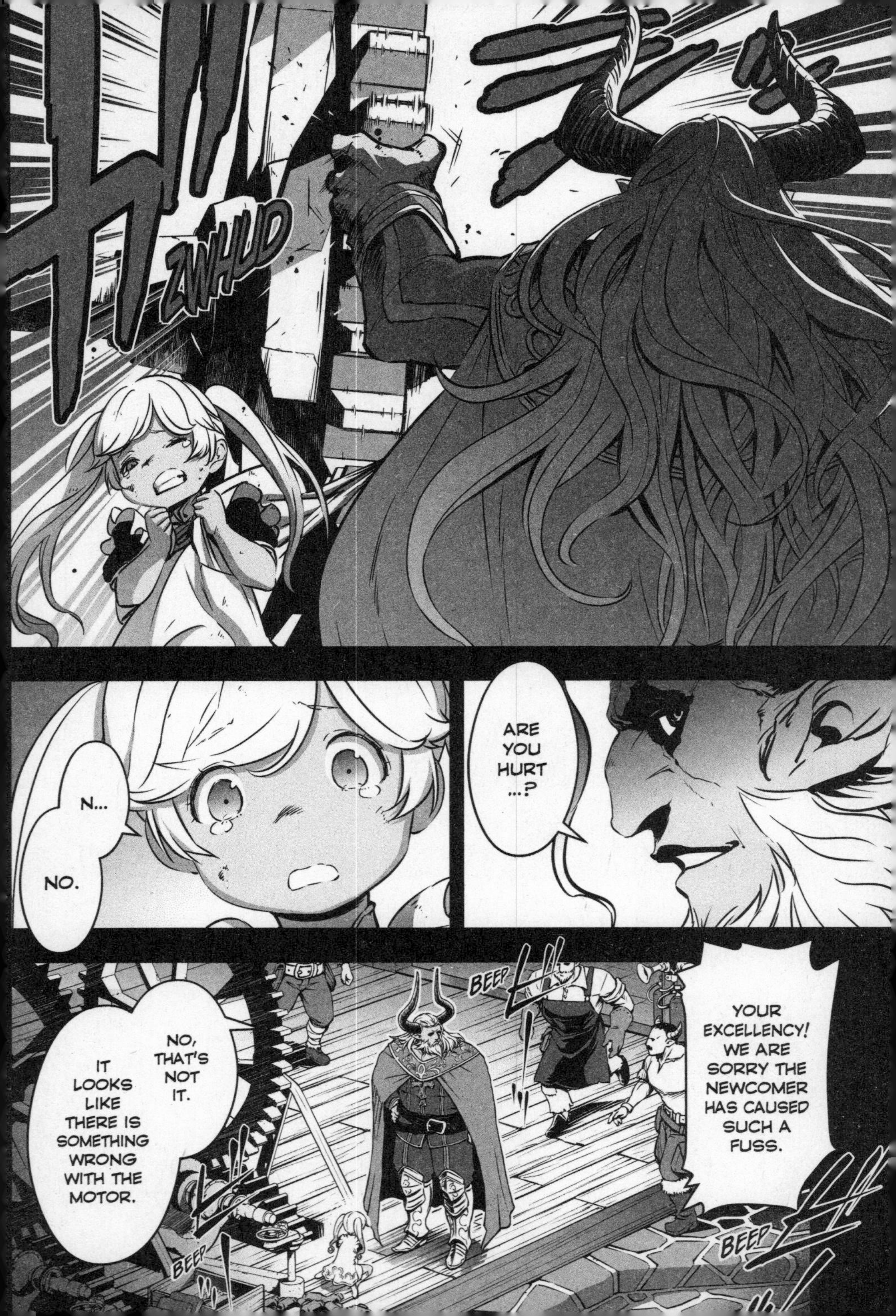
ZWHUD
ARE YOU HURT ...?
N...
NO.
YOUR EXCELLENCY! WE ARE SORRY THE NEWCOMER HAS CAUSED SUCH A FUSS.
BEEP
BEEP
NO, THAT'S NOT IT.
IT LOOKS LIKE THERE IS SOMETHING WRONG WITH THE MOTOR.
BEEP

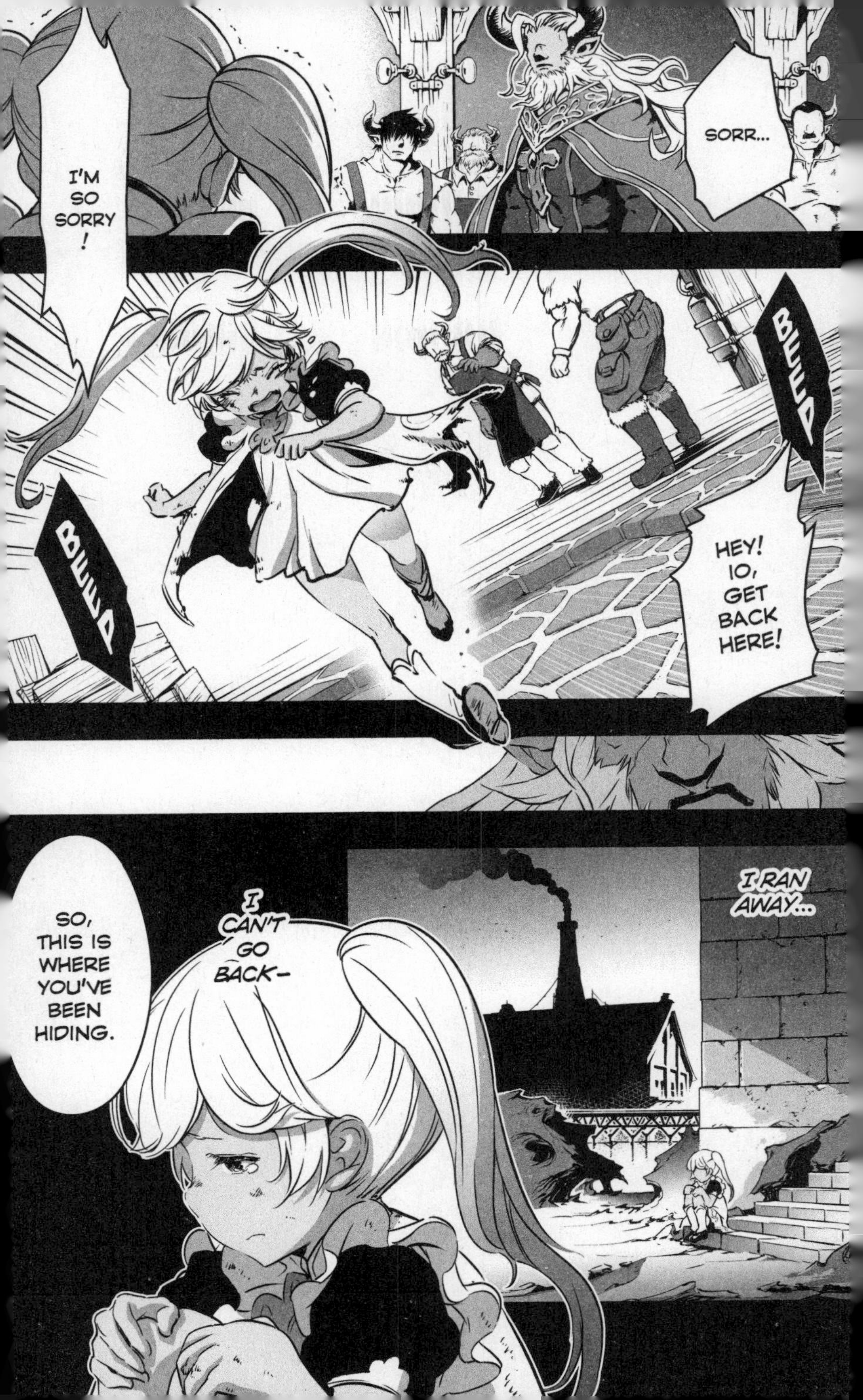
SORR...
I'M SO SORRY!
HEY! IO, GET BACK HERE!
I RAN AWAY...
I CAN'T GO BACK-
SO, THIS IS WHERE YOU'VE BEEN HIDING.

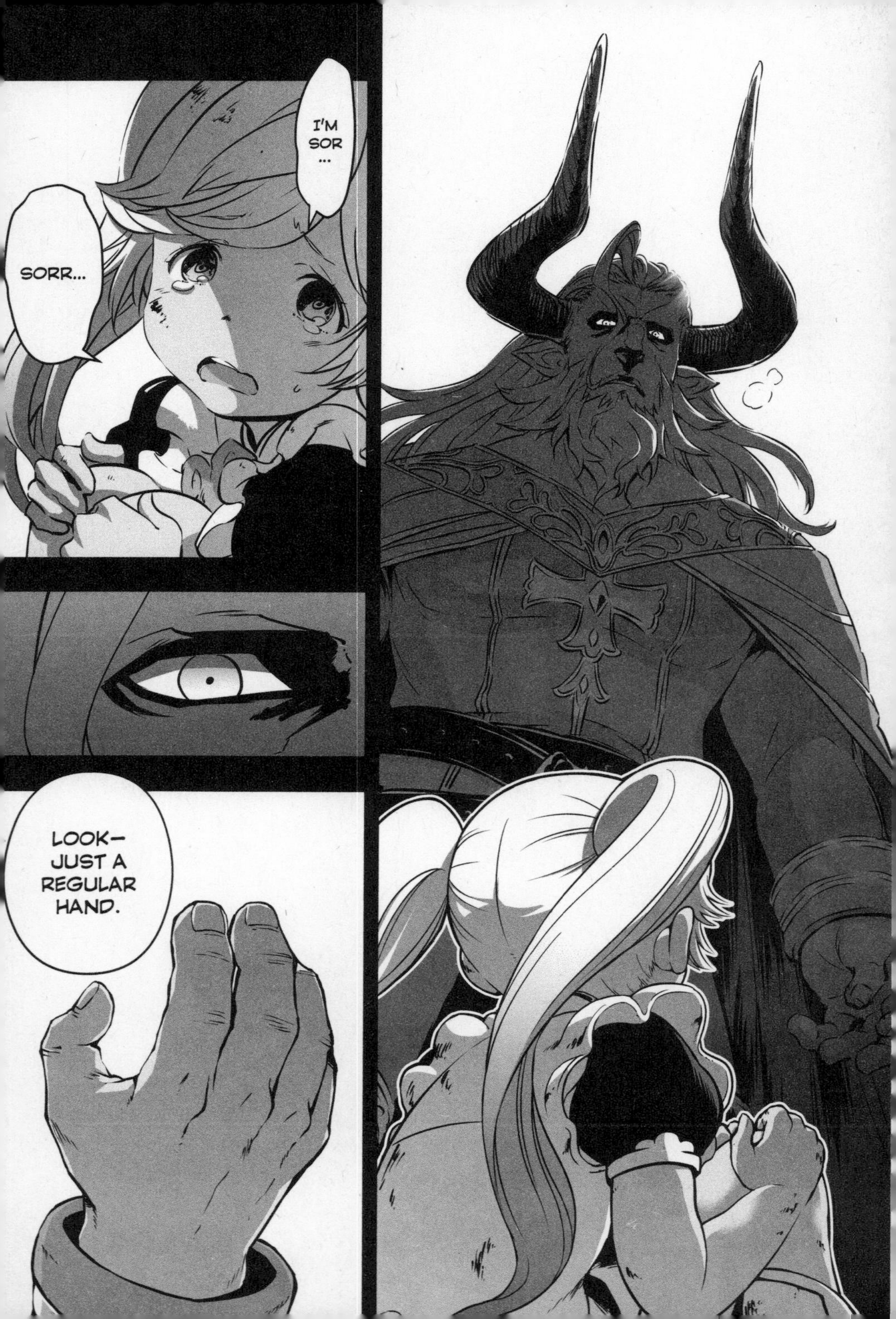
I'M SOR ...
SORR...
LOOK— JUST A REGULAR HAND.

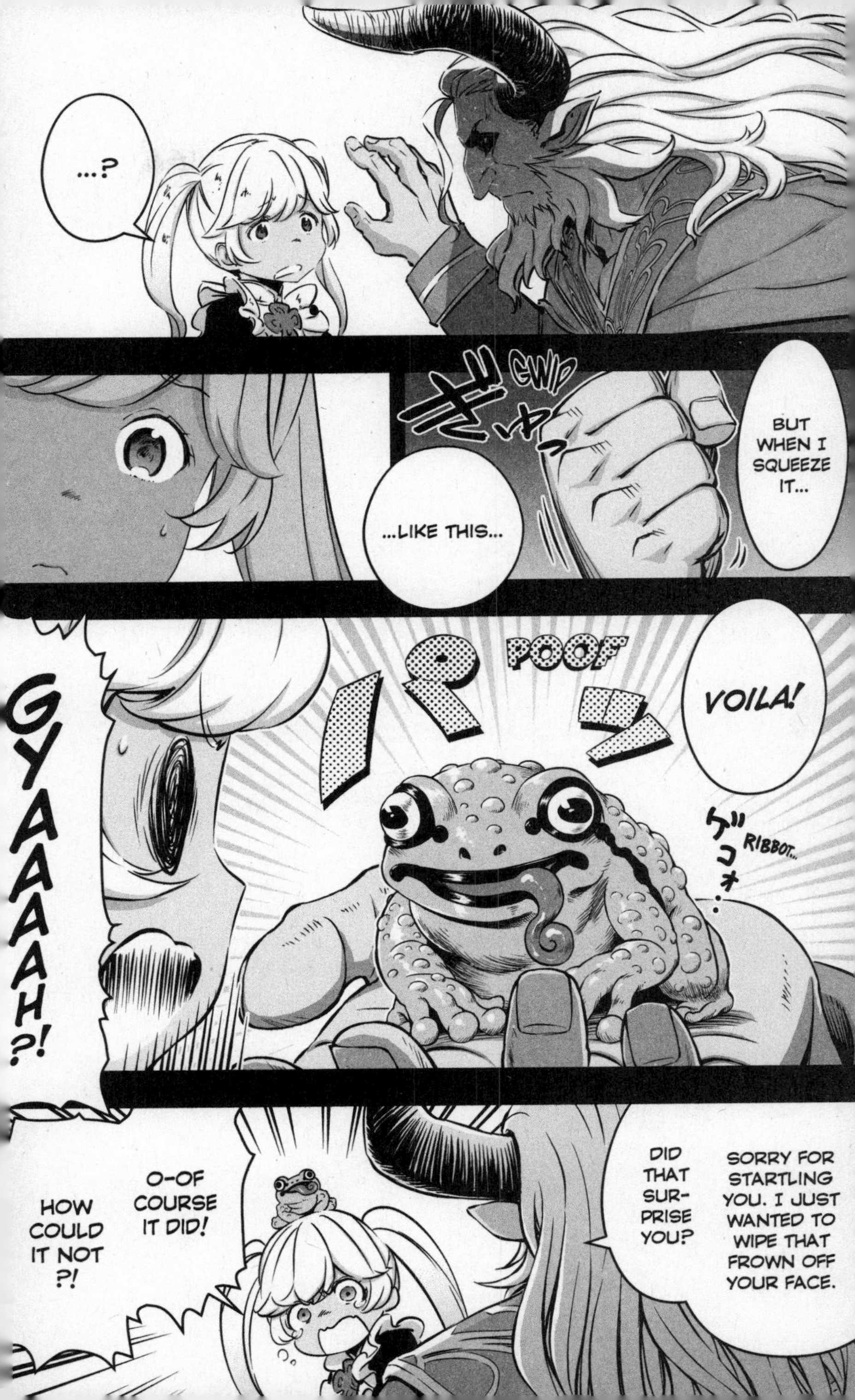
...?
ぎゅっ
GWID
BUT WHEN I SQUEEZE IT...
...LIKE THIS...
パッ
POOF
VOILA!
ゲコォ...
RIBBOT...
GYAAAAAH?!
SORRY FOR STARTLING YOU. I JUST WANTED TO WIPE THAT FROWN OFF YOUR FACE.
DID THAT SUR-PRISE YOU?
O-OF COURSE IT DID!
HOW COULD IT NOT?!

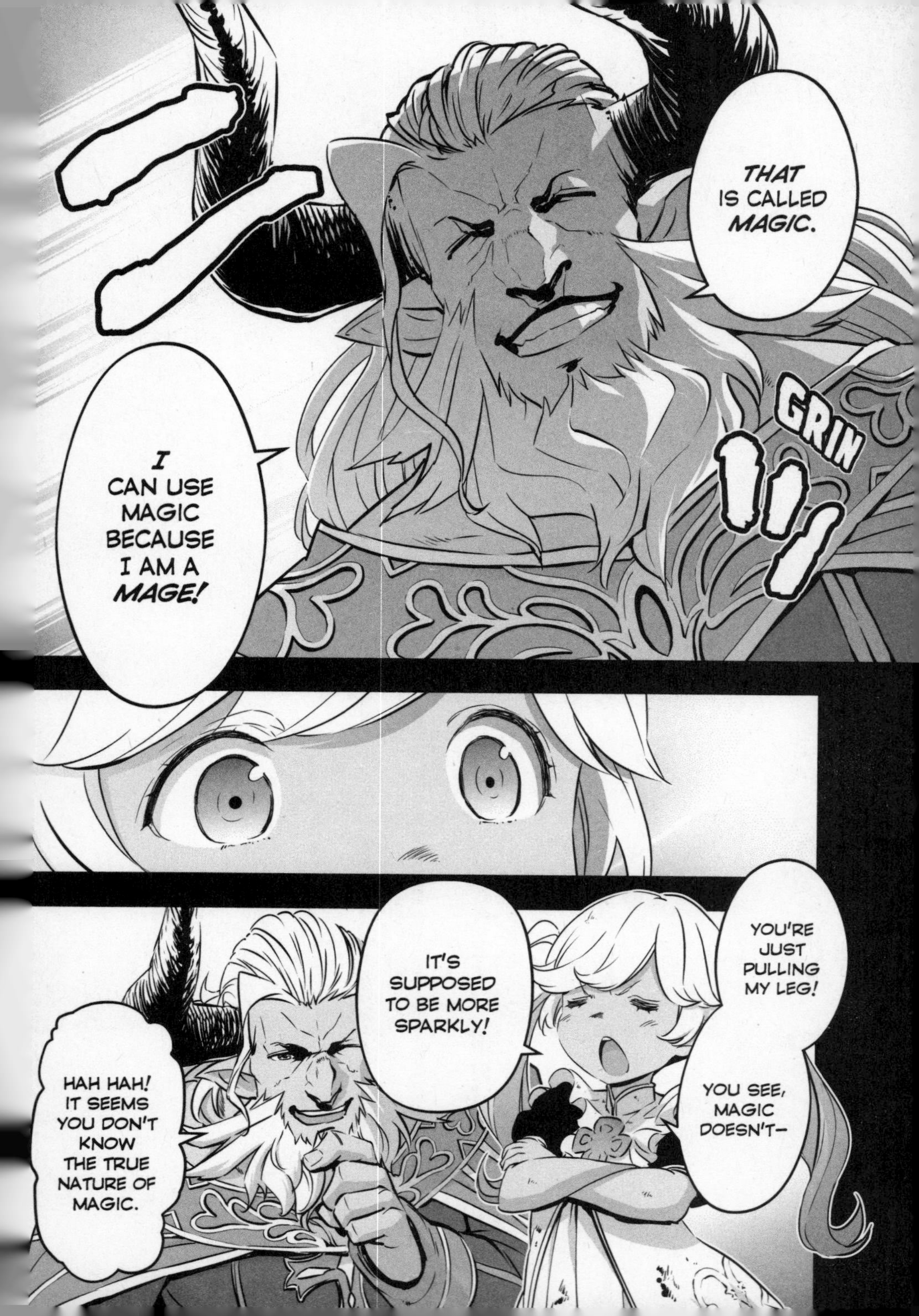

THAT IS CALLED MAGIC.
GRIN
I CAN USE MAGIC BECAUSE I AM A MAGE!
YOU'RE JUST PULLING MY LEG!
IT'S SUPPOSED TO BE MORE SPARKLY!
YOU SEE, MAGIC DOESN'T—
HAH HAH! IT SEEMS YOU DON'T KNOW THE TRUE NATURE OF MAGIC.

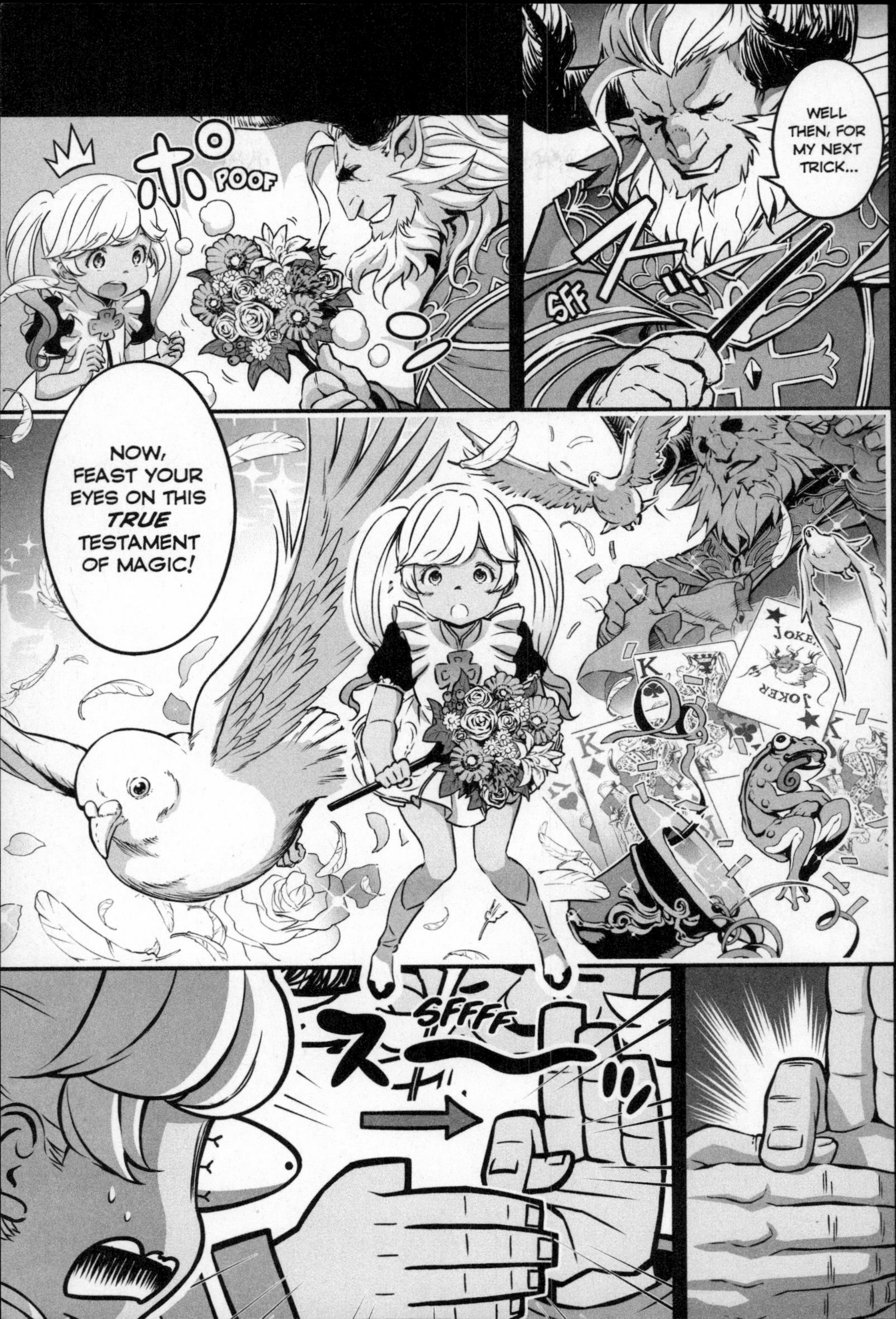
WELL THEN, FOR MY NEXT TRICK...
SFF
POOF
NOW, FEAST YOUR EYES ON THIS *TRUE* TESTAMENT OF MAGIC!
JOKER
SFFFF

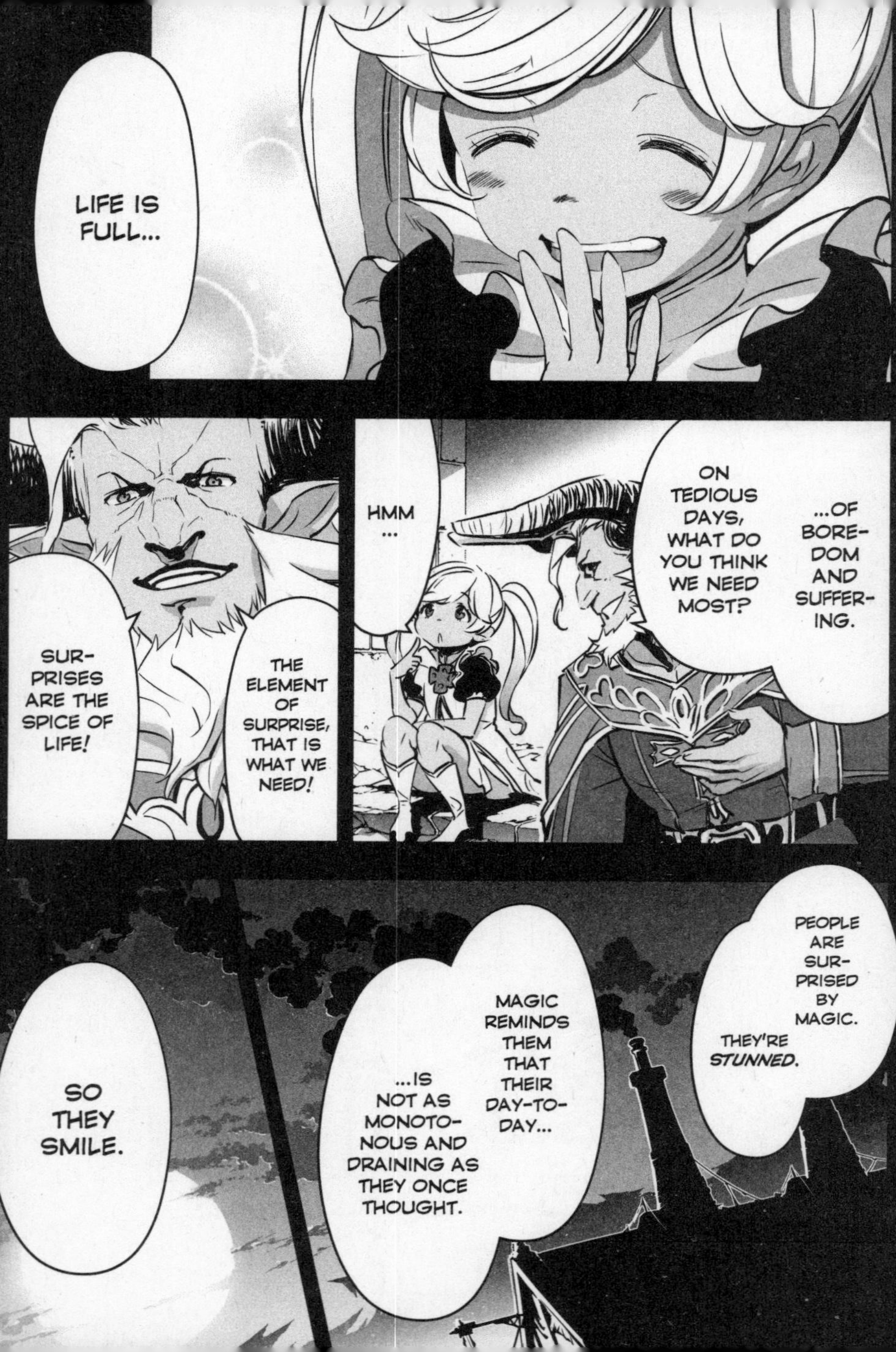

LIFE IS FULL...
...OF BORE-DOM AND SUFFER-ING.
ON TEDIOUS DAYS, WHAT DO YOU THINK WE NEED MOST?
HMM ...
THE ELEMENT OF SURPRISE, THAT IS WHAT WE NEED!
SUR-PRISES ARE THE SPICE OF LIFE!
PEOPLE ARE SUR-PRISED BY MAGIC.
THEY'RE *STUNNED*.
MAGIC REMINDS THEM THAT THEIR DAY-TO-DAY...
...IS NOT AS MONOTO-NOUS AND DRAINING AS THEY ONCE THOUGHT.
SO THEY SMILE.

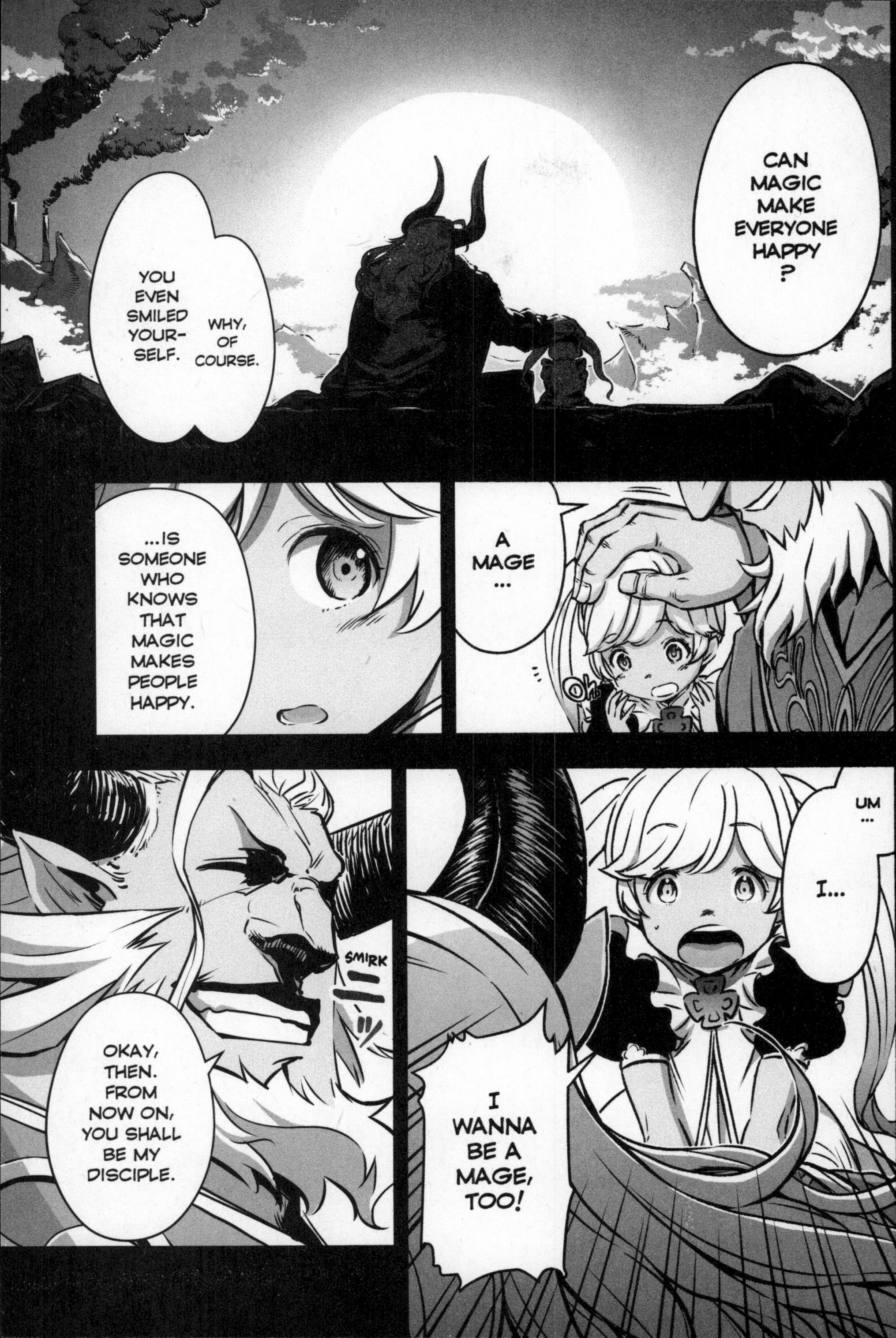
CAN MAGIC MAKE EVERYONE HAPPY?
WHY, OF COURSE.
YOU EVEN SMILED YOURSELF.
A MAGE...
...IS SOMEONE WHO KNOWS THAT MAGIC MAKES PEOPLE HAPPY.
UM...
I...
I WANNA BE A MAGE, TOO!
SMIRK
OKAY, THEN. FROM NOW ON, YOU SHALL BE MY DISCIPLE.

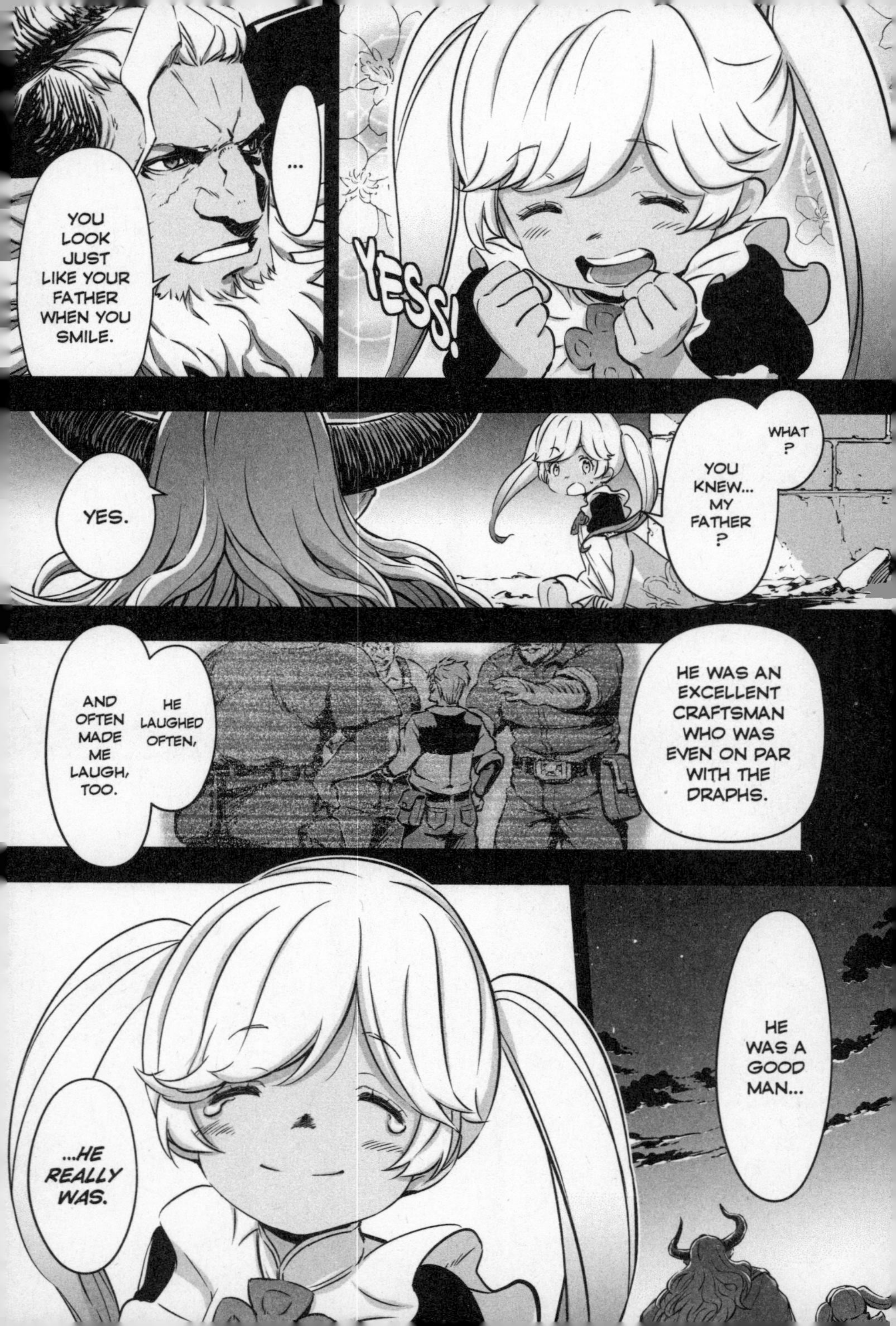
YESS!
...
YOU LOOK JUST LIKE YOUR FATHER WHEN YOU SMILE.
WHAT?
YOU KNEW... MY FATHER?
YES.
HE WAS AN EXCELLENT CRAFTSMAN WHO WAS EVEN ON PAR WITH THE DRAPHS.
HE LAUGHED OFTEN,
AND OFTEN MADE ME LAUGH, TOO.
HE WAS A GOOD MAN...
...HE REALLY WAS.

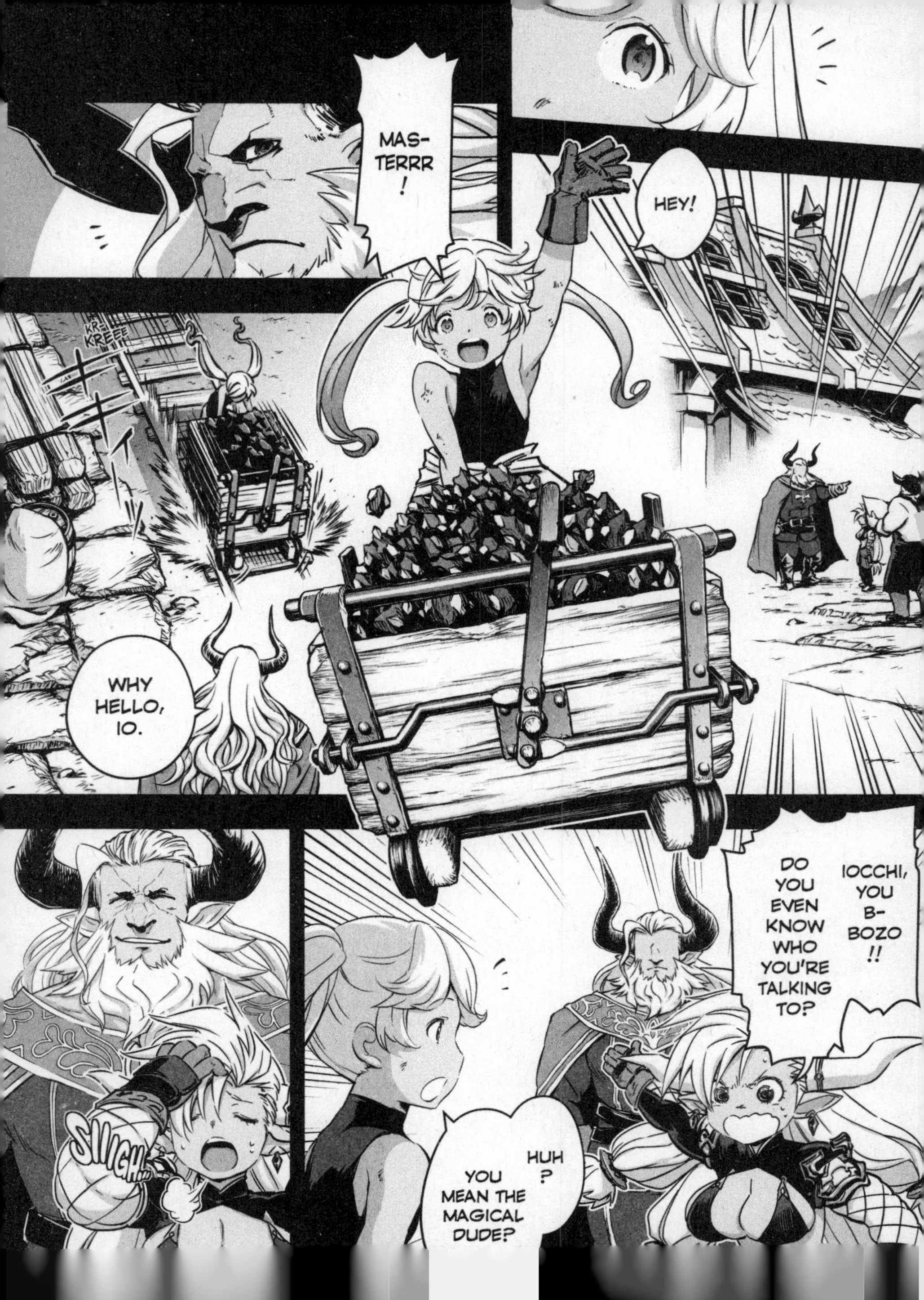
MAS-TERRR!
HEY!
KR-KREEE
WHY HELLO, IO.
IOCCHI, YOU B-BOZO!!
DO YOU EVEN KNOW WHO YOU'RE TALKING TO?
HUH?
YOU MEAN THE MAGICAL DUDE?
SIIGH...

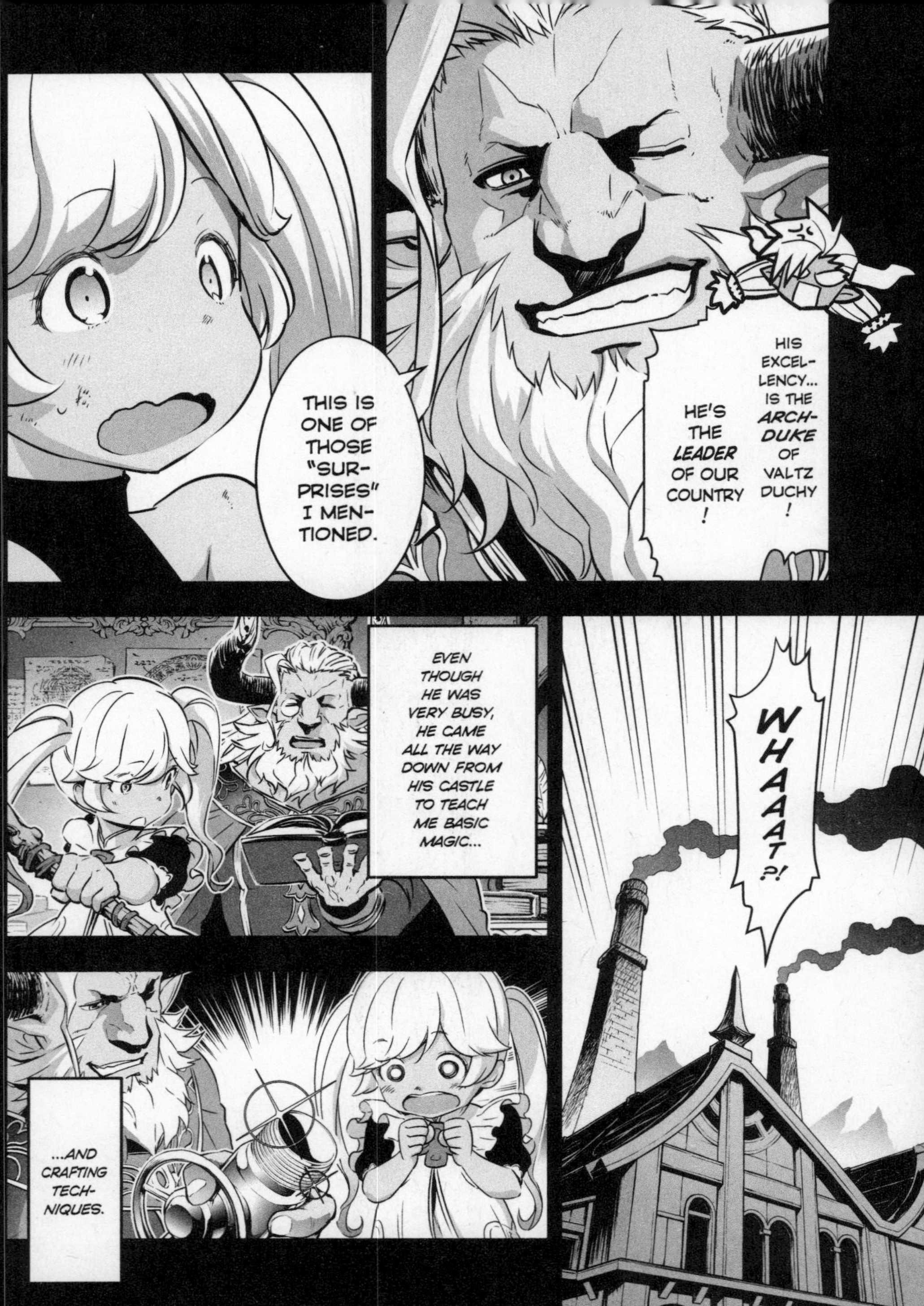
HIS EXCELLENCY... IS THE ARCHDUKE OF VALTZ DUCHY!
HE'S THE LEADER OF OUR COUNTRY!
THIS IS ONE OF THOSE "SURPRISES" I MENTIONED.
WHAAAAT?!
EVEN THOUGH HE WAS VERY BUSY, HE CAME ALL THE WAY DOWN FROM HIS CASTLE TO TEACH ME BASIC MAGIC...
...AND CRAFTING TECHNIQUES.

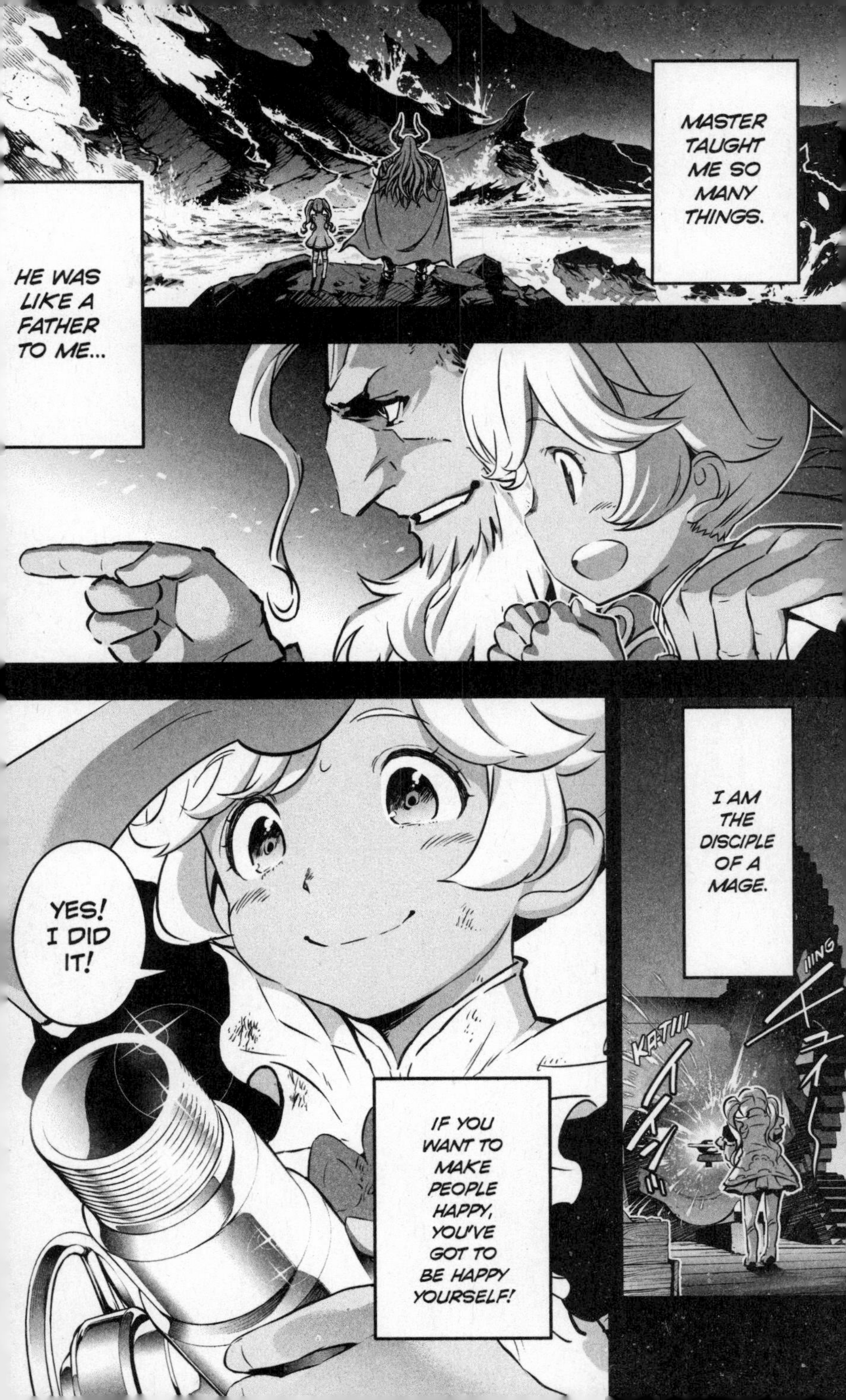
MASTER TAUGHT ME SO MANY THINGS.
HE WAS LIKE A FATHER TO ME...
I AM THE DISCIPLE OF A MAGE.
IIING
KA-TIII
YES! I DID IT!
IF YOU WANT TO MAKE PEOPLE HAPPY, YOU'VE GOT TO BE HAPPY YOURSELF!

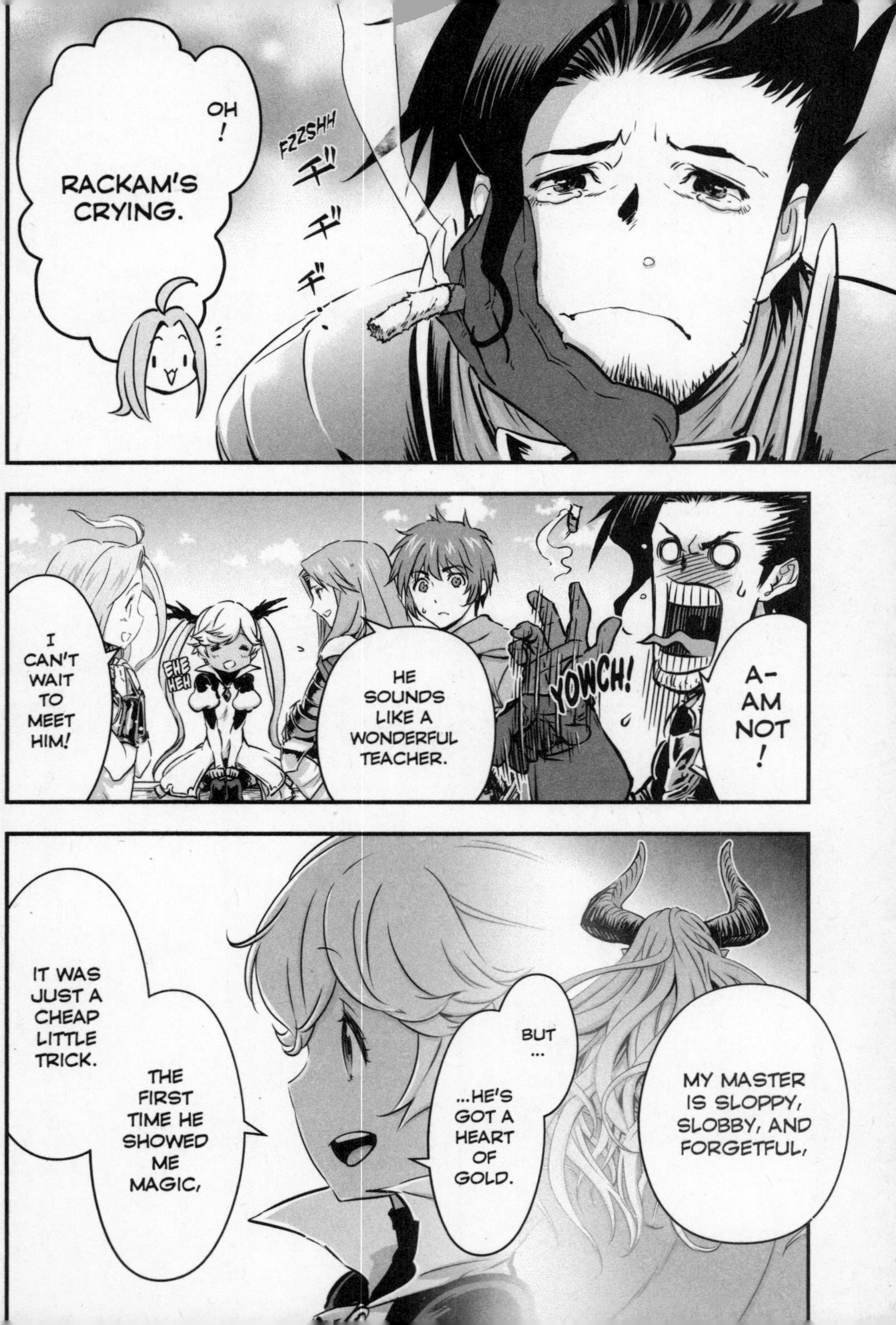
FZZSHH
ギギギ…
OH! RACKAM'S CRYING.
A- AM NOT!
YOWCH!
HE SOUNDS LIKE A WONDERFUL TEACHER.
EHE HEH
I CAN'T WAIT TO MEET HIM!
MY MASTER IS SLOPPY, SLOBBY, AND FORGETFUL,
BUT...
...HE'S GOT A HEART OF GOLD.
THE FIRST TIME HE SHOWED ME MAGIC,
IT WAS JUST A CHEAP LITTLE TRICK.

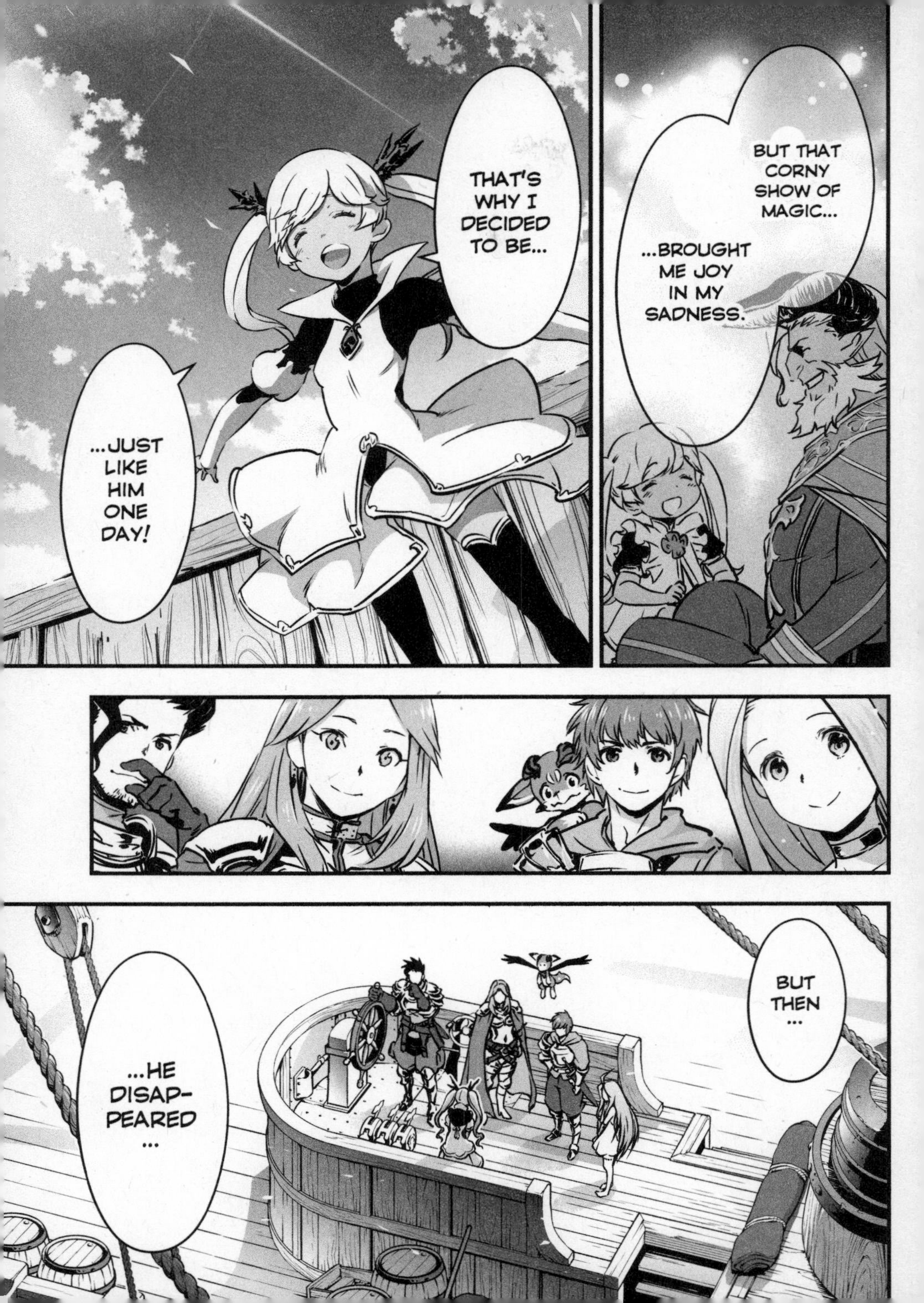
BUT THAT CORNY SHOW OF MAGIC...
...BROUGHT ME JOY IN MY SADNESS.
THAT'S WHY I DECIDED TO BE...
...JUST LIKE HIM ONE DAY!
BUT THEN...
...HE DISAP-PEARED...

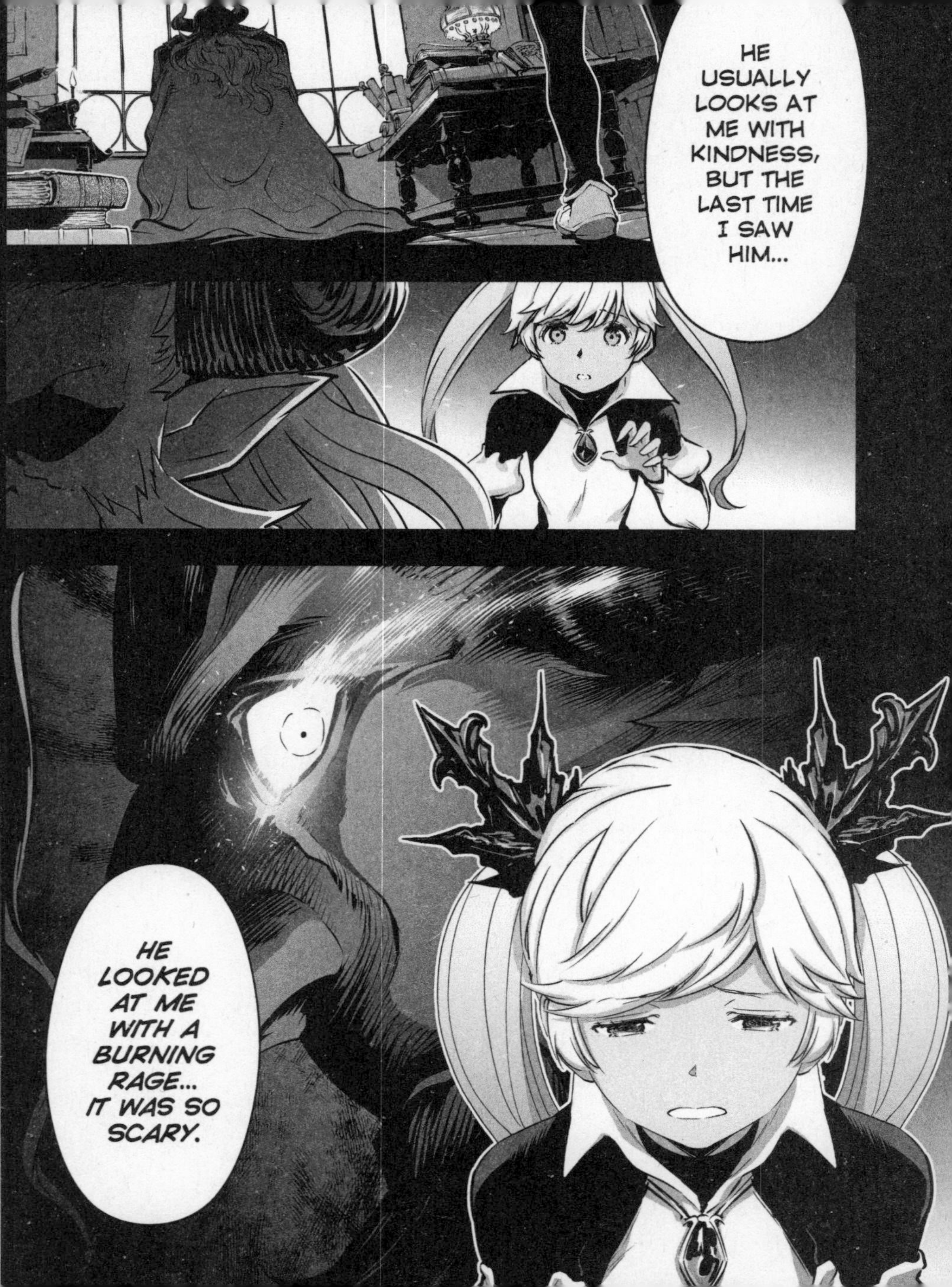
HE USUALLY LOOKS AT ME WITH KINDNESS, BUT THE LAST TIME I SAW HIM...
HE LOOKED AT ME WITH A BURNING RAGE... IT WAS SO SCARY.

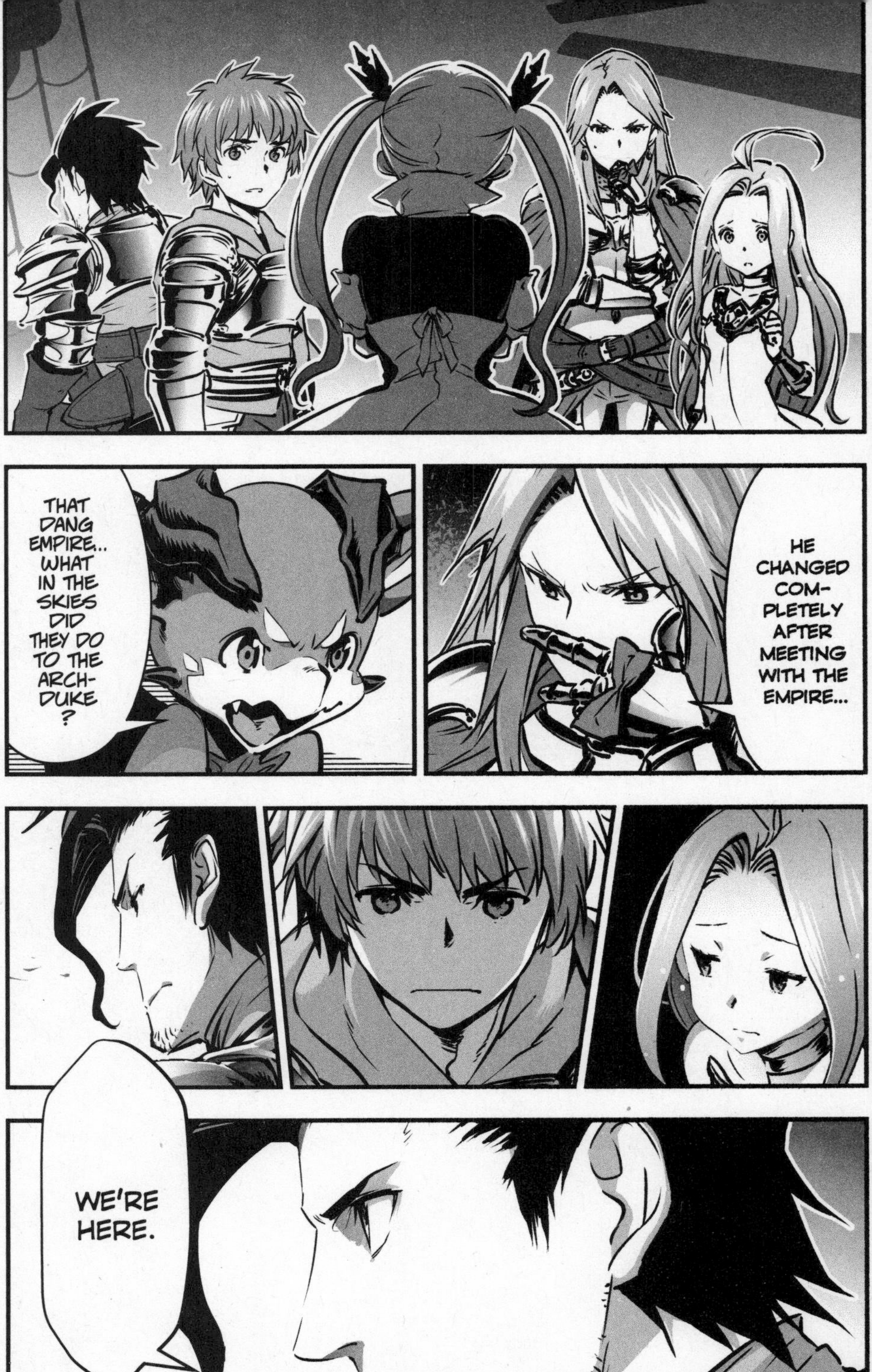
HE CHANGED COMPLETELY AFTER MEETING WITH THE EMPIRE...
THAT DANG EMPIRE... WHAT IN THE SKIES DID THEY DO TO THE ARCHDUKE?
WE'RE HERE.

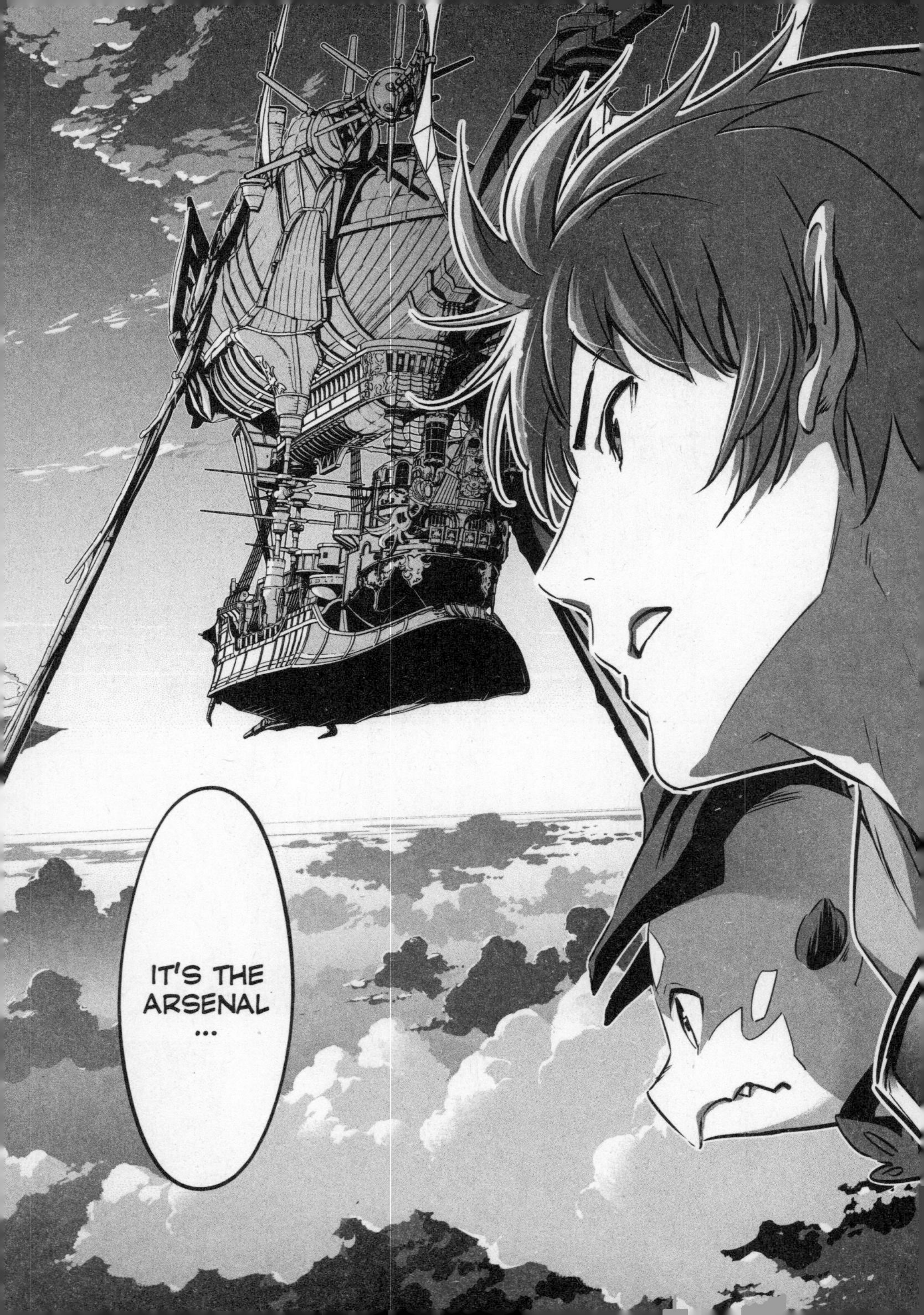
IT'S THE ARSENAL ...

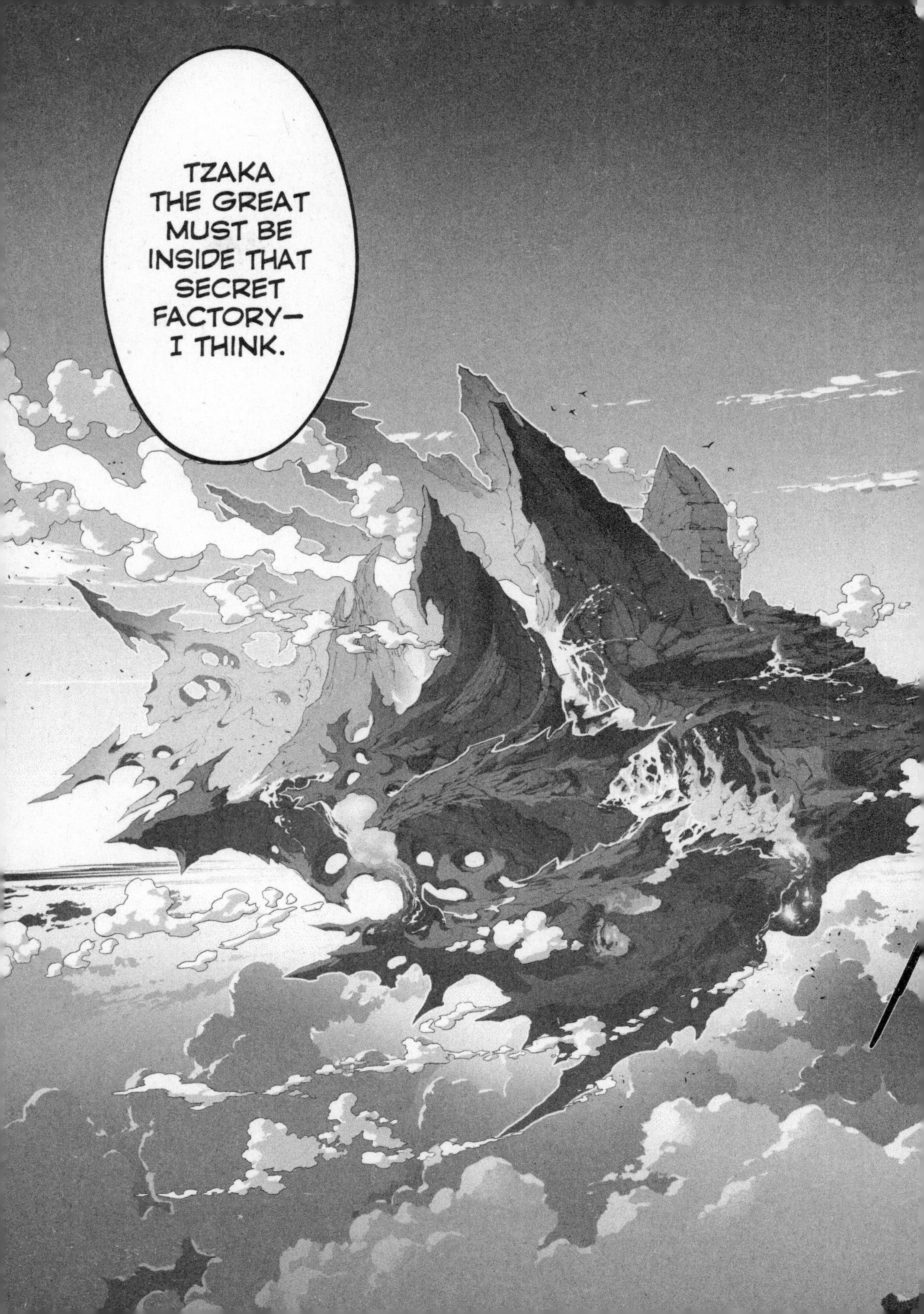
TZAKA THE GREAT MUST BE INSIDE THAT SECRET FACTORY— I THINK.

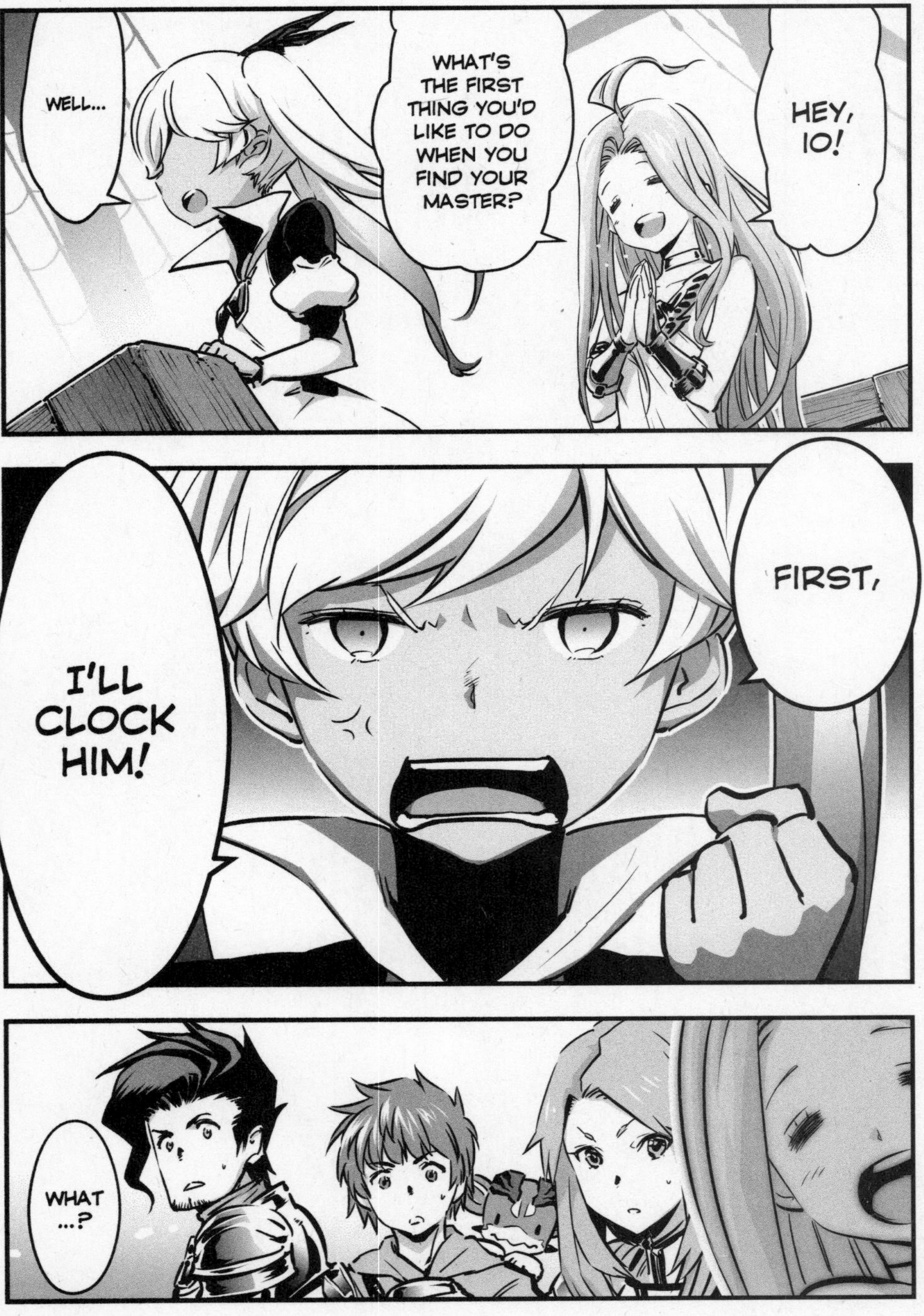
HEY, IO!
WHAT'S THE FIRST THING YOU'D LIKE TO DO WHEN YOU FIND YOUR MASTER?
WELL...
FIRST,
I'LL CLOCK HIM!
WHAT ...?

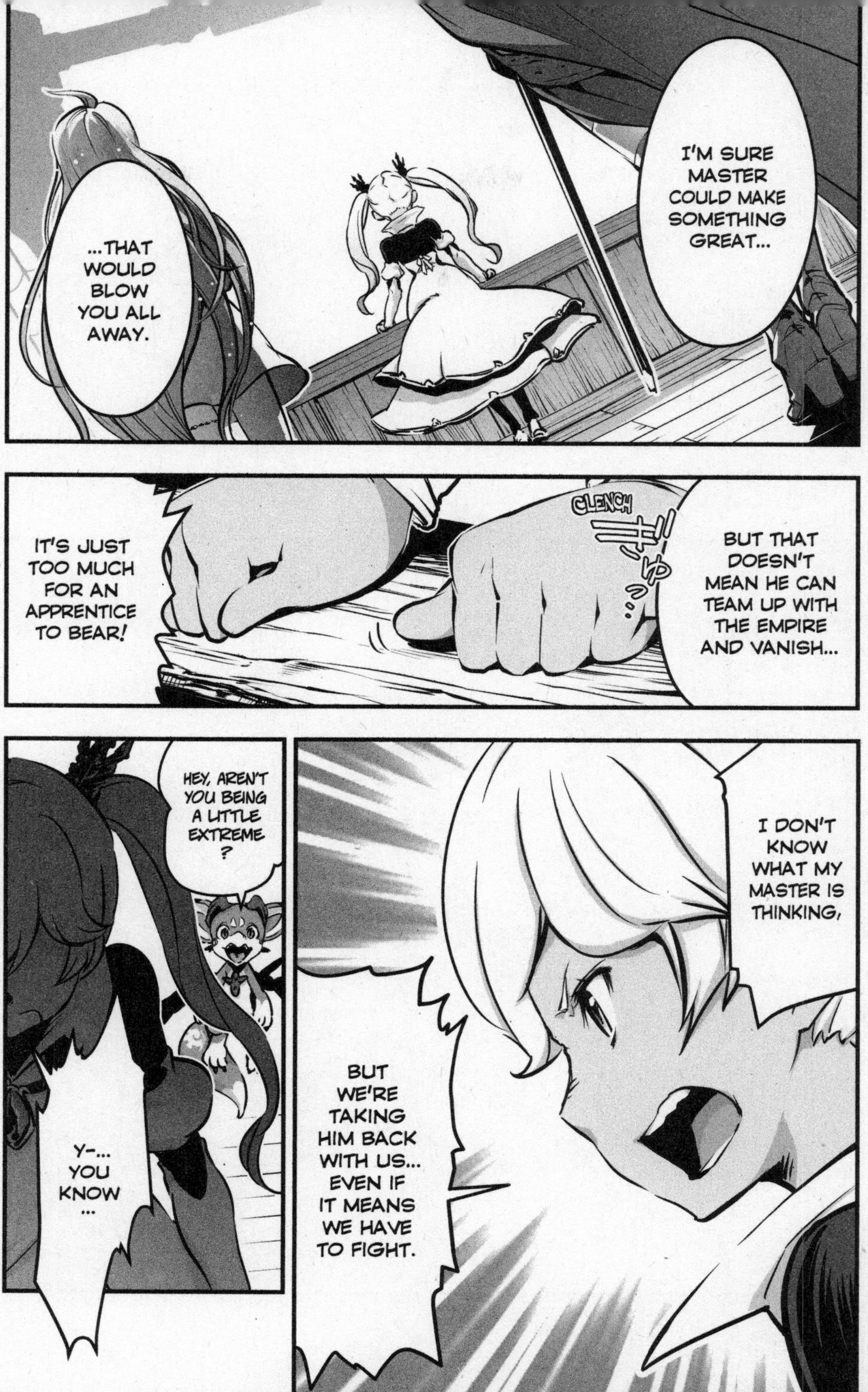
I'M SURE MASTER COULD MAKE SOMETHING GREAT...
...THAT WOULD BLOW YOU ALL AWAY.
CLENCH
ぎゅっ
BUT THAT DOESN'T MEAN HE CAN TEAM UP WITH THE EMPIRE AND VANISH...
IT'S JUST TOO MUCH FOR AN APPRENTICE TO BEAR!
I DON'T KNOW WHAT MY MASTER IS THINKING,
BUT WE'RE TAKING HIM BACK WITH US... EVEN IF IT MEANS WE HAVE TO FIGHT.
HEY, AREN'T YOU BEING A LITTLE EXTREME?
Y-... YOU KNOW ...

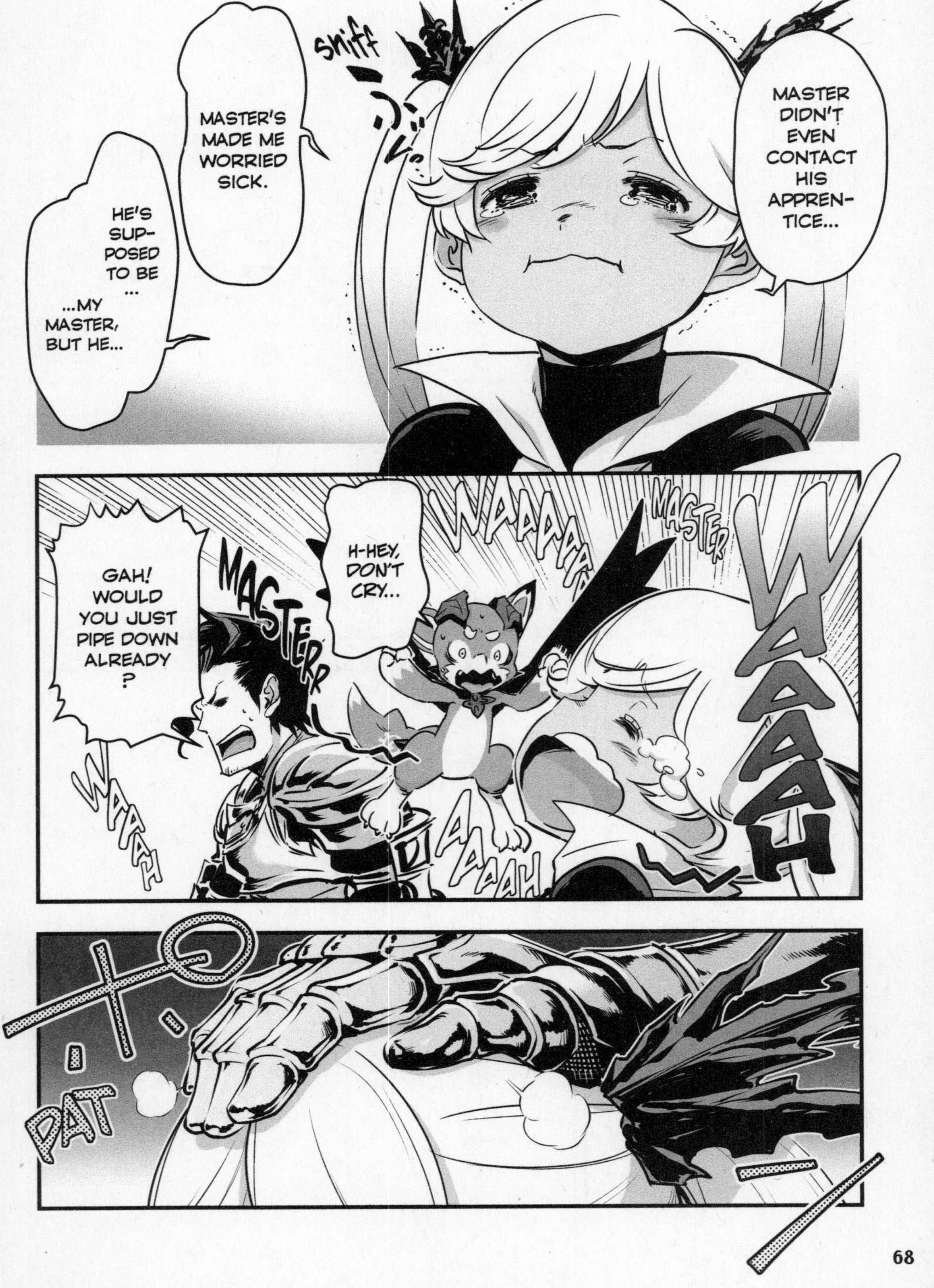

MASTER DIDN'T EVEN CONTACT HIS APPREN-TICE...
sniff
MASTER'S MADE ME WORRIED SICK.
HE'S SUP-POSED TO BE ...
...MY MASTER, BUT HE...
WAAAAH
MASTER
WAAAAAAA
H-HEY, DON'T CRY...
MASTERRR
AAAAH
GAH! WOULD YOU JUST PIPE DOWN ALREADY ?
WAAAH
PAT

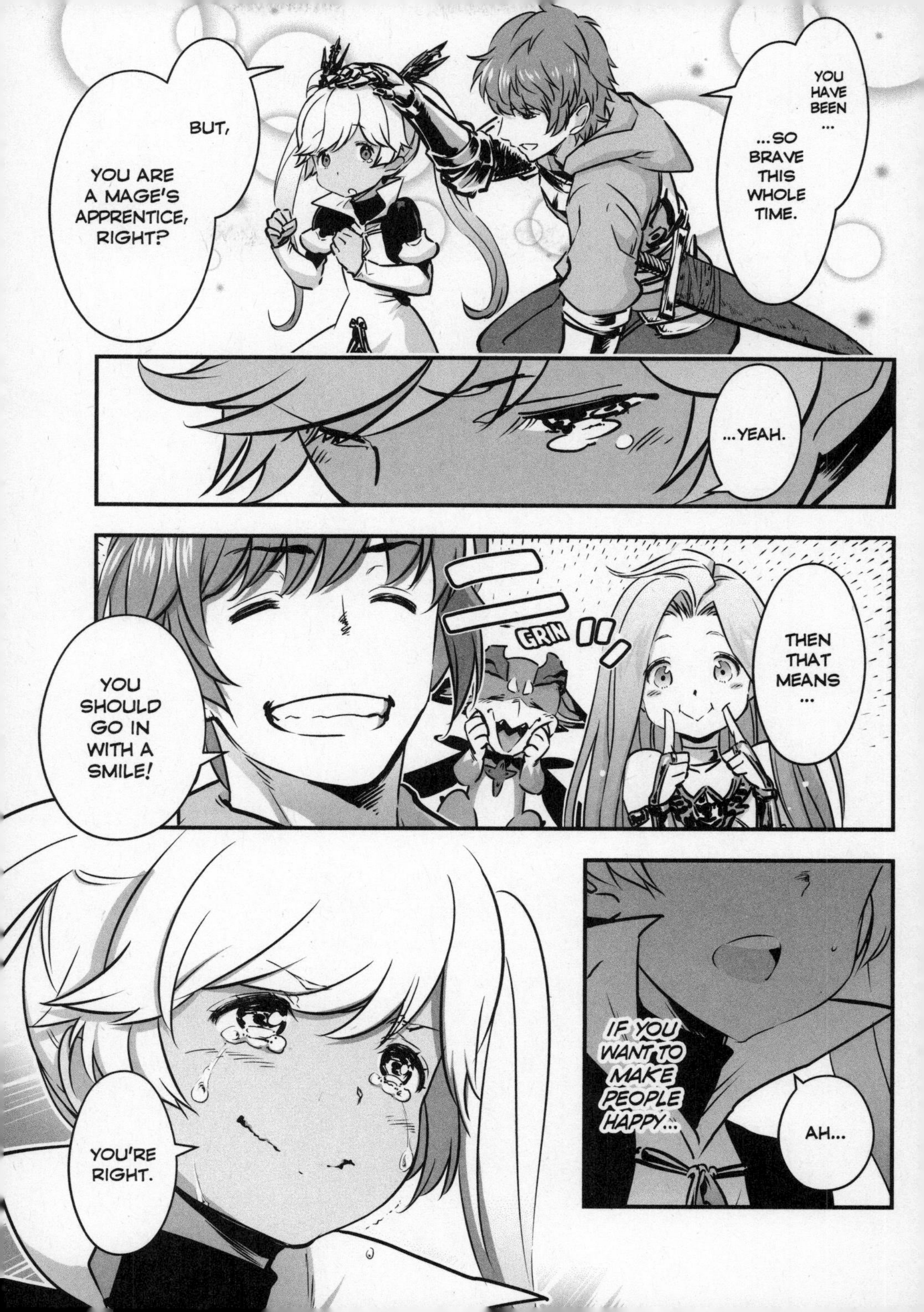
YOU HAVE BEEN ...
...SO BRAVE THIS WHOLE TIME.
BUT, YOU ARE A MAGE'S APPRENTICE, RIGHT?
...YEAH.
THEN THAT MEANS ...
GRIN
YOU SHOULD GO IN WITH A SMILE!
IF YOU WANT TO MAKE PEOPLE HAPPY...
AH...
YOU'RE RIGHT.

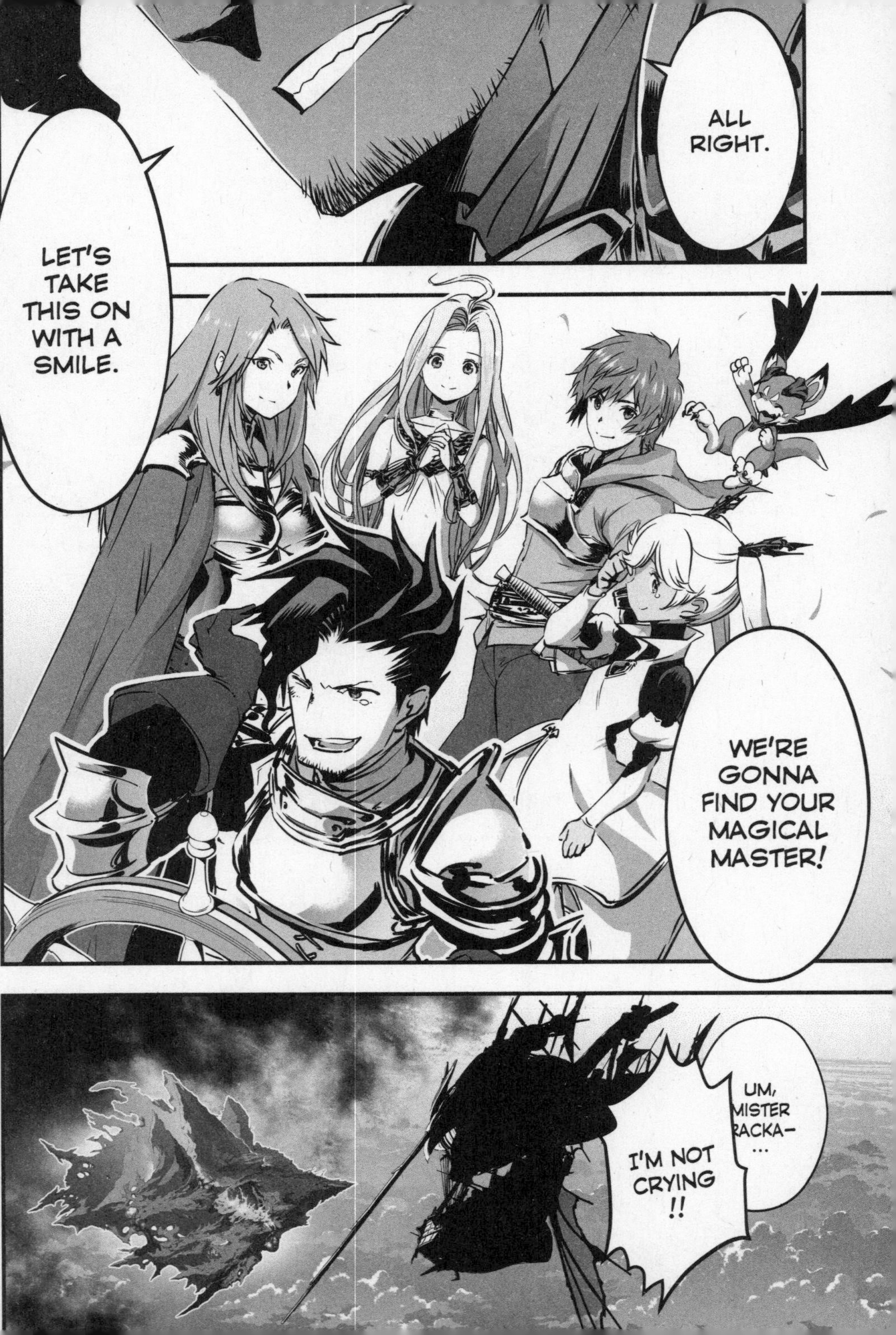
ALL RIGHT.
LET'S TAKE THIS ON WITH A SMILE.
WE'RE GONNA FIND YOUR MAGICAL MASTER!
UM, MISTER RACKA— ...
I'M NOT CRYING!!

GRANBLUE FANTASY
グランブルーファンタジー

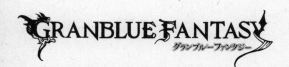

GRANBLUE FANTASY
グランブルーファンタジー

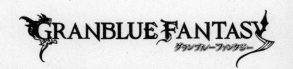

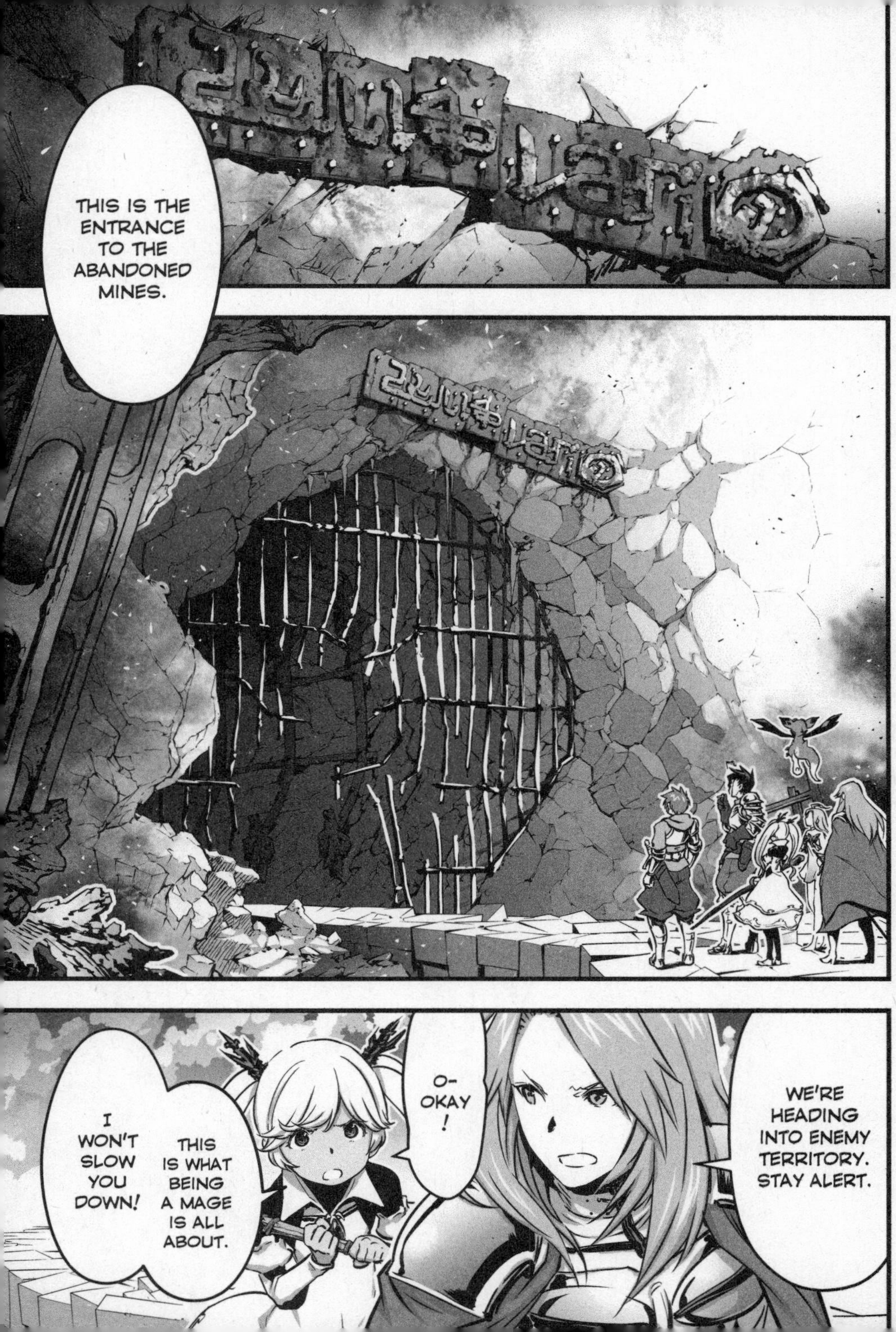
THIS IS THE ENTRANCE TO THE ABANDONED MINES.
WE'RE HEADING INTO ENEMY TERRITORY. STAY ALERT.
O-OKAY!
I WON'T SLOW YOU DOWN! THIS IS WHAT BEING A MAGE IS ALL ABOUT.

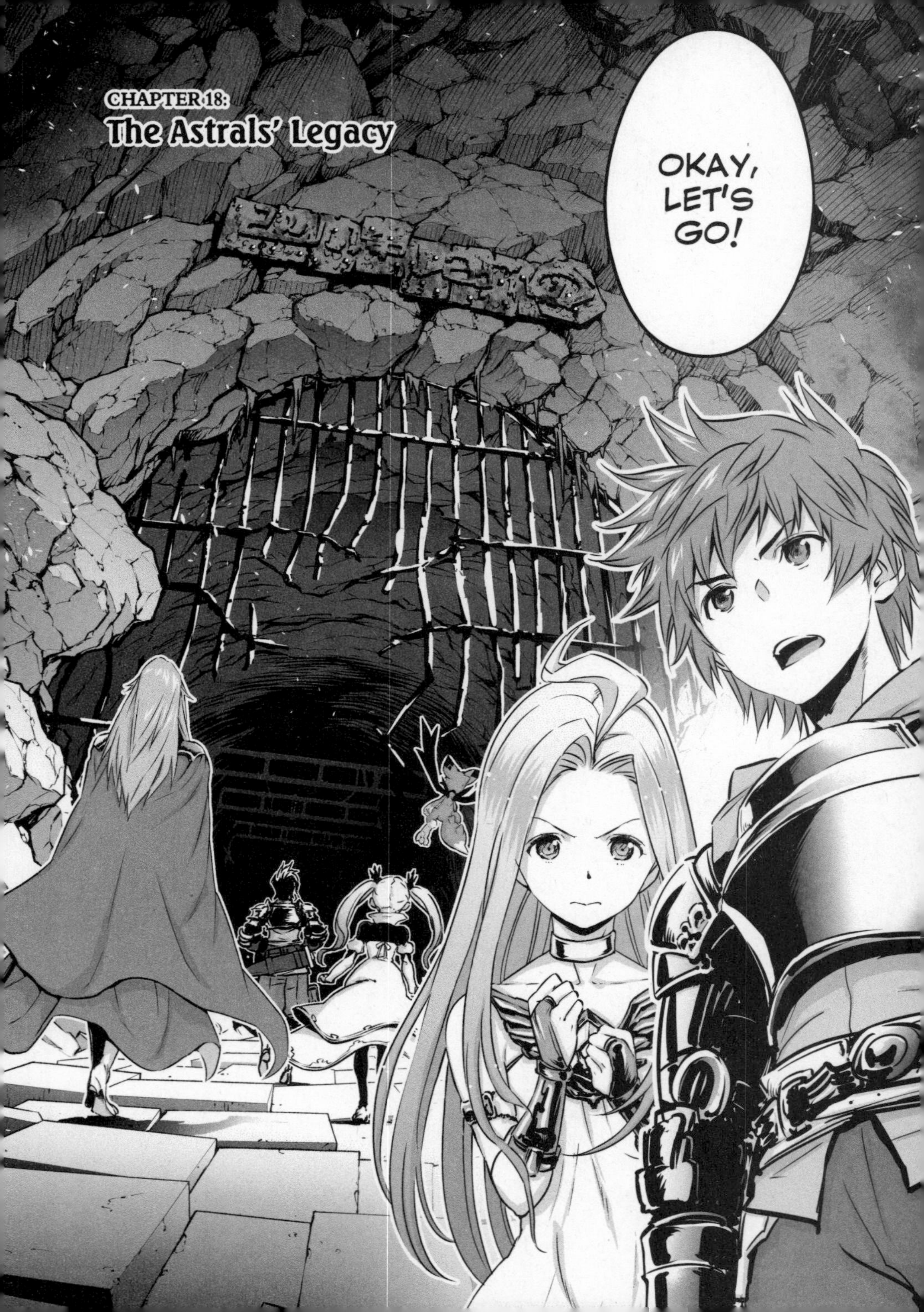
CHAPTER 18:
The Astrals' Legacy
OKAY, LET'S GO!

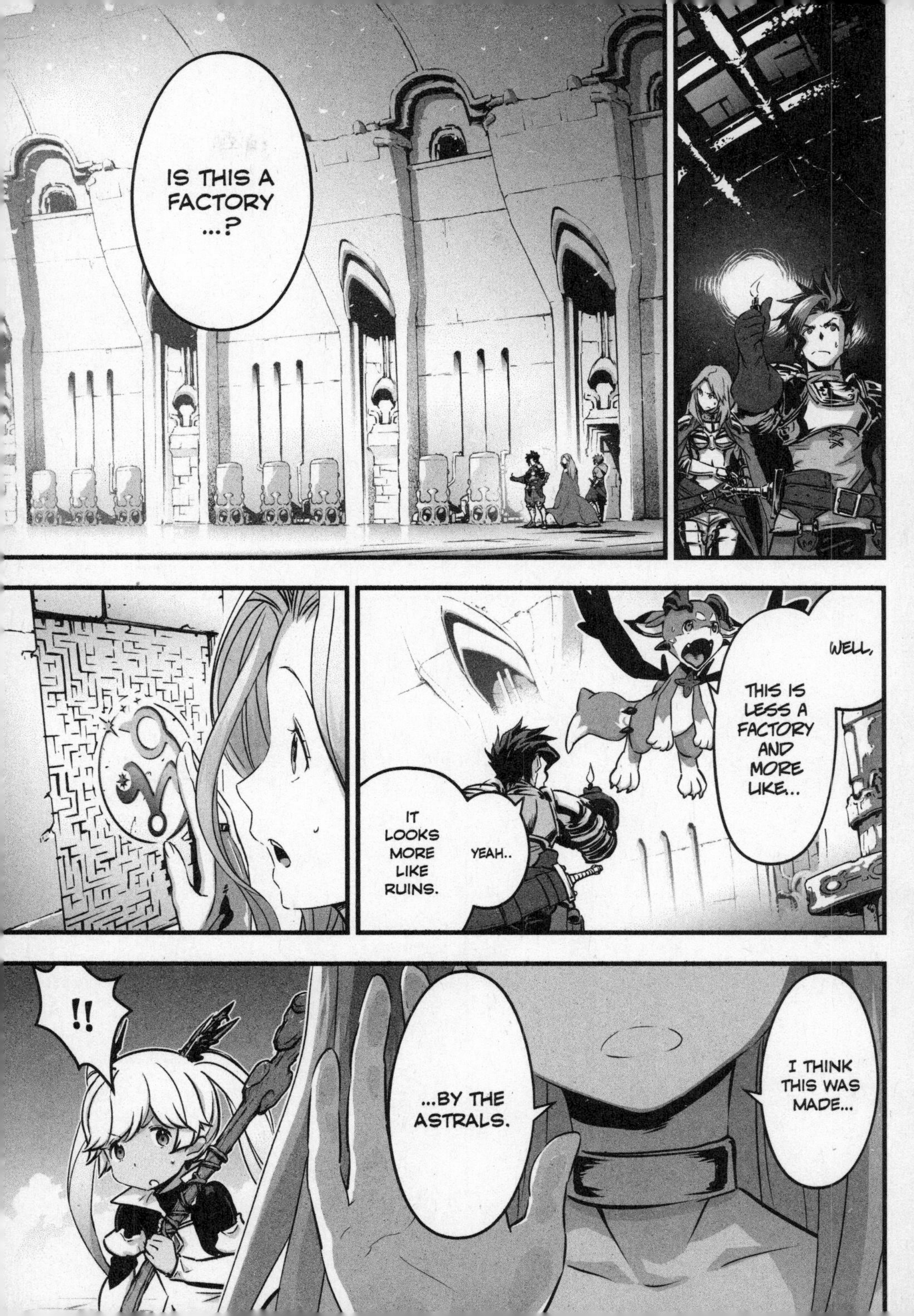
IS THIS A FACTORY ...?
WELL,
THIS IS LESS A FACTORY AND MORE LIKE...
YEAH..
IT LOOKS MORE LIKE RUINS.
I THINK THIS WAS MADE...
...BY THE ASTRALS.
!!

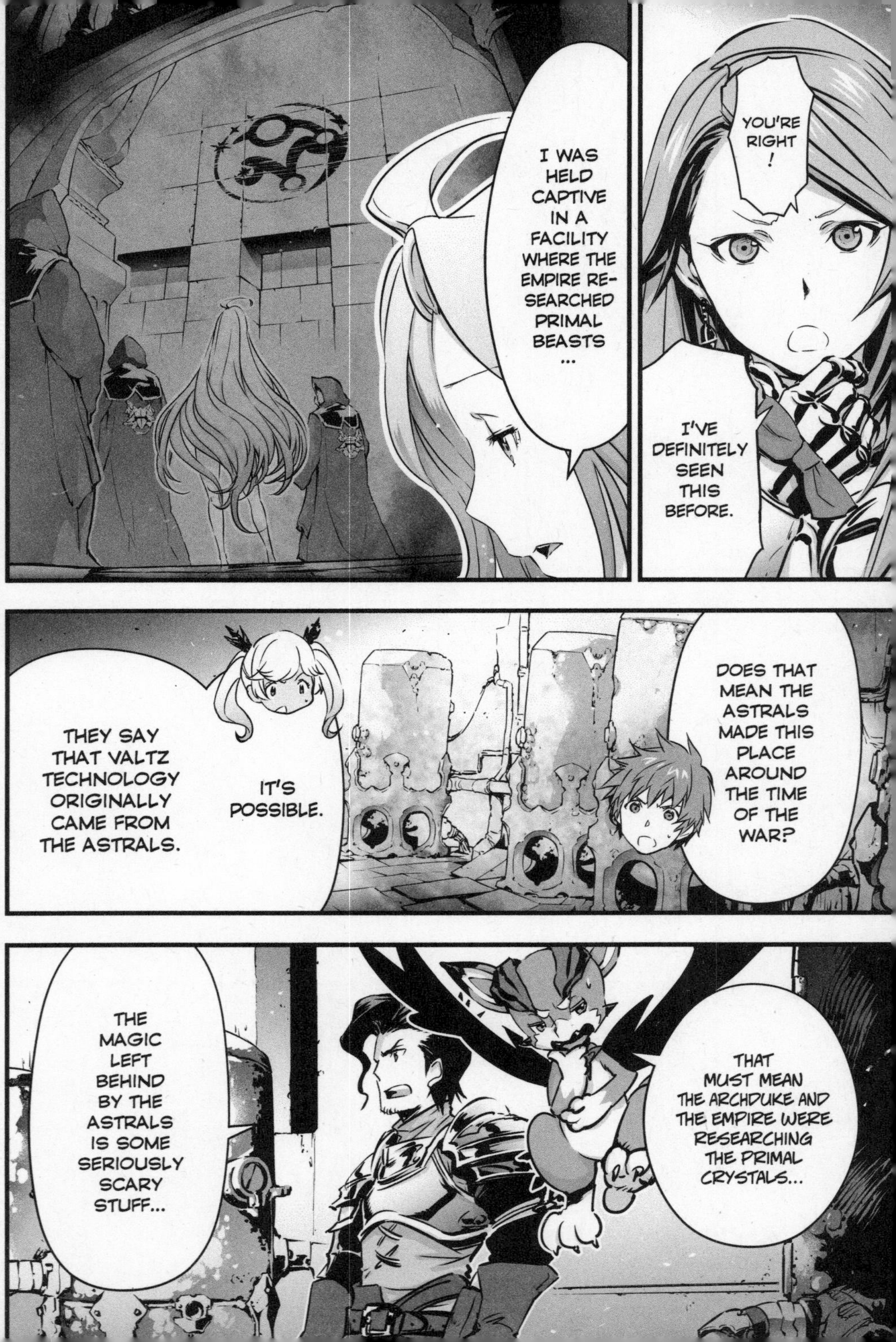
YOU'RE RIGHT!
I'VE DEFINITELY SEEN THIS BEFORE.
I WAS HELD CAPTIVE IN A FACILITY WHERE THE EMPIRE RE-SEARCHED PRIMAL BEASTS...
DOES THAT MEAN THE ASTRALS MADE THIS PLACE AROUND THE TIME OF THE WAR?
IT'S POSSIBLE.
THEY SAY THAT VALTZ TECHNOLOGY ORIGINALLY CAME FROM THE ASTRALS.
THAT MUST MEAN THE ARCHDUKE AND THE EMPIRE WERE RESEARCHING THE PRIMAL CRYSTALS...
THE MAGIC LEFT BEHIND BY THE ASTRALS IS SOME SERIOUSLY SCARY STUFF...

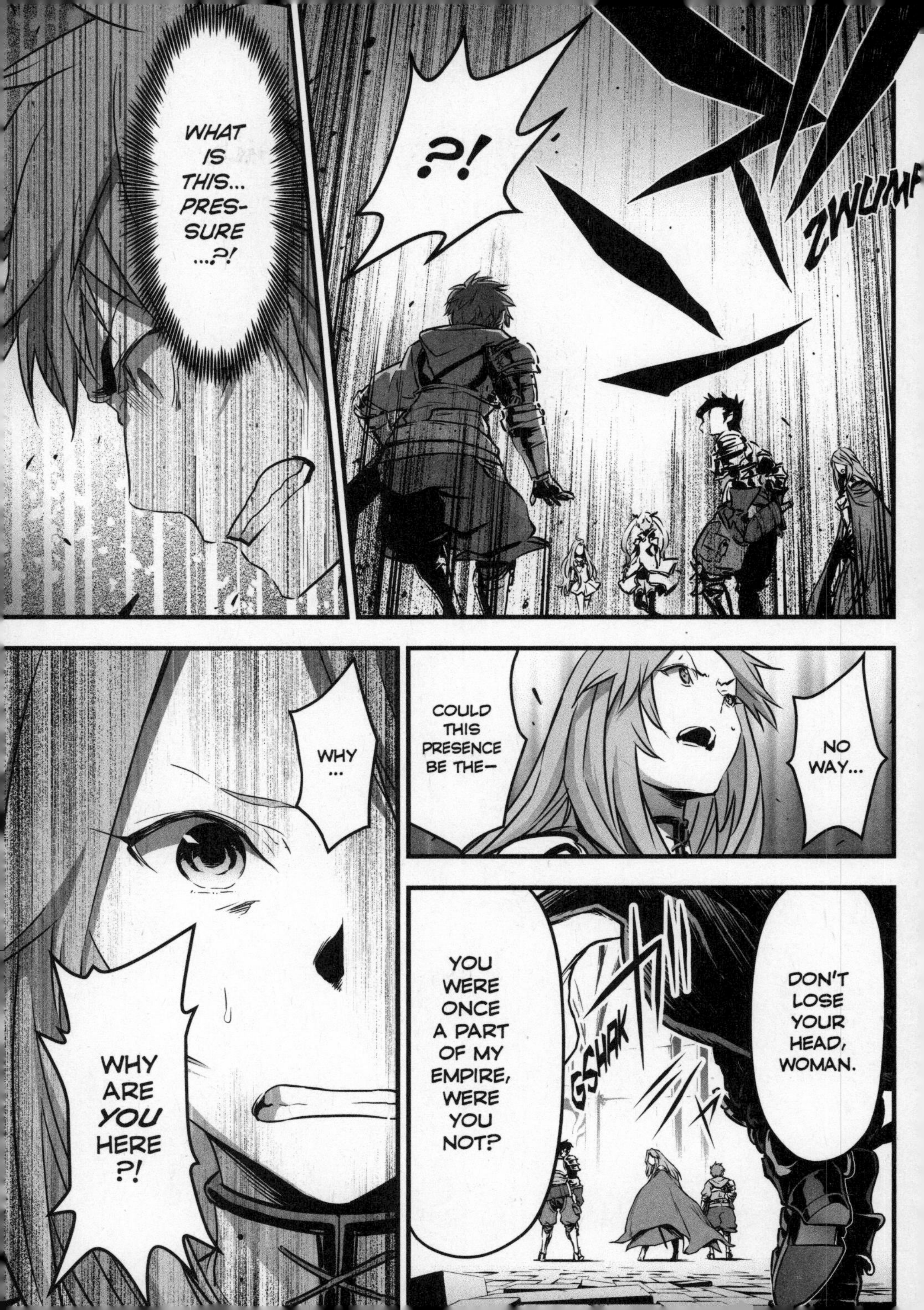
ZWUMF
?!
WHAT IS THIS... PRESSURE...?!
NO WAY...
COULD THIS PRESENCE BE THE—
DON'T LOSE YOUR HEAD, WOMAN.
GSHAK
YOU WERE ONCE A PART OF MY EMPIRE, WERE YOU NOT?
WHY...
WHY ARE *YOU* HERE?!

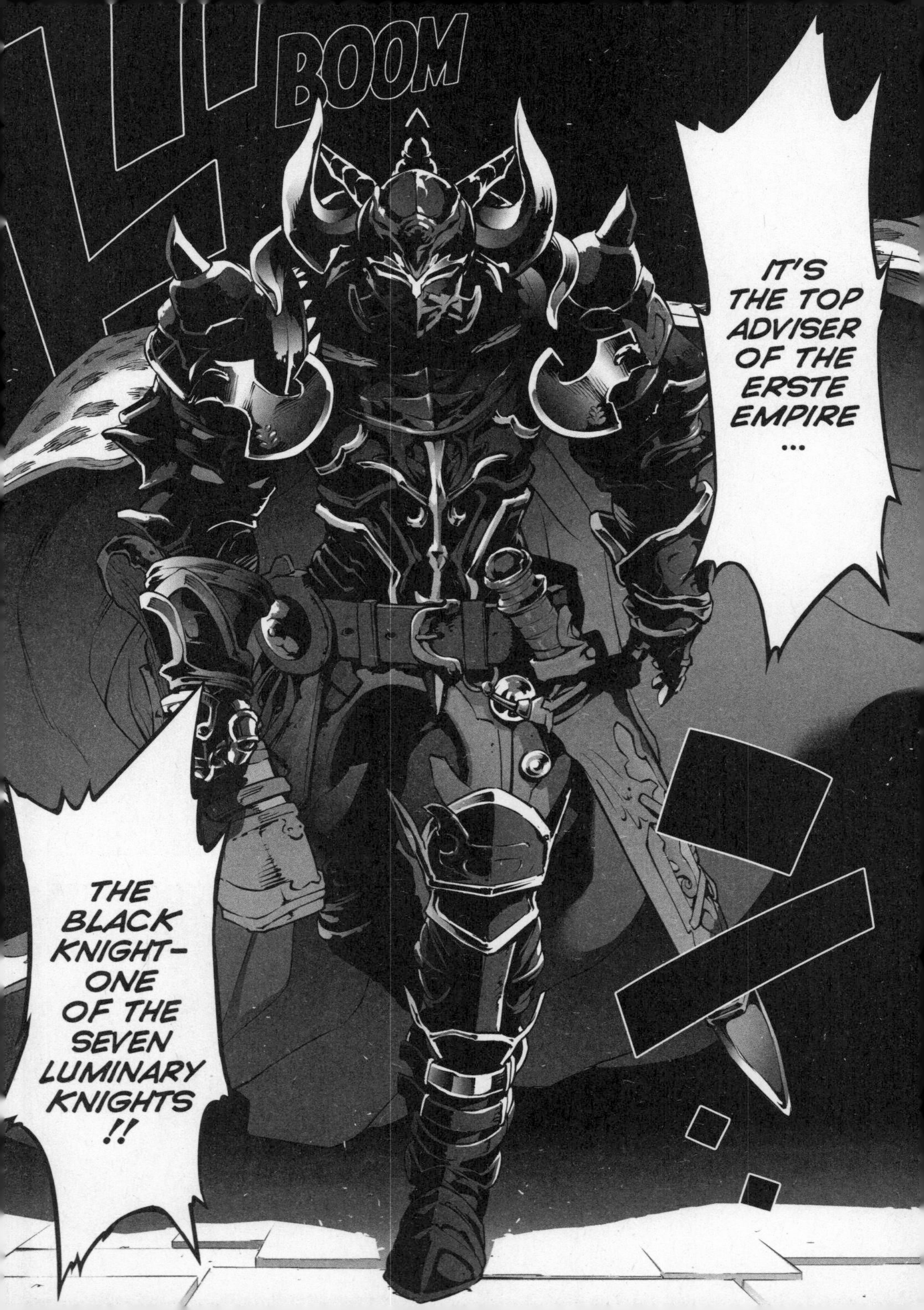
BOOM
IT'S THE TOP ADVISER OF THE ERSTE EMPIRE ...
THE BLACK KNIGHT- ONE OF THE SEVEN LUMINARY KNIGHTS !!

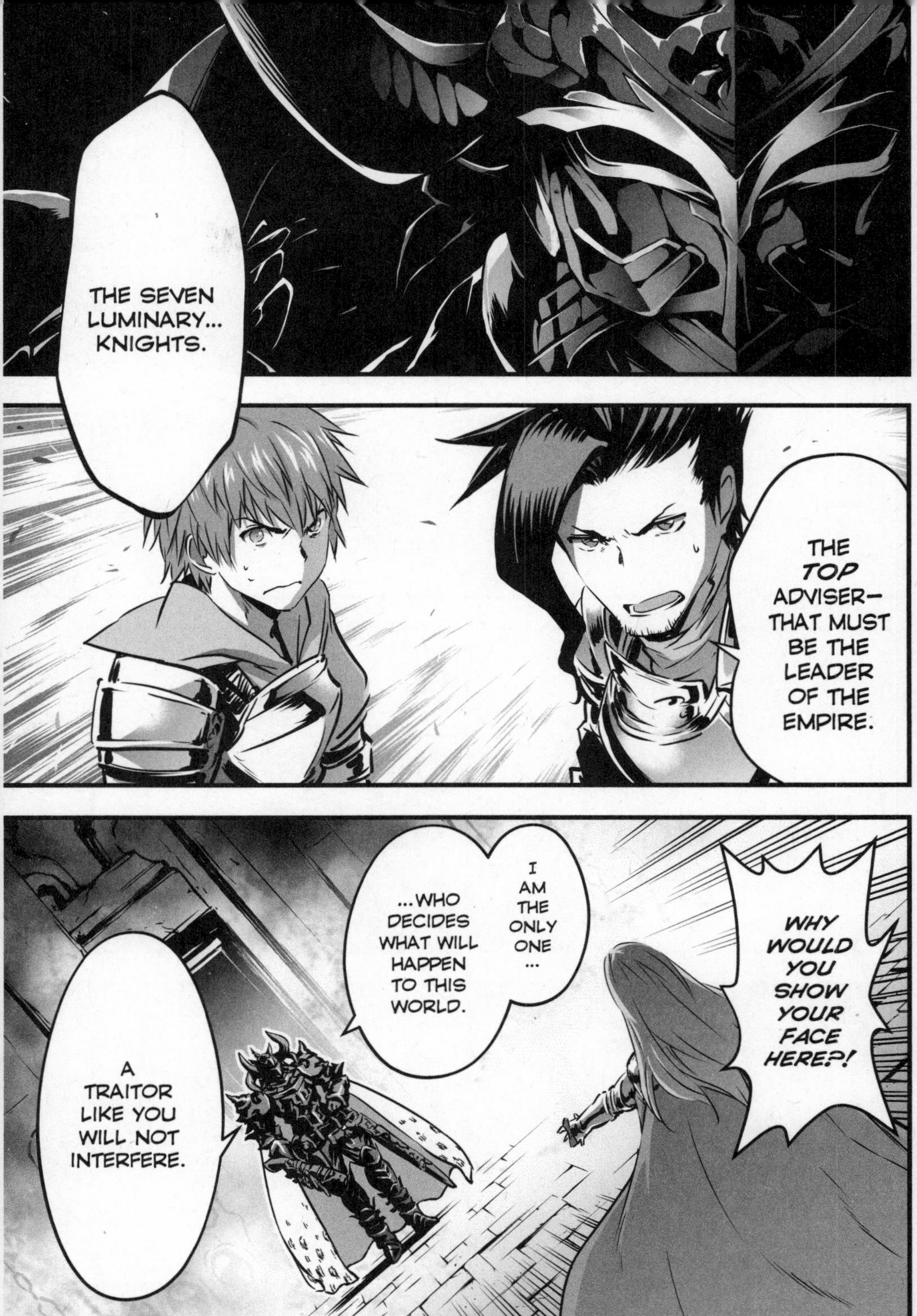
THE SEVEN LUMINARY... KNIGHTS.
THE TOP ADVISER— THAT MUST BE THE LEADER OF THE EMPIRE.
WHY WOULD YOU SHOW YOUR FACE HERE?!
I AM THE ONLY ONE ...
...WHO DECIDES WHAT WILL HAPPEN TO THIS WORLD.
A TRAITOR LIKE YOU WILL NOT INTERFERE.

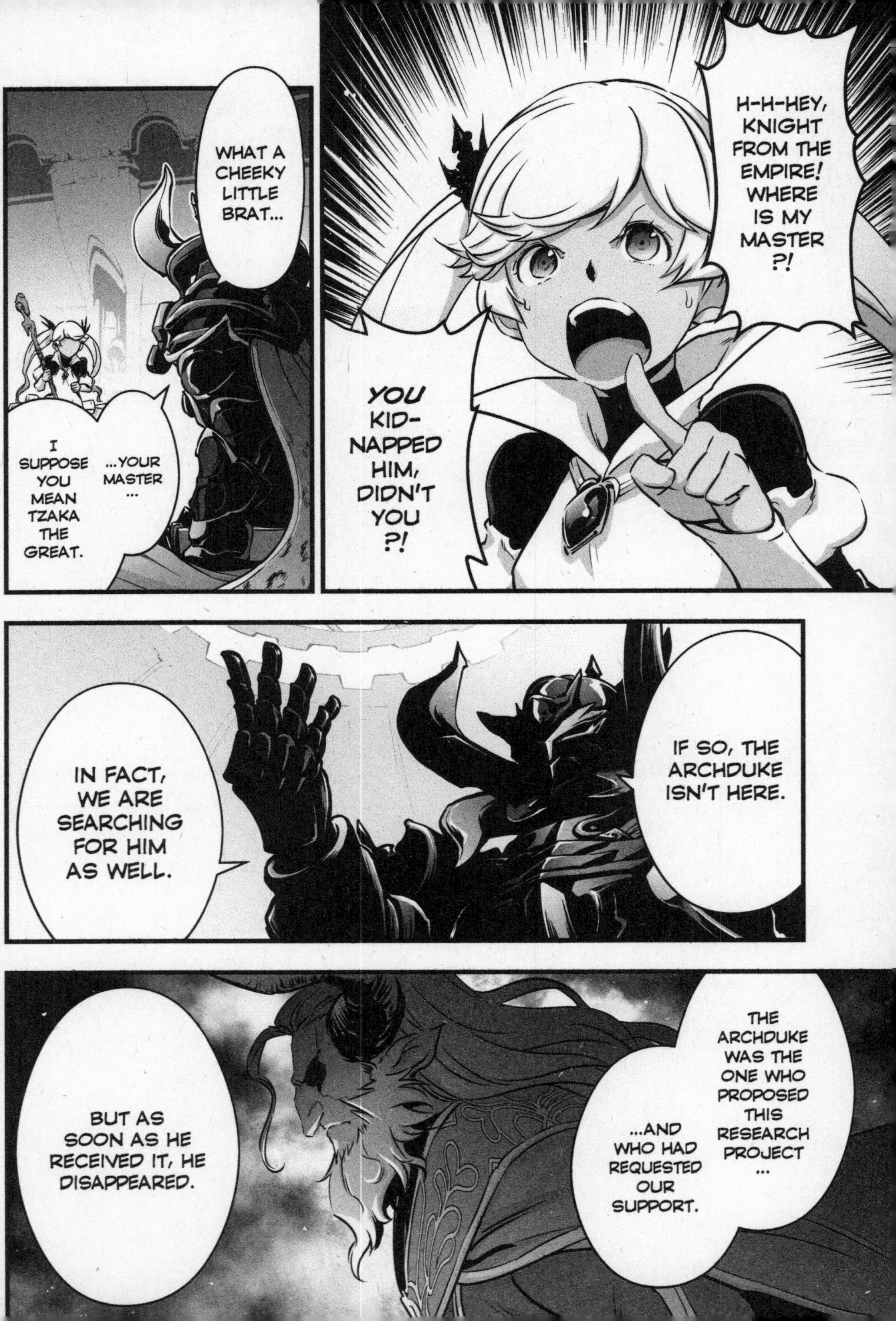
H-H-HEY, KNIGHT FROM THE EMPIRE! WHERE IS MY MASTER?!
YOU KID-NAPPED HIM, DIDN'T YOU?!
WHAT A CHEEKY LITTLE BRAT...
...YOUR MASTER...
I SUPPOSE YOU MEAN TZAKA THE GREAT.
IF SO, THE ARCHDUKE ISN'T HERE.
IN FACT, WE ARE SEARCHING FOR HIM AS WELL.
THE ARCHDUKE WAS THE ONE WHO PROPOSED THIS RESEARCH PROJECT...
...AND WHO HAD REQUESTED OUR SUPPORT.
BUT AS SOON AS HE RECEIVED IT, HE DISAPPEARED.

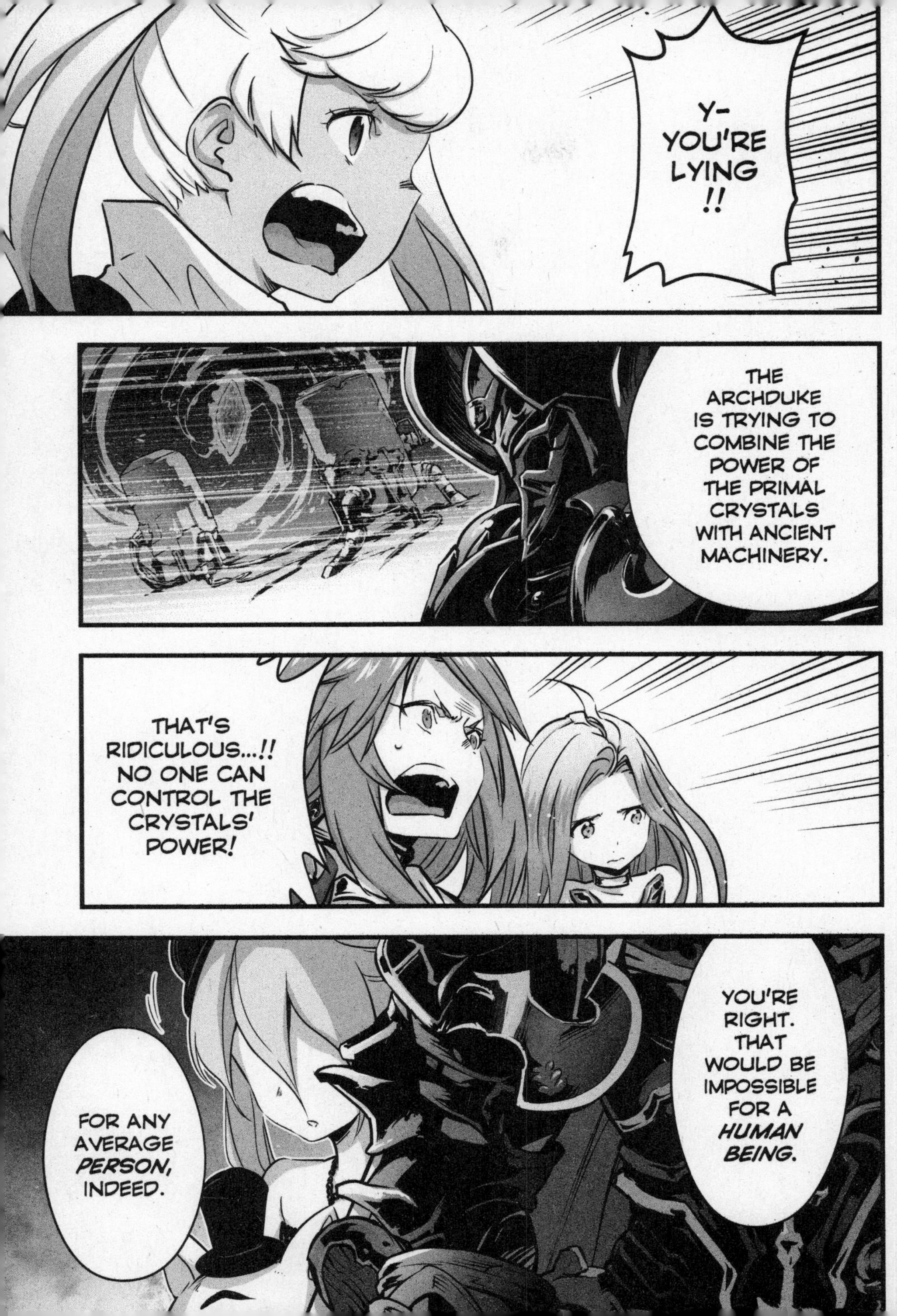
Y- YOU'RE LYING !!
THE ARCHDUKE IS TRYING TO COMBINE THE POWER OF THE PRIMAL CRYSTALS WITH ANCIENT MACHINERY.
THAT'S RIDICULOUS...!! NO ONE CAN CONTROL THE CRYSTALS' POWER!
YOU'RE RIGHT. THAT WOULD BE IMPOSSIBLE FOR A *HUMAN BEING*.
FOR ANY AVERAGE *PERSON*, INDEED.

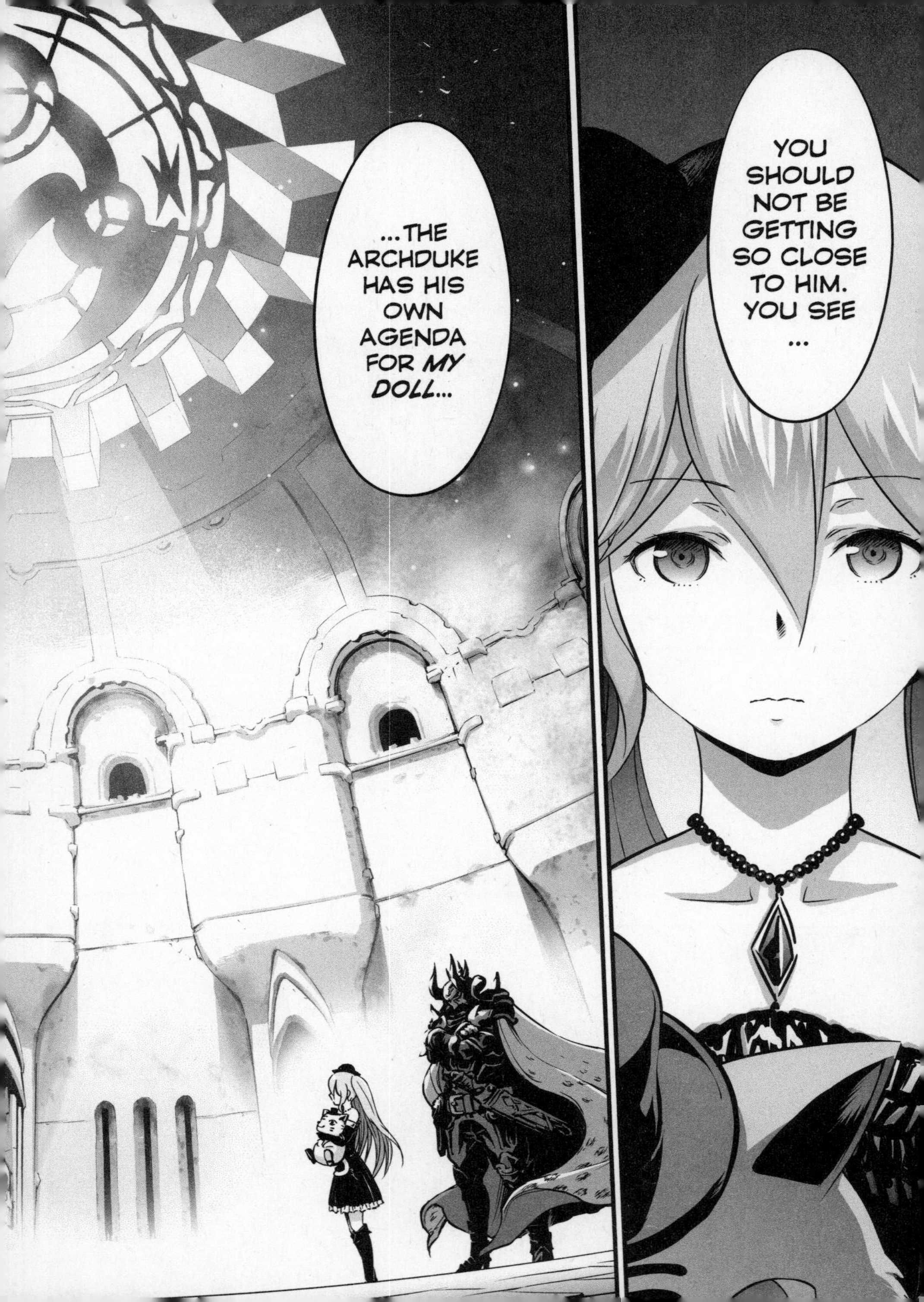
YOU SHOULD NOT BE GETTING SO CLOSE TO HIM. YOU SEE ...
...THE ARCHDUKE HAS HIS OWN AGENDA FOR *MY DOLL*...

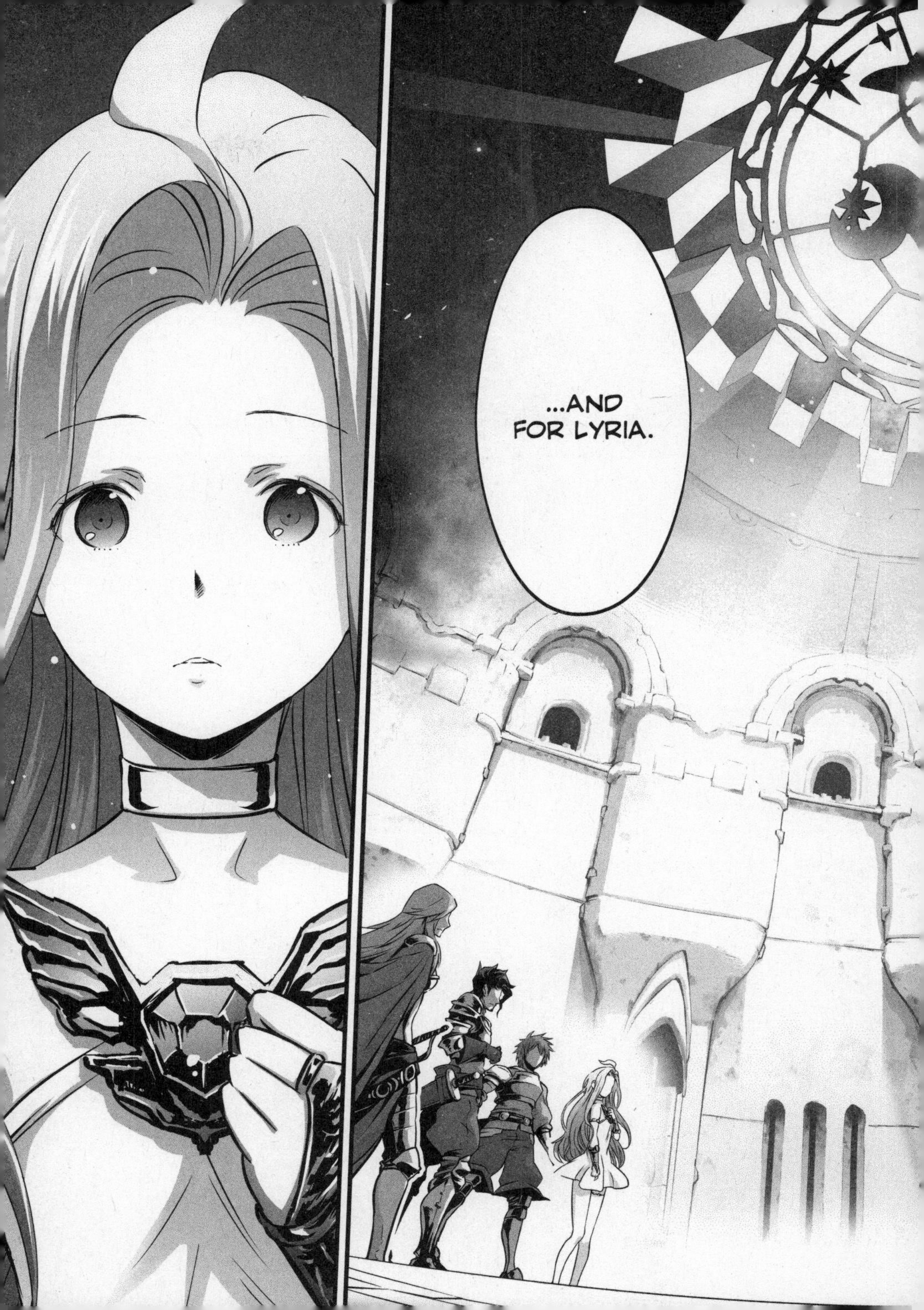
...AND FOR LYRIA.

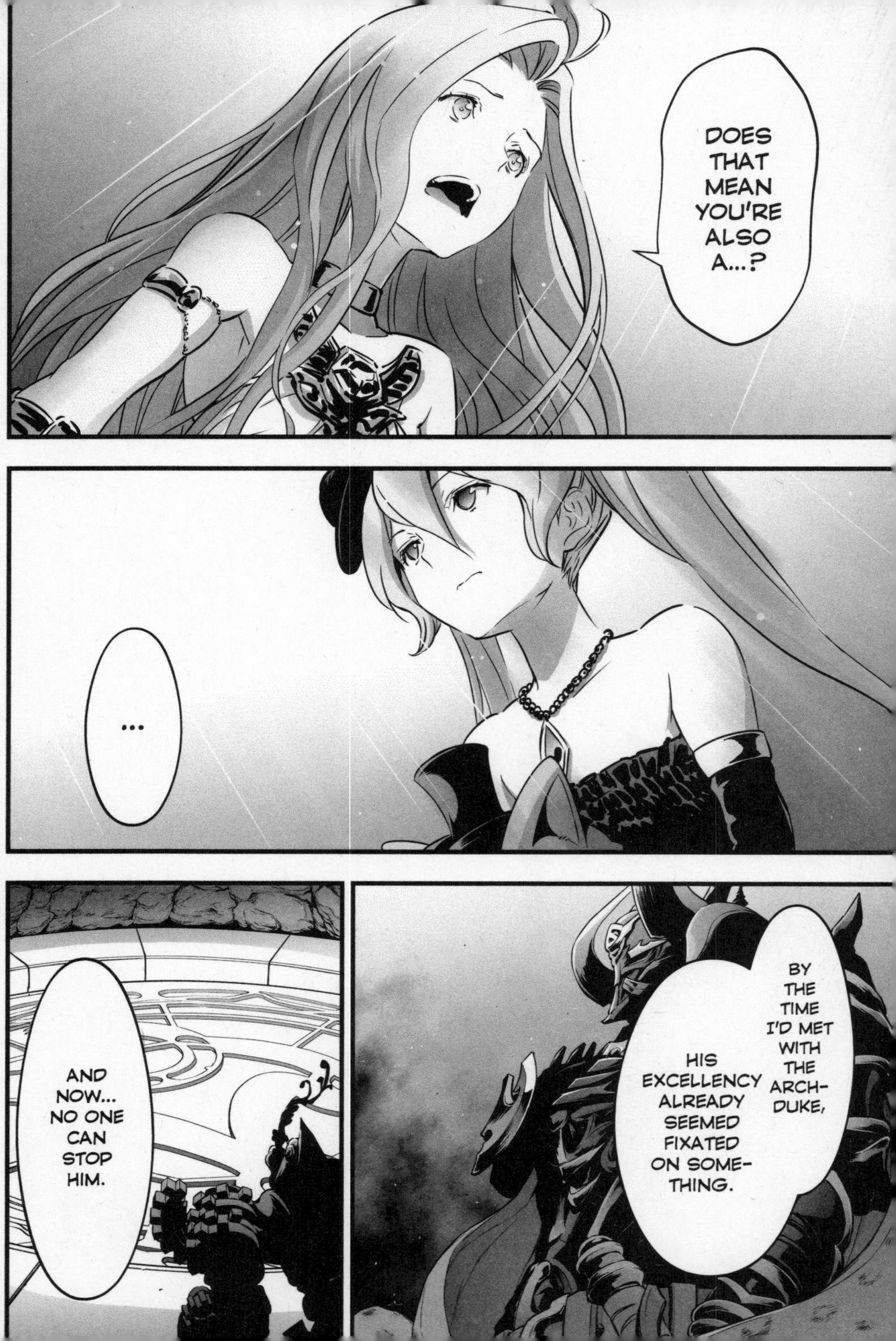
DOES THAT MEAN YOU'RE ALSO A...?
...
BY THE TIME I'D MET WITH THE ARCH-DUKE,
HIS EXCELLENCY ALREADY SEEMED FIXATED ON SOME-THING.
AND NOW... NO ONE CAN STOP HIM.

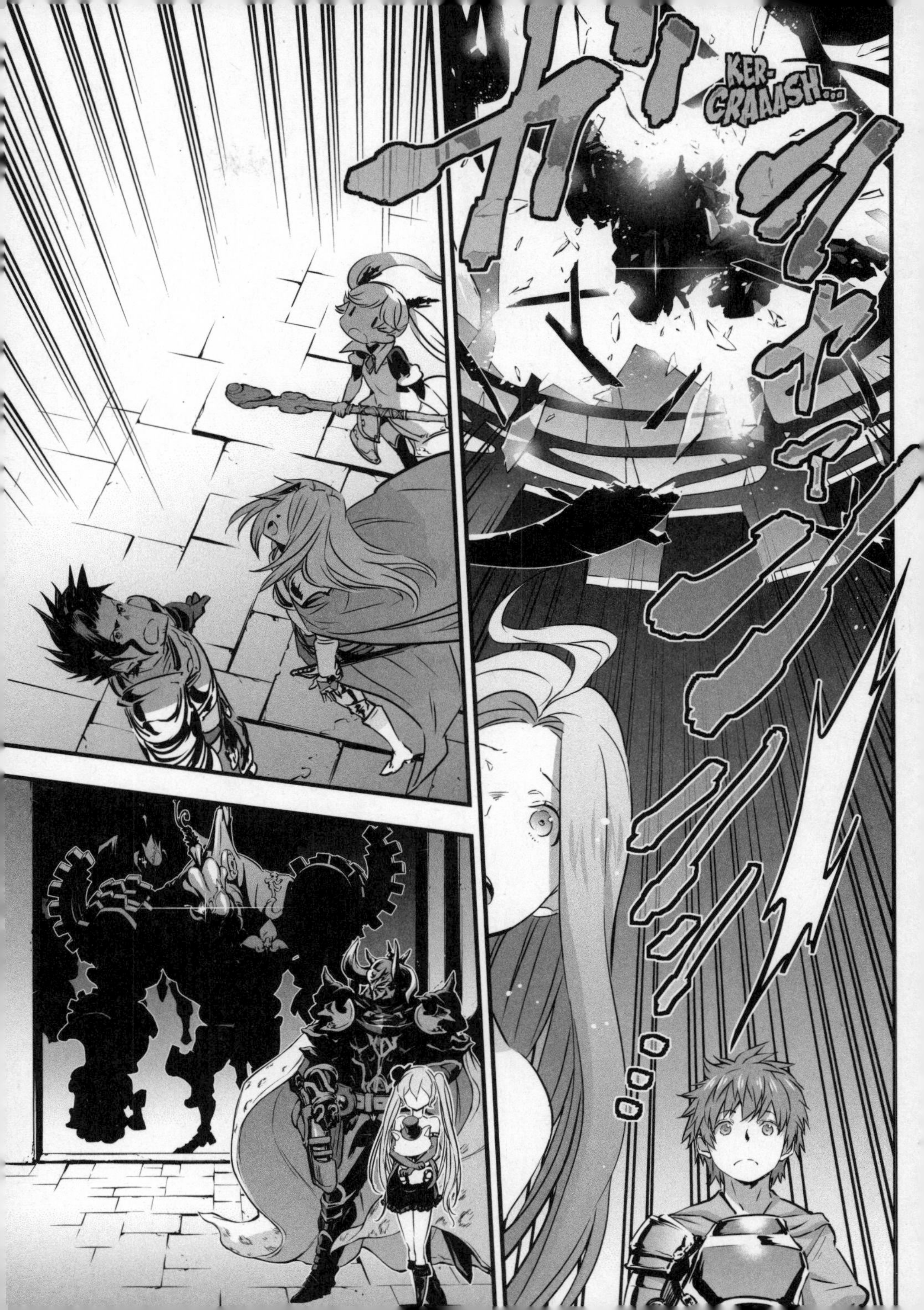
KER-CRAAASH...

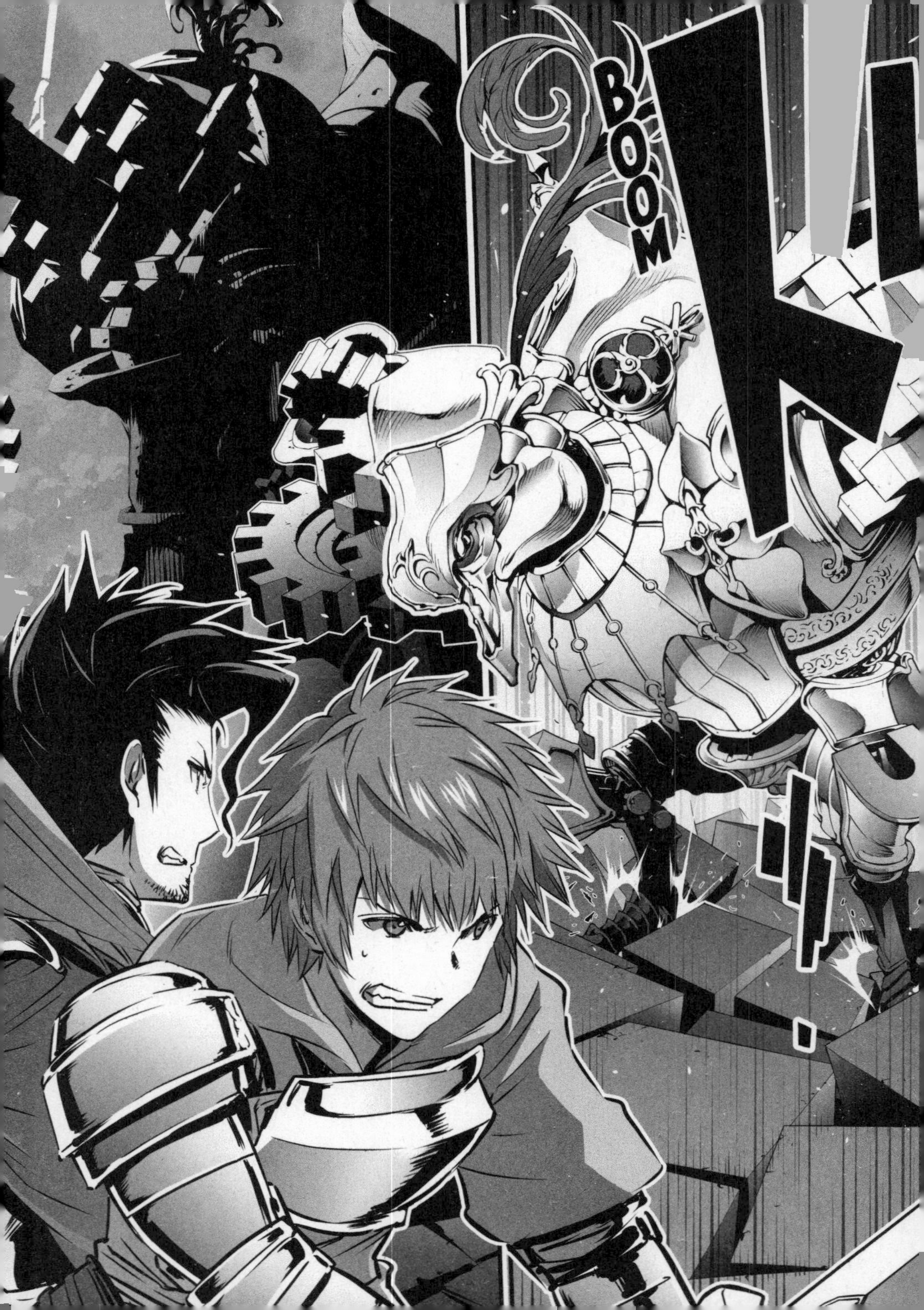
BOOM

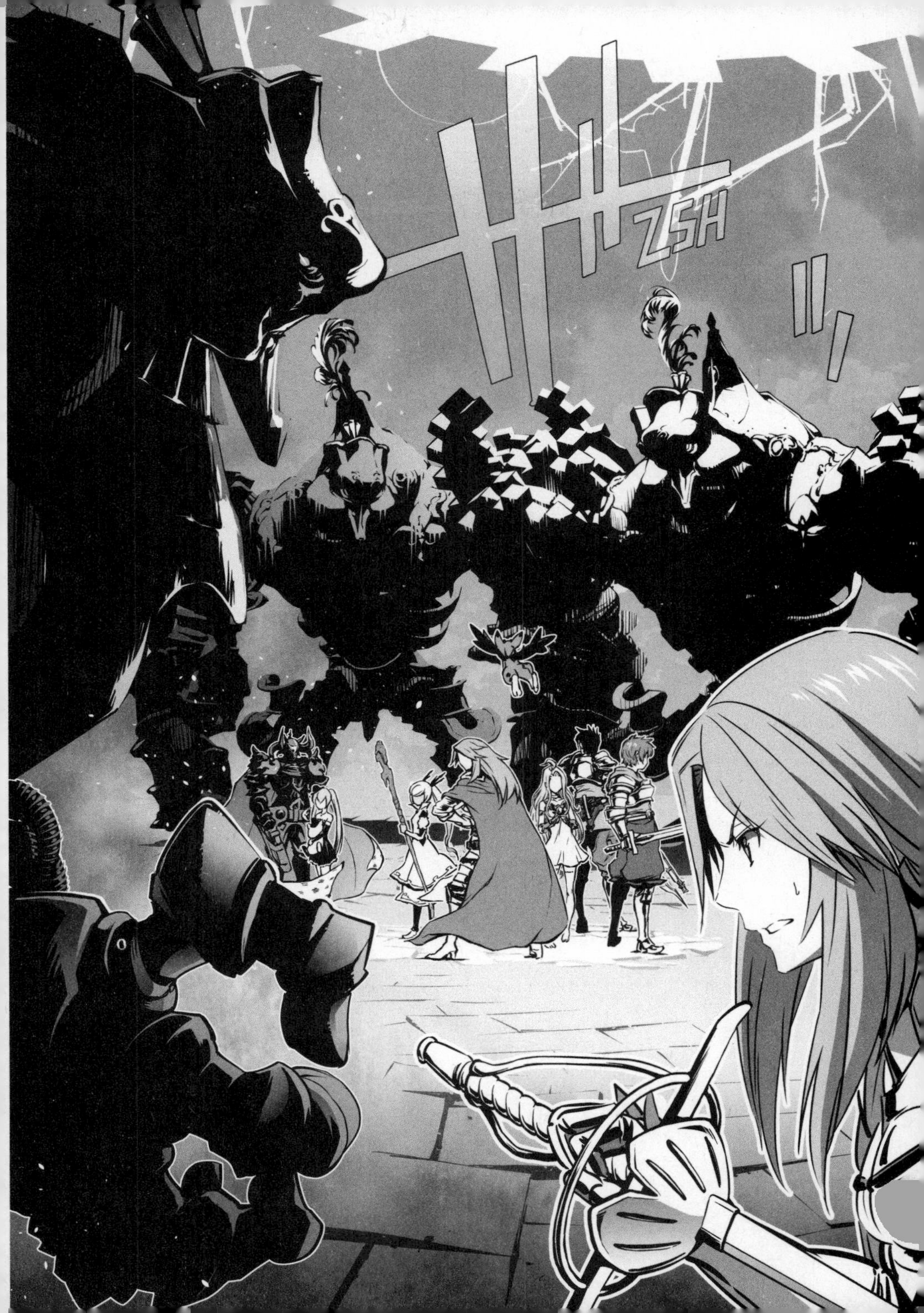
ZSH

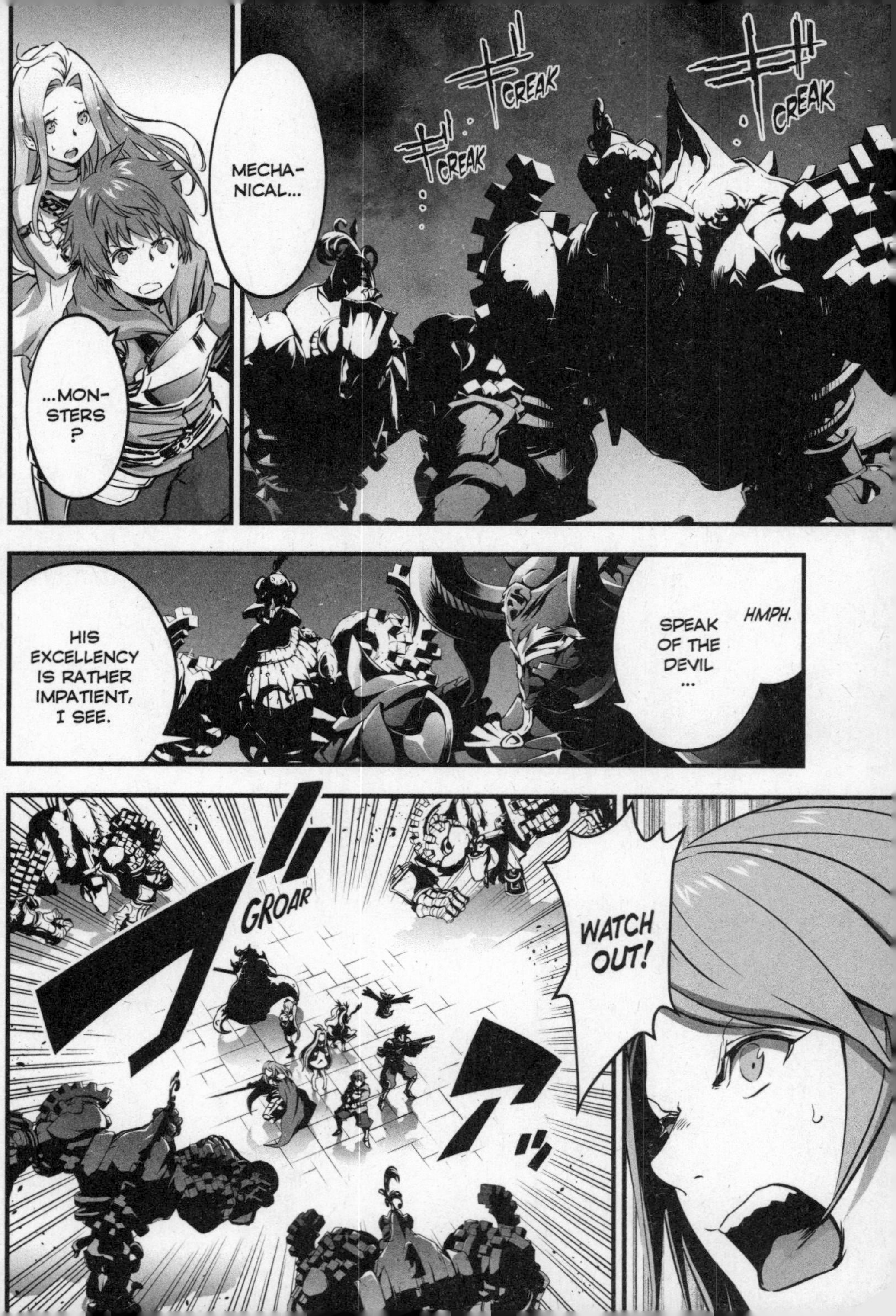
CREAK
CREAK
CREAK
MECHA-NICAL...
...MON-STERS?
HMPH.
SPEAK OF THE DEVIL...
HIS EXCELLENCY IS RATHER IMPATIENT, I SEE.
WATCH OUT!
GROAR

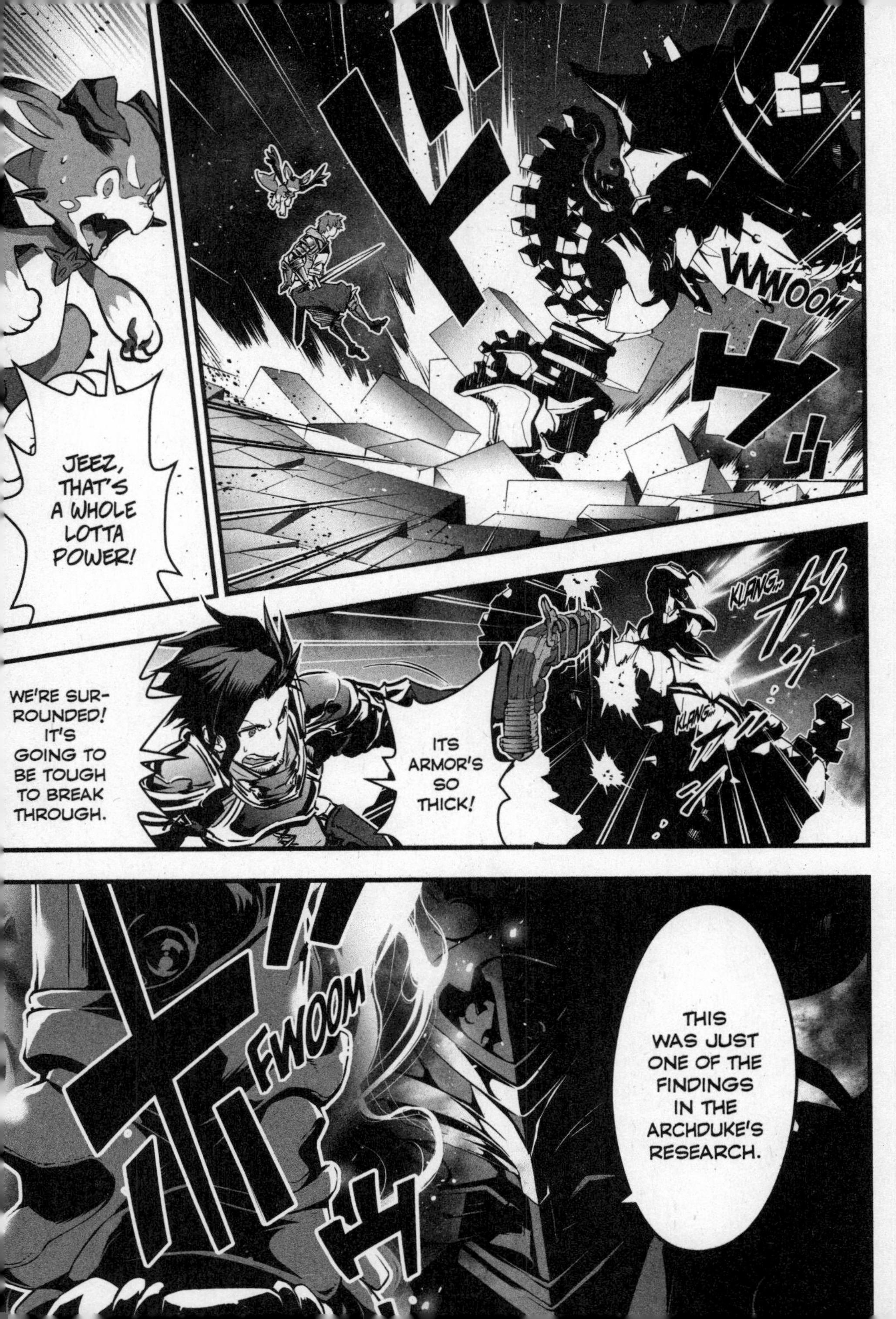
WWOOM
JEEZ, THAT'S A WHOLE LOTTA POWER!
KLANG
KLANG
ITS ARMOR'S SO THICK!
WE'RE SURROUNDED! IT'S GOING TO BE TOUGH TO BREAK THROUGH.
THIS WAS JUST ONE OF THE FINDINGS IN THE ARCHDUKE'S RESEARCH.
FWOOM

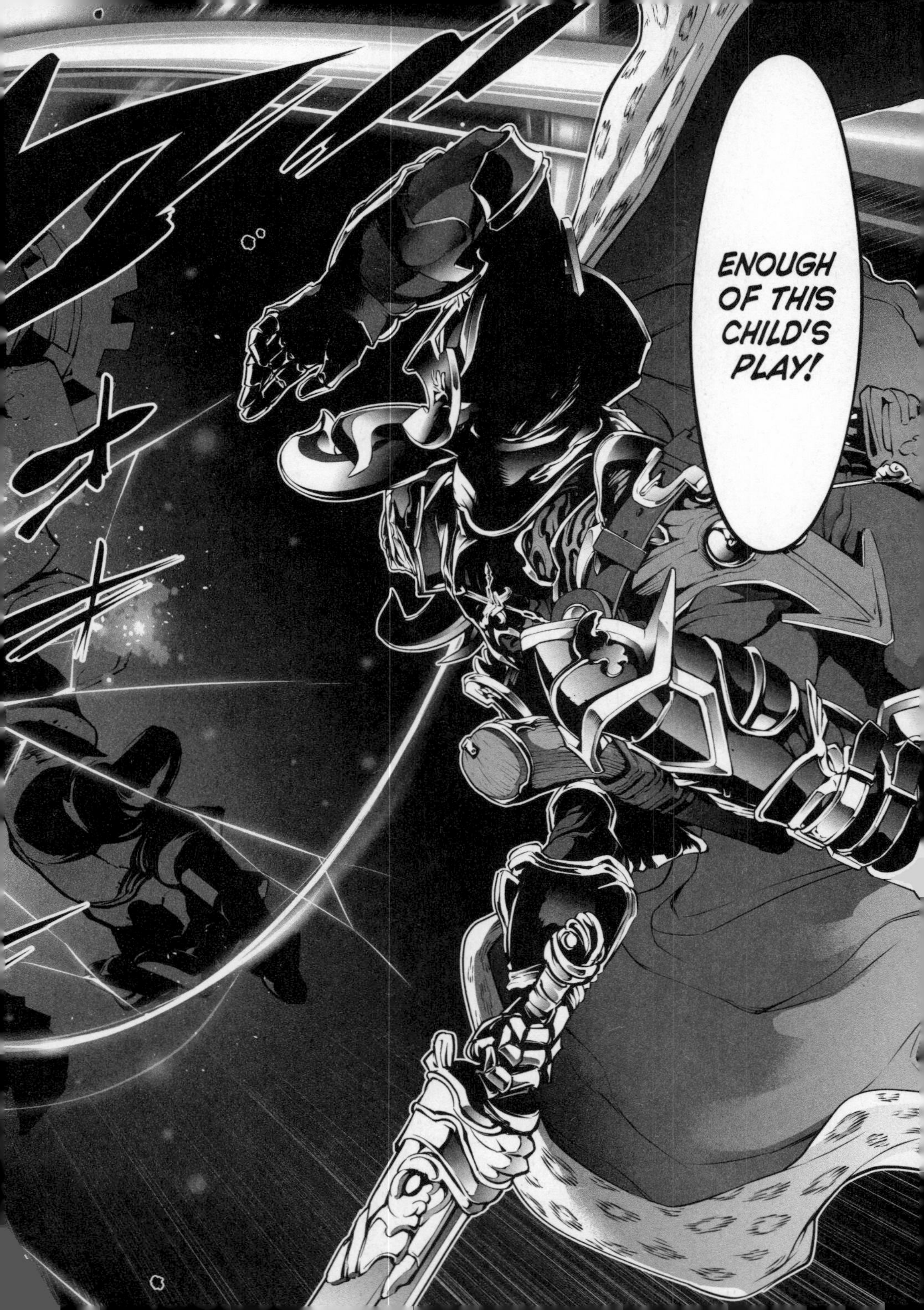
ENOUGH OF THIS CHILD'S PLAY!

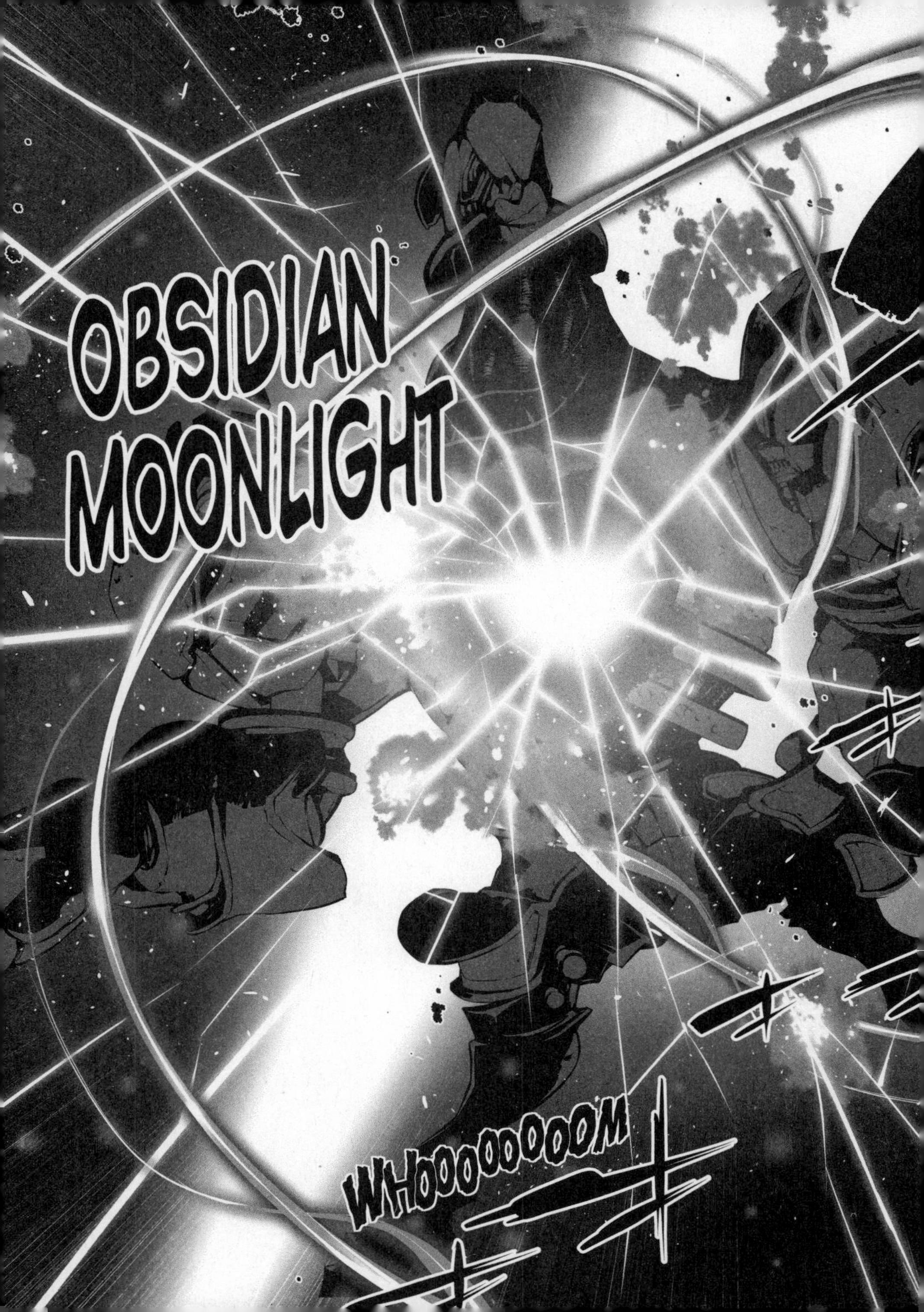
OBSIDIAN MOONLIGHT
WHOOOOOOOOM

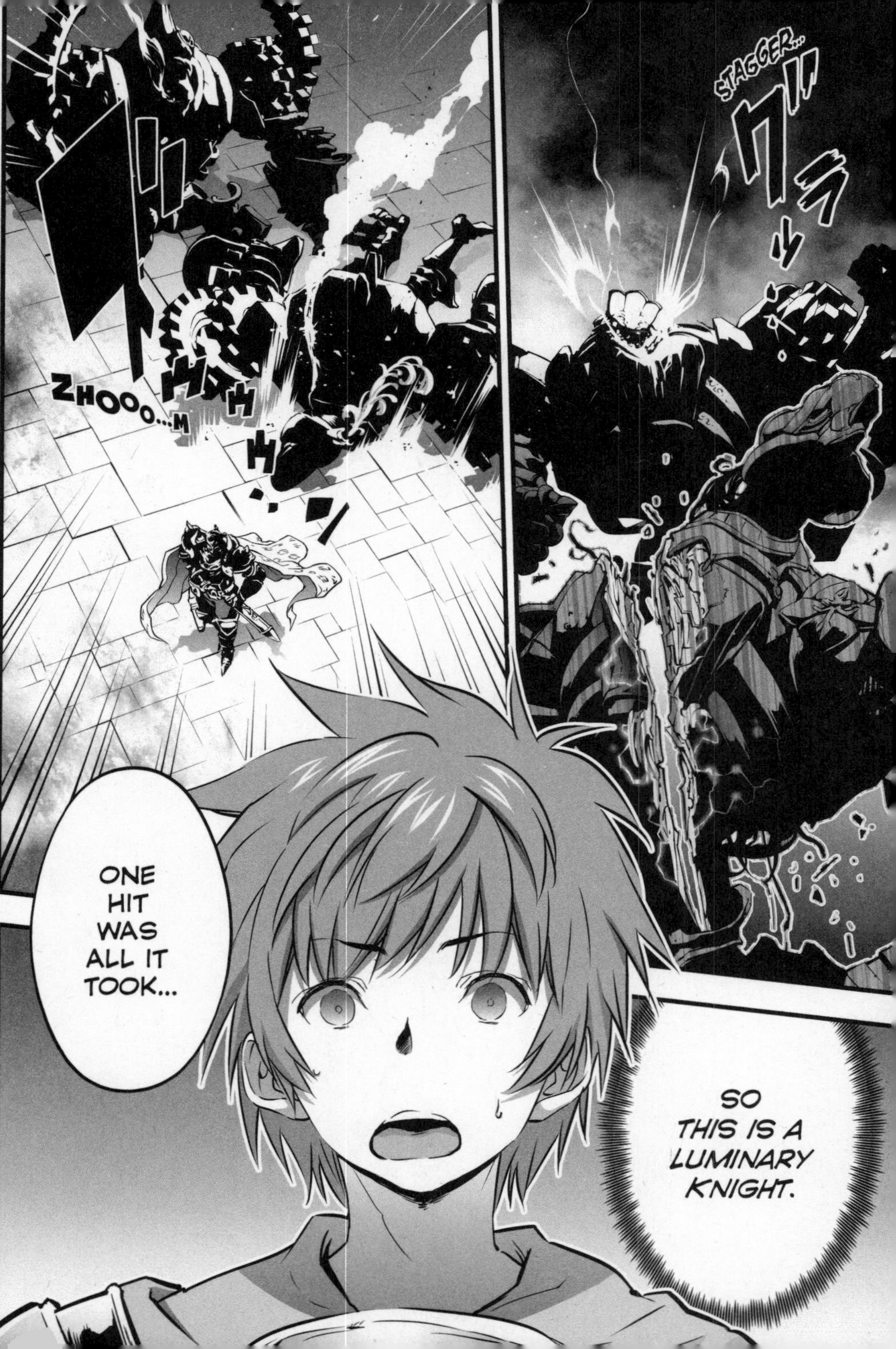
STAGGER...
ZHOOO...M
SO THIS IS A LUMINARY KNIGHT.
ONE HIT WAS ALL IT TOOK...

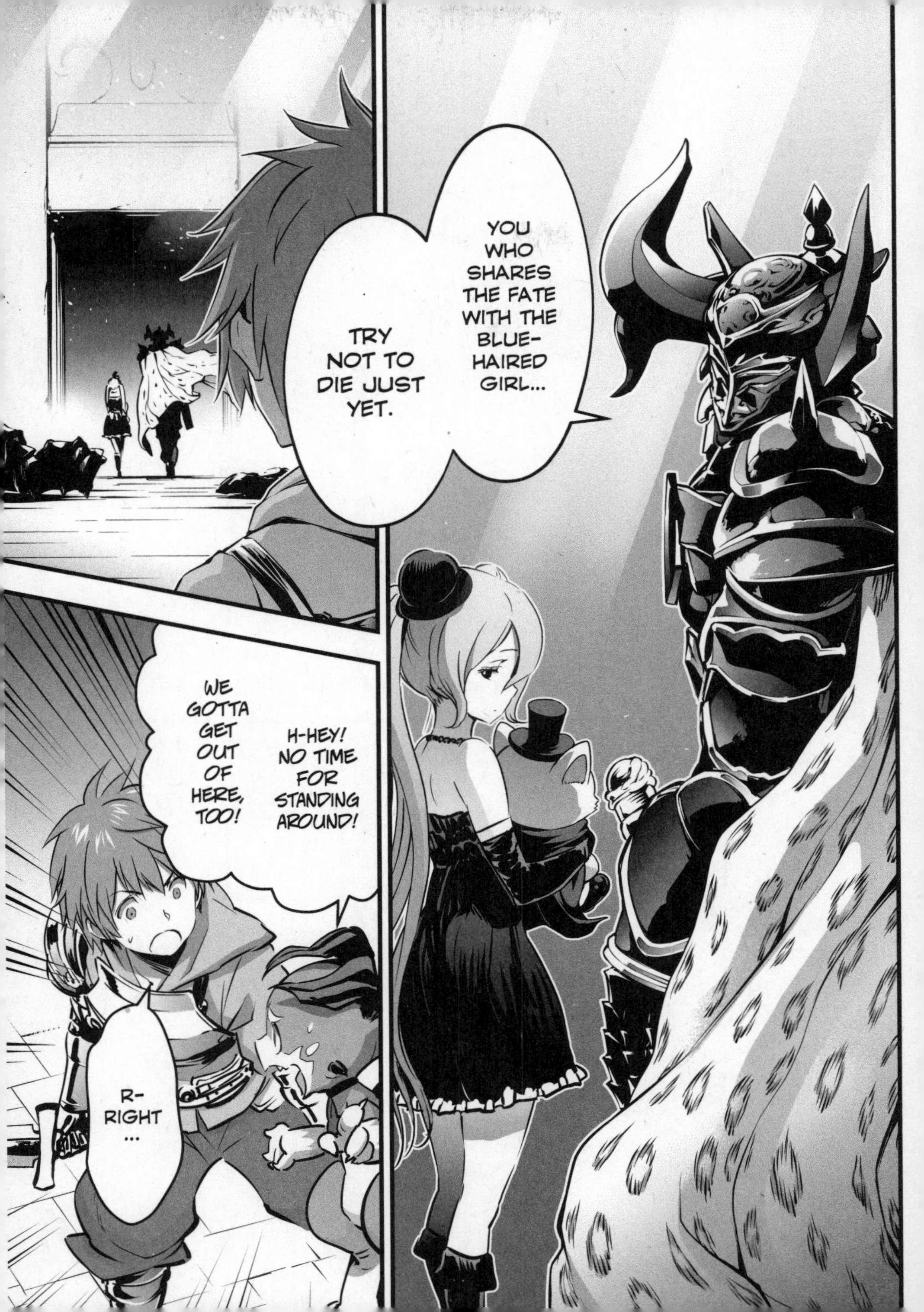
YOU WHO SHARES THE FATE WITH THE BLUE-HAIRED GIRL...
TRY NOT TO DIE JUST YET.
H-HEY! NO TIME FOR STANDING AROUND!
WE GOTTA GET OUT OF HERE, TOO!
R-RIGHT ...

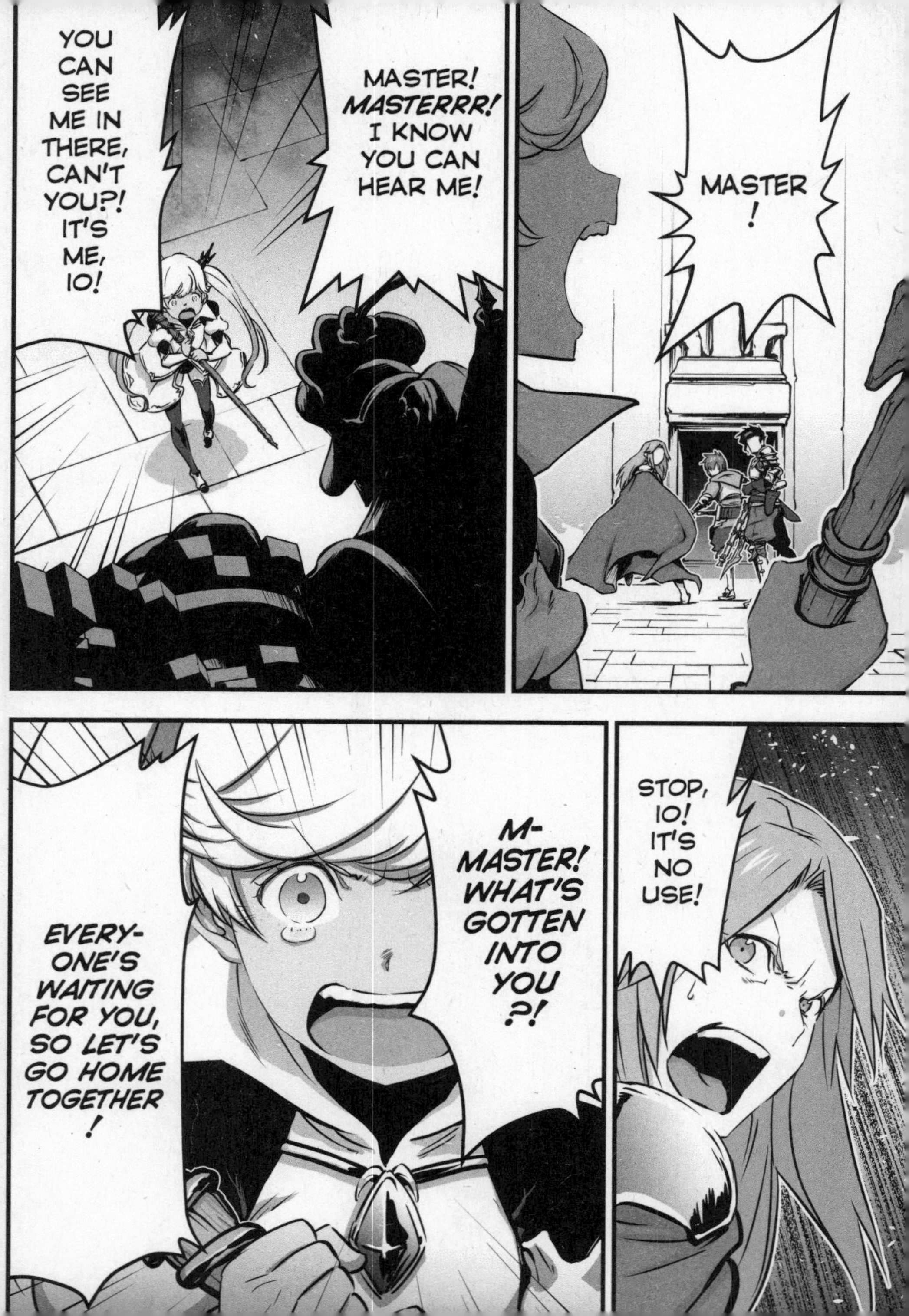
MASTER!
MASTER! MASTERRR! I KNOW YOU CAN HEAR ME!
YOU CAN SEE ME IN THERE, CAN'T YOU?! IT'S ME, IO!
STOP, IO! IT'S NO USE!
M-MASTER! WHAT'S GOTTEN INTO YOU?!
EVERYONE'S WAITING FOR YOU, SO LET'S GO HOME TOGETHER!

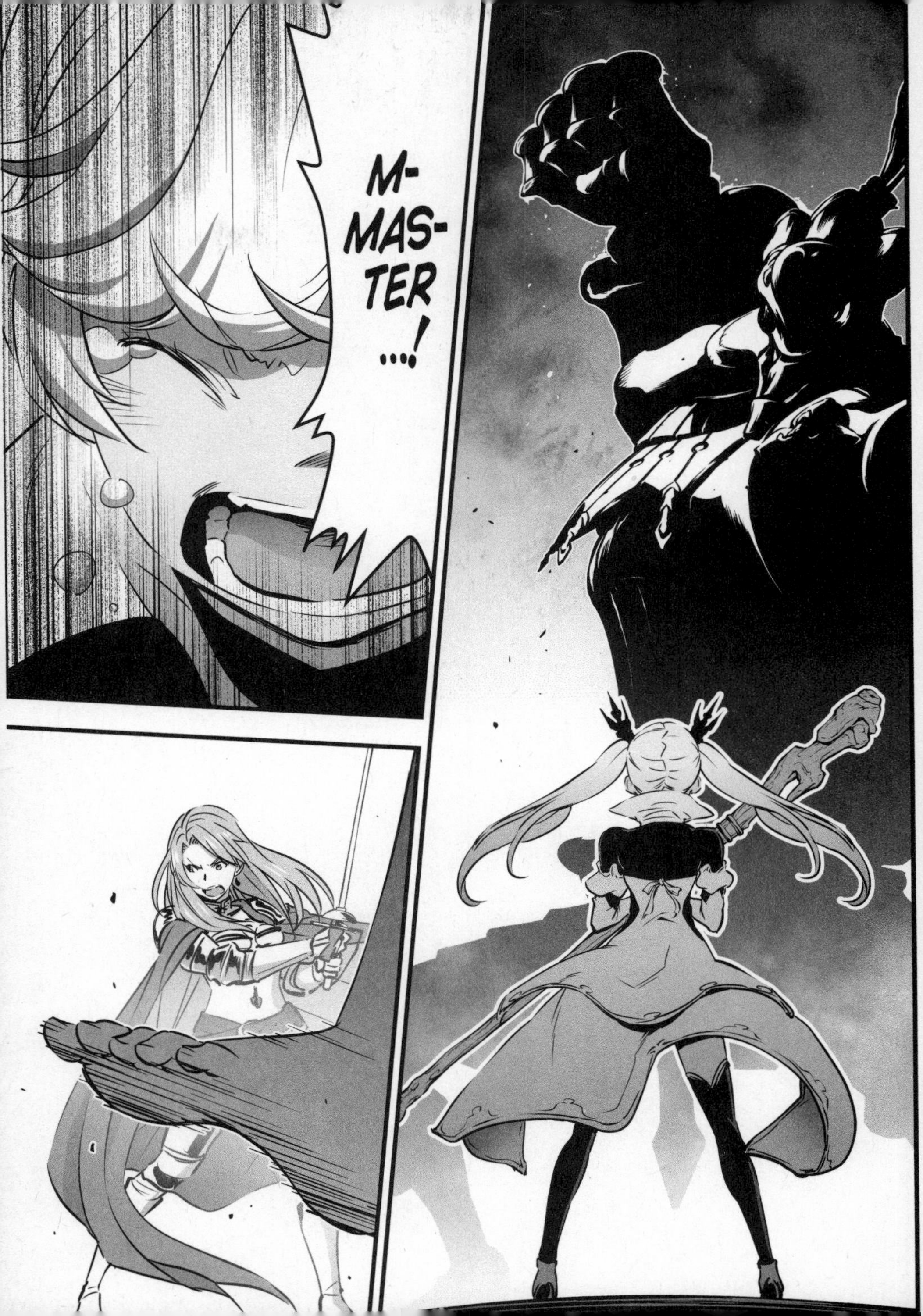
M-MAS-TER ...!

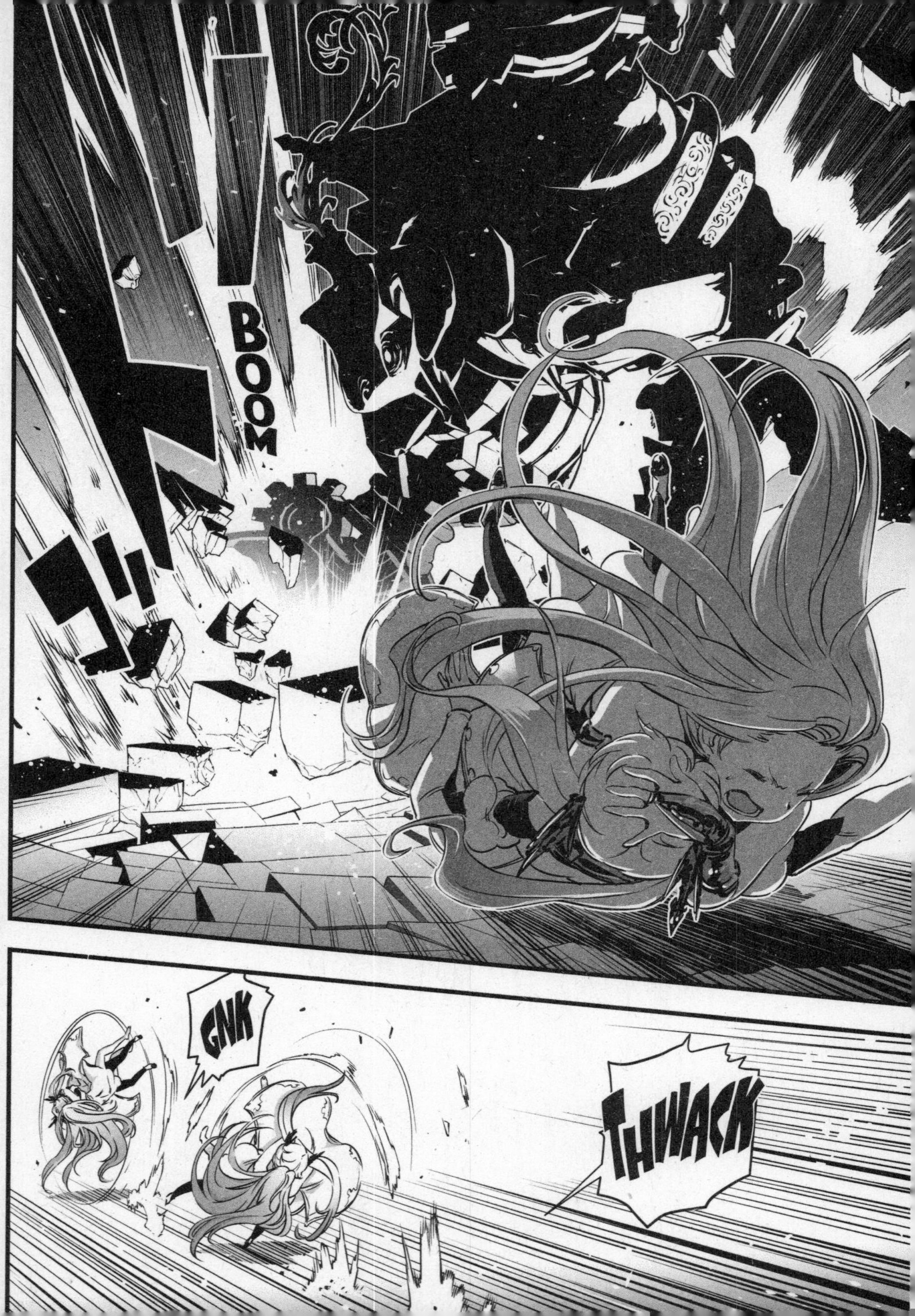
BOOM
THWACK
GNK

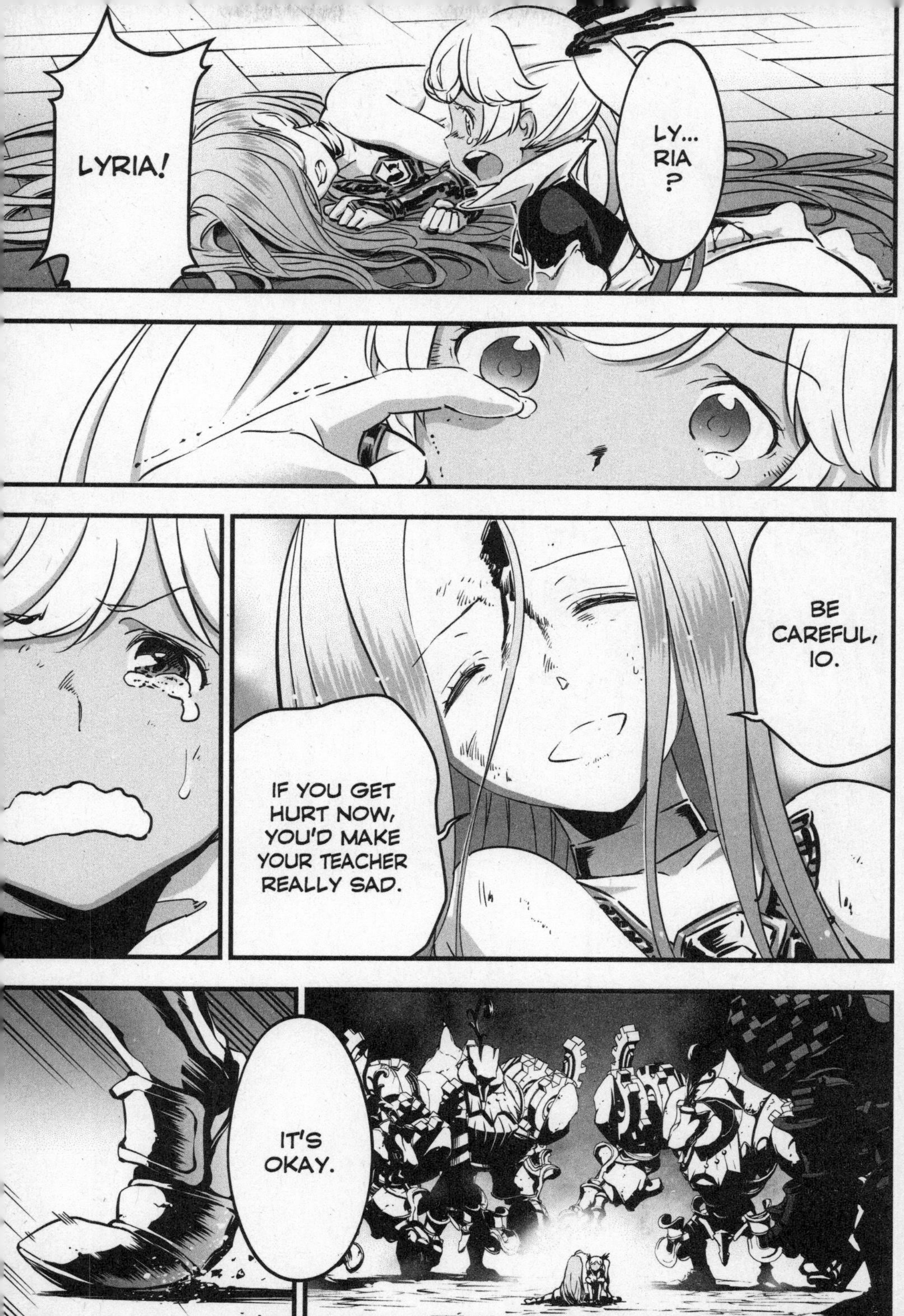
LY... RIA ?
LYRIA!
BE CAREFUL, IO.
IF YOU GET HURT NOW, YOU'D MAKE YOUR TEACHER REALLY SAD.
IT'S OKAY.

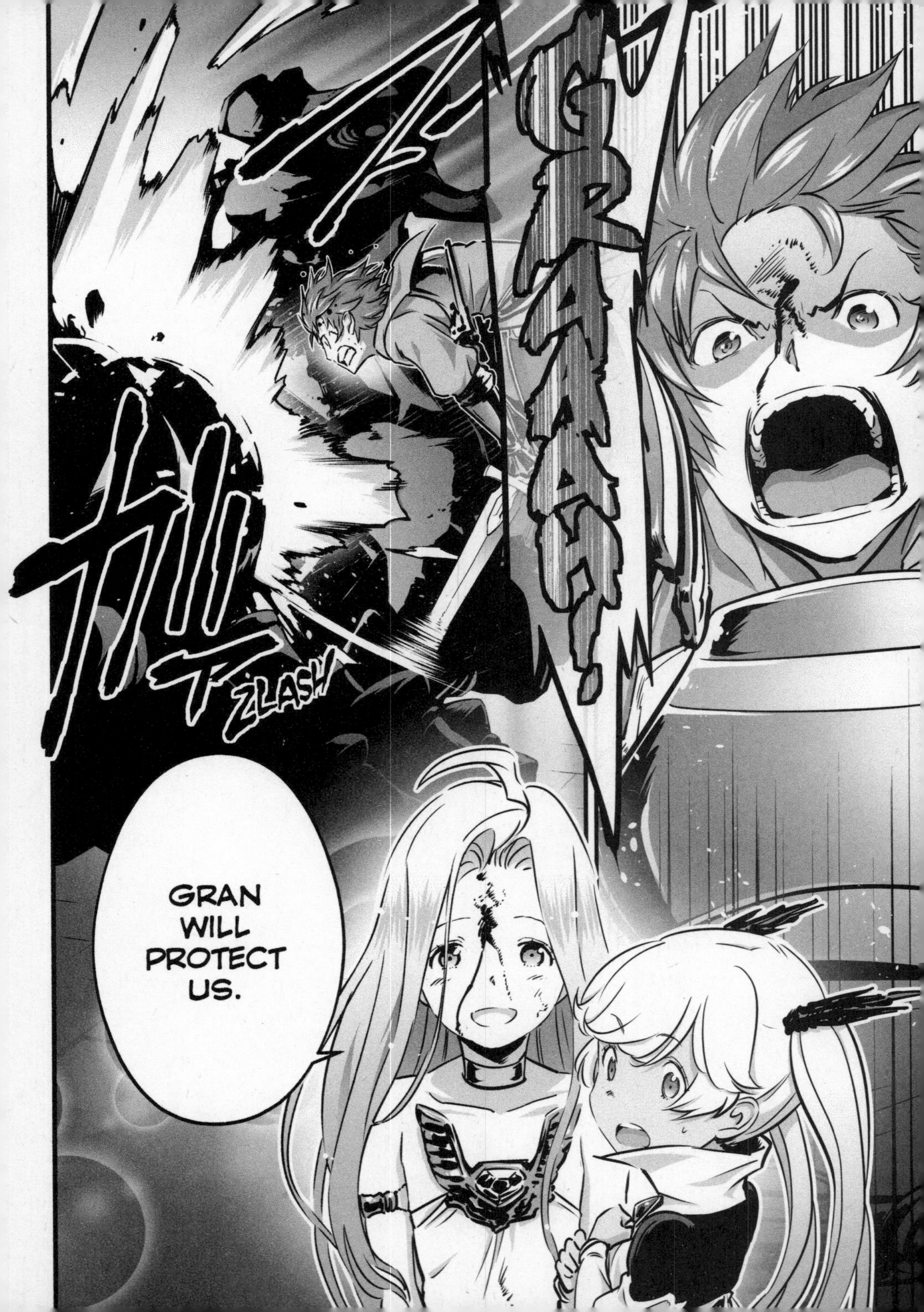
GRAAAH!
ガッ
ZLASH
GRAN WILL PROTECT US.

LYRIA
!!

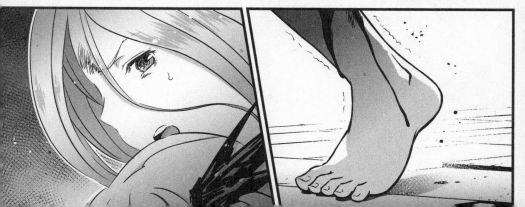

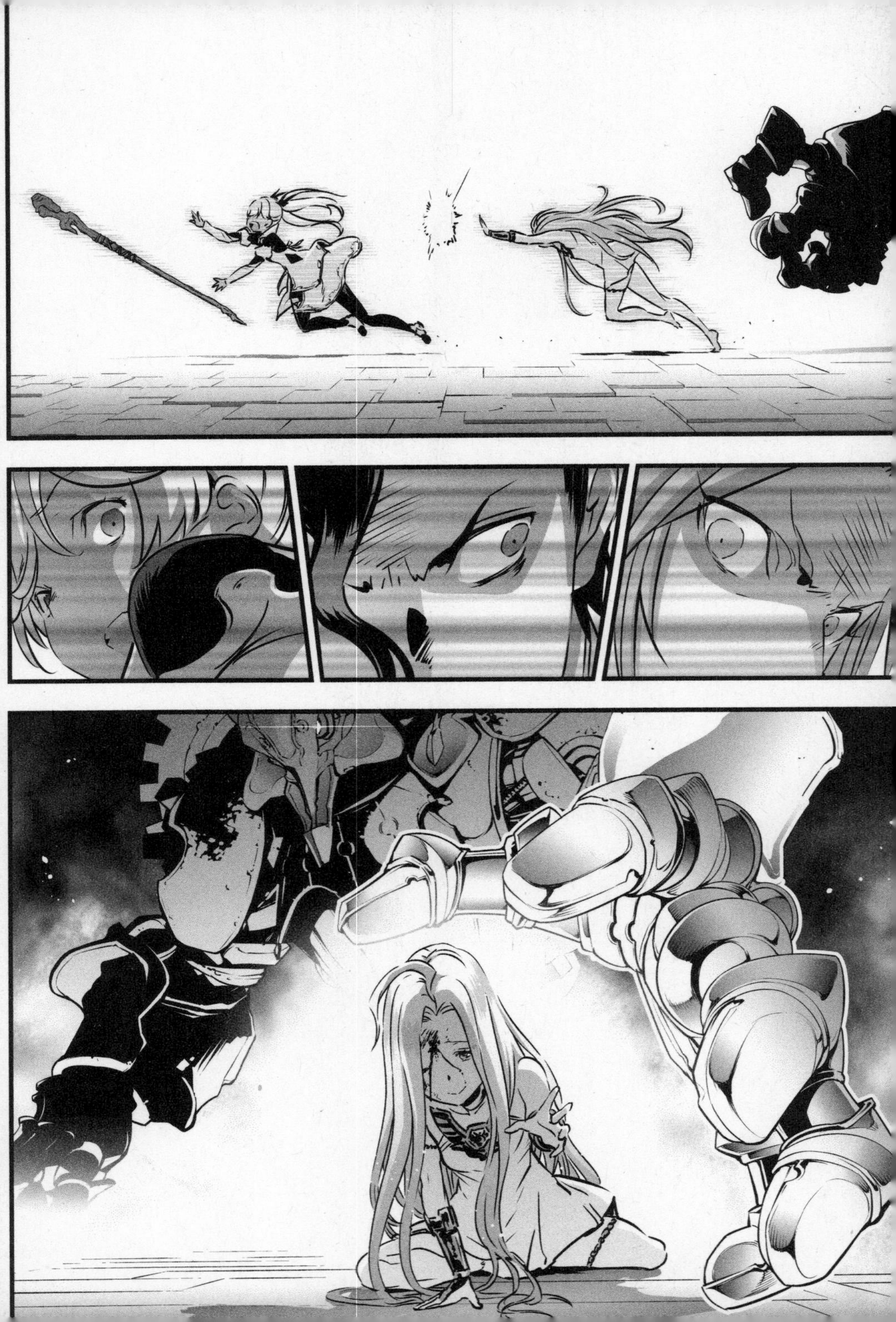

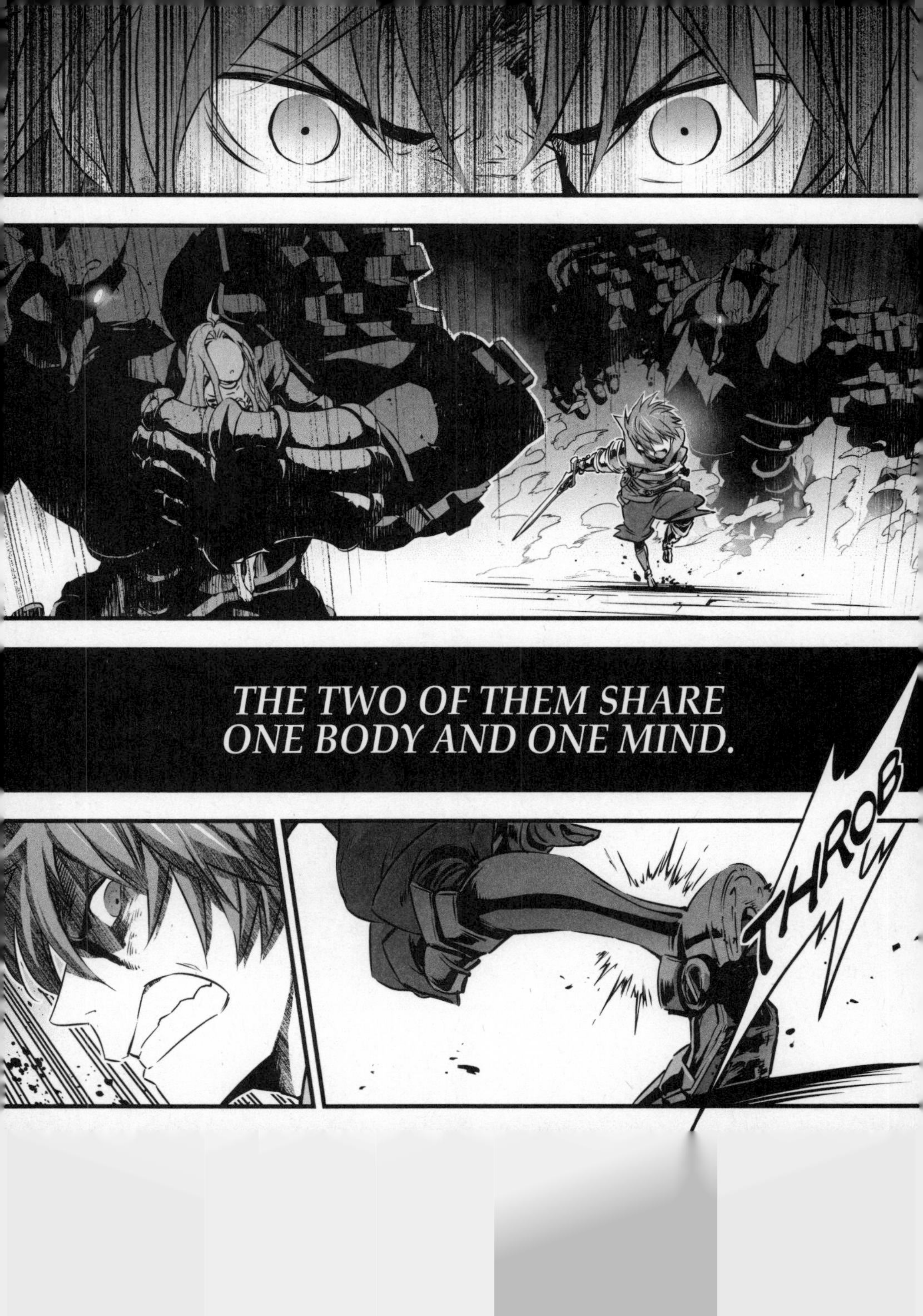
THE TWO OF THEM SHARE
ONE BODY AND ONE MIND.
THROB

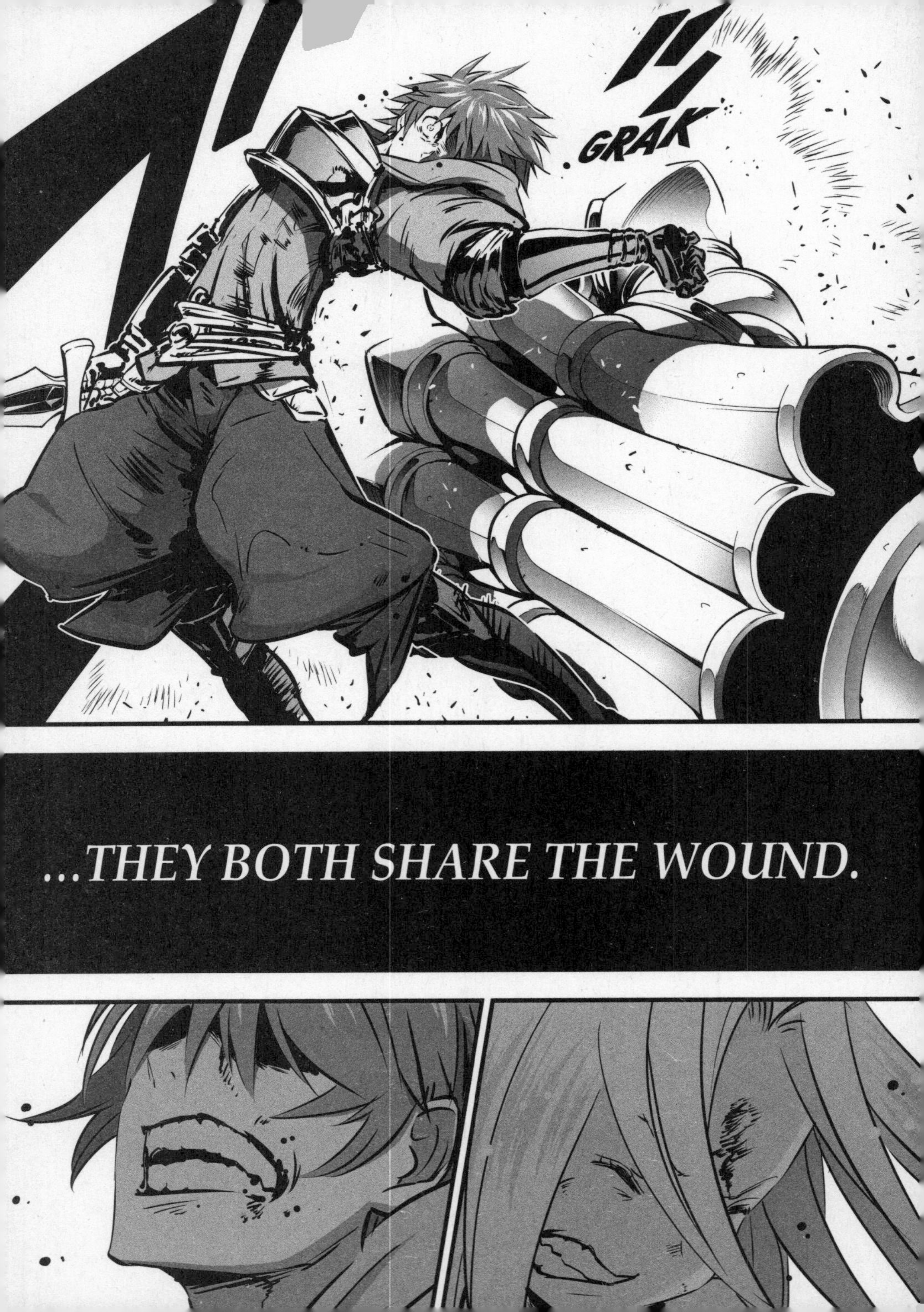
GRAK
...THEY BOTH SHARE THE WOUND.

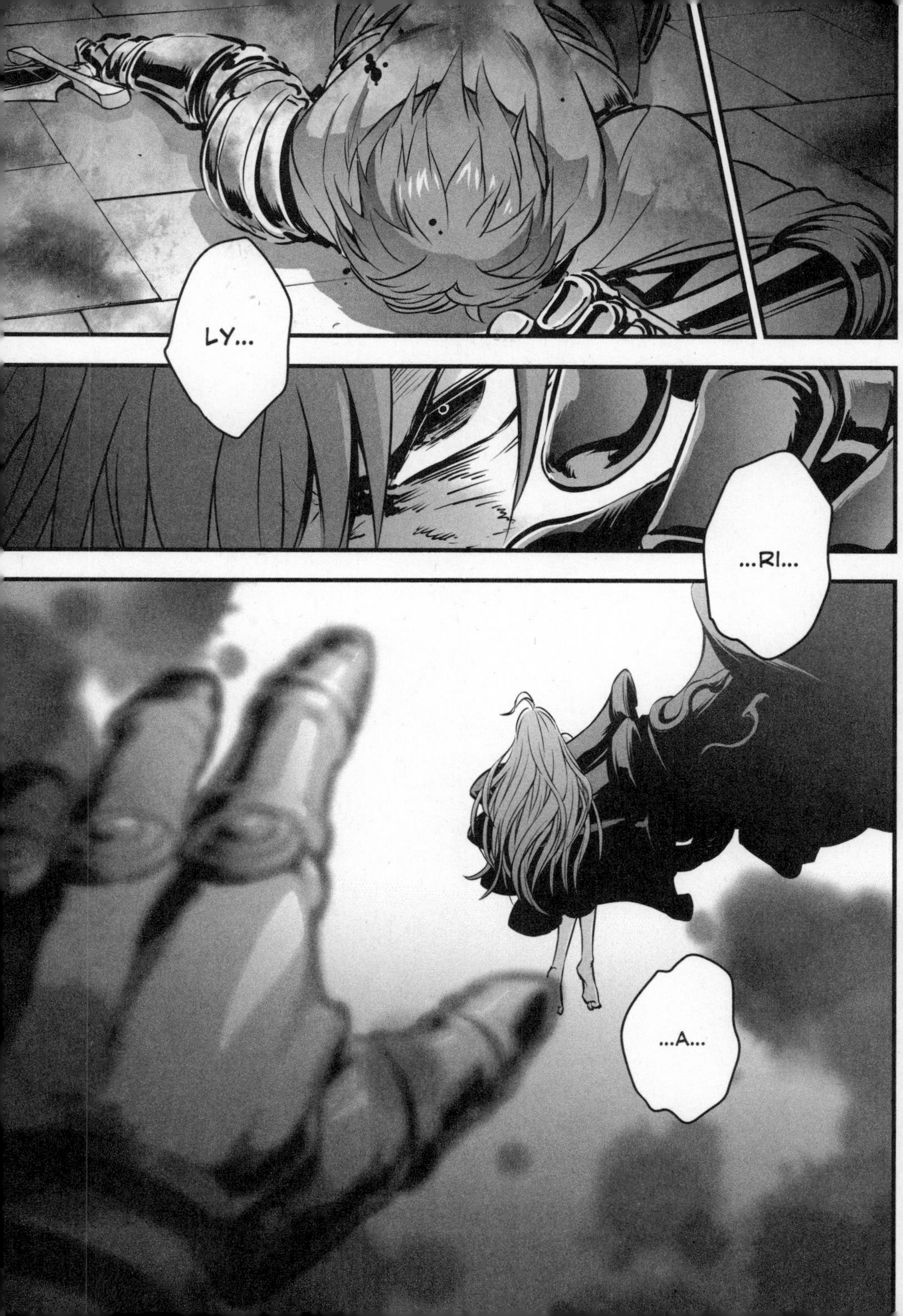
LY...
...RI...
...A...

GRANBLUE FANTASY
グランブルーファンタジー

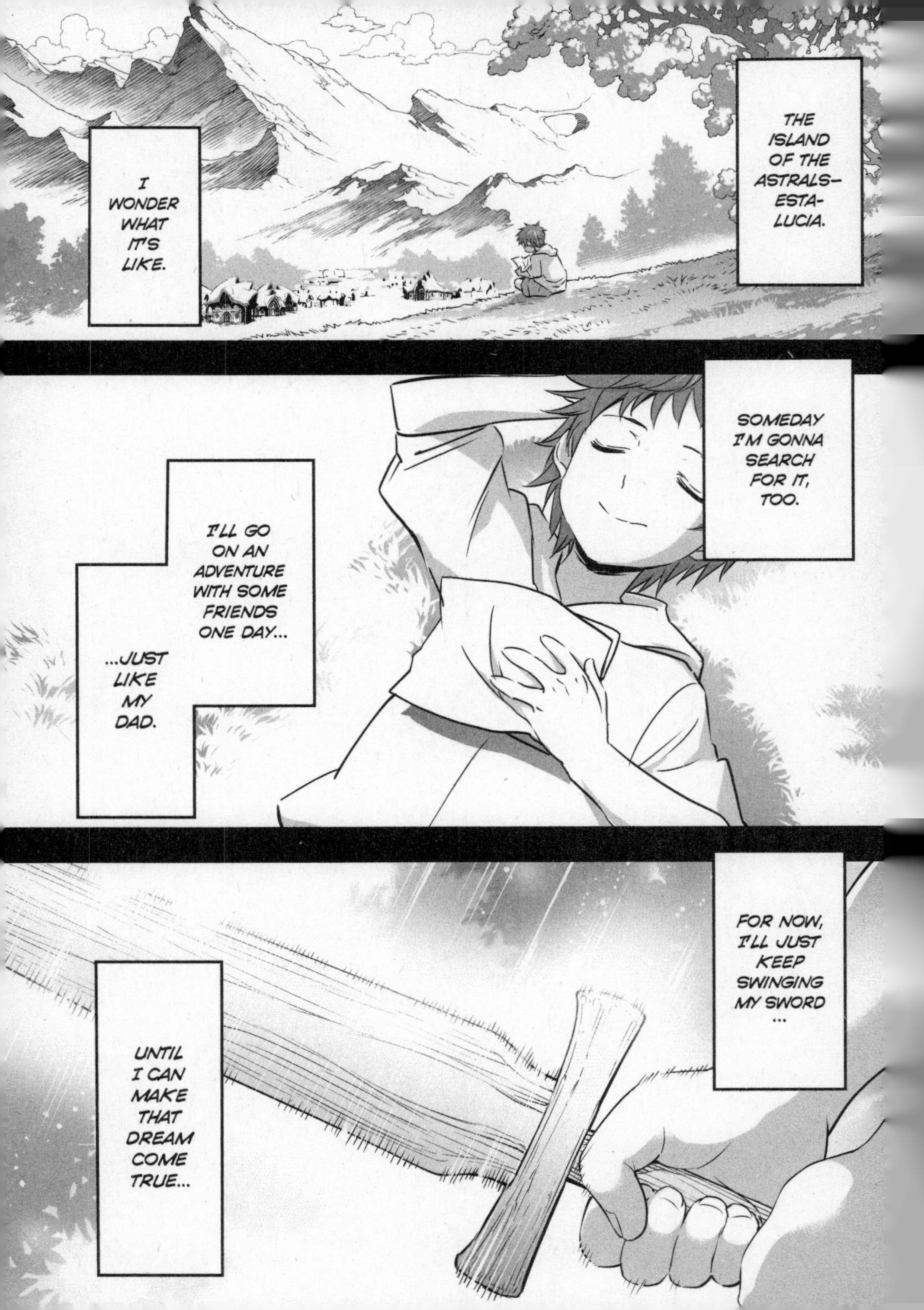
THE ISLAND OF THE ASTRALS—ESTA-LUCIA.
I WONDER WHAT IT'S LIKE.
SOMEDAY I'M GONNA SEARCH FOR IT, TOO.
I'LL GO ON AN ADVENTURE WITH SOME FRIENDS ONE DAY...
...JUST LIKE MY DAD.
FOR NOW, I'LL JUST KEEP SWINGING MY SWORD...
UNTIL I CAN MAKE THAT DREAM COME TRUE...

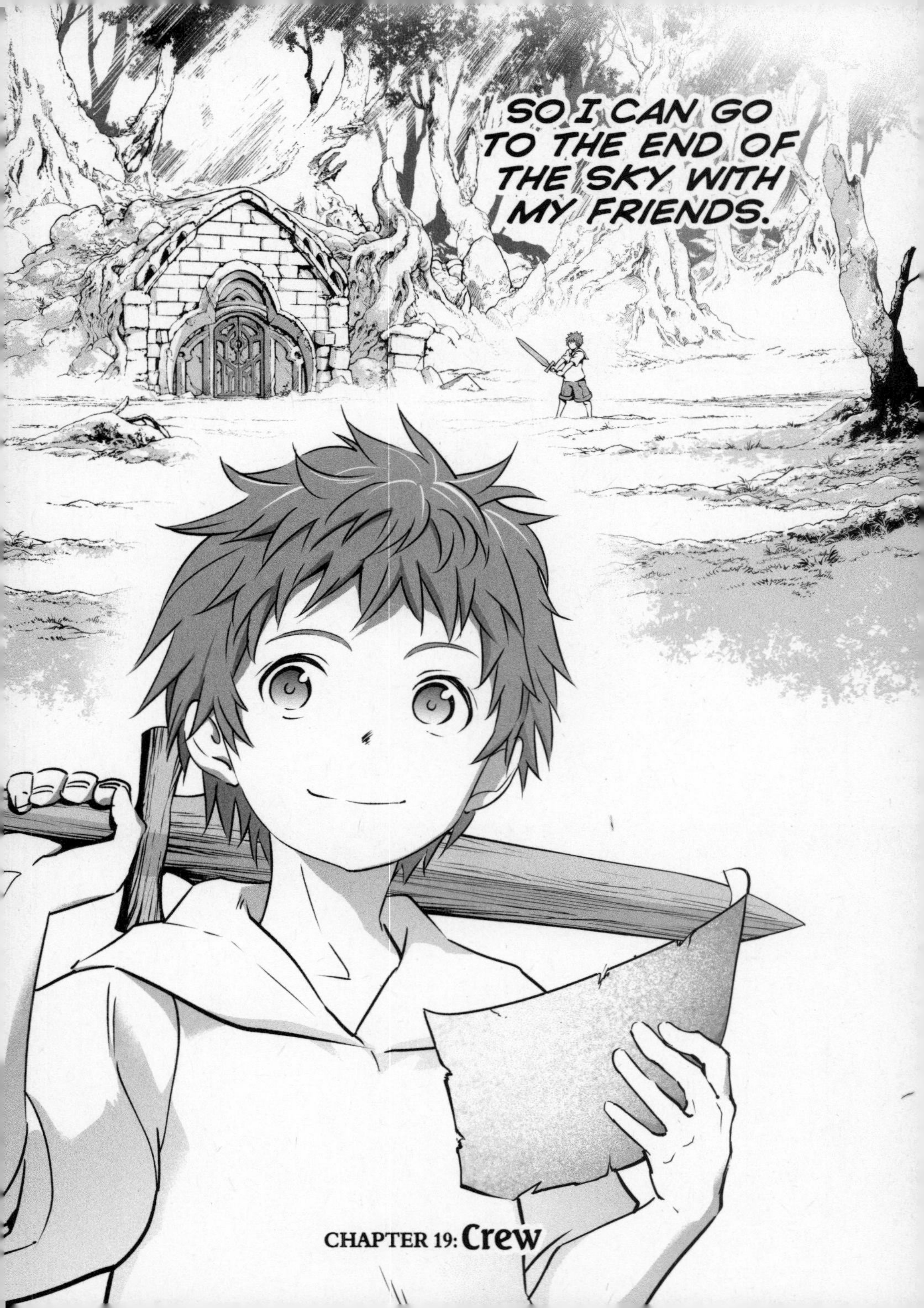
SO I CAN GO TO THE END OF THE SKY WITH MY FRIENDS.
CHAPTER 19: Crew

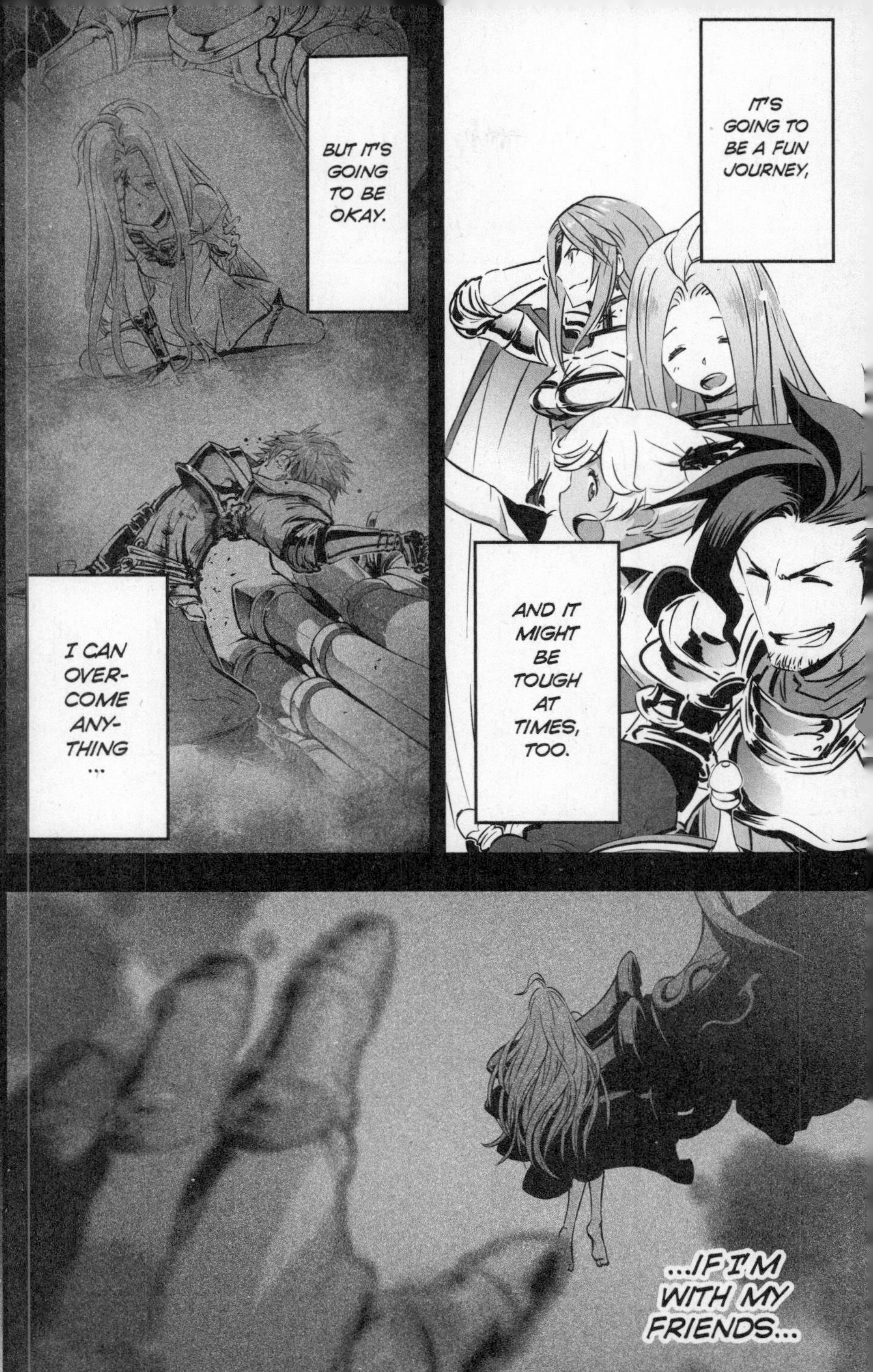
IT'S GOING TO BE A FUN JOURNEY,
AND IT MIGHT BE TOUGH AT TIMES, TOO.
BUT IT'S GOING TO BE OKAY.
I CAN OVERCOME ANYTHING...
...IF I'M WITH MY FRIENDS...

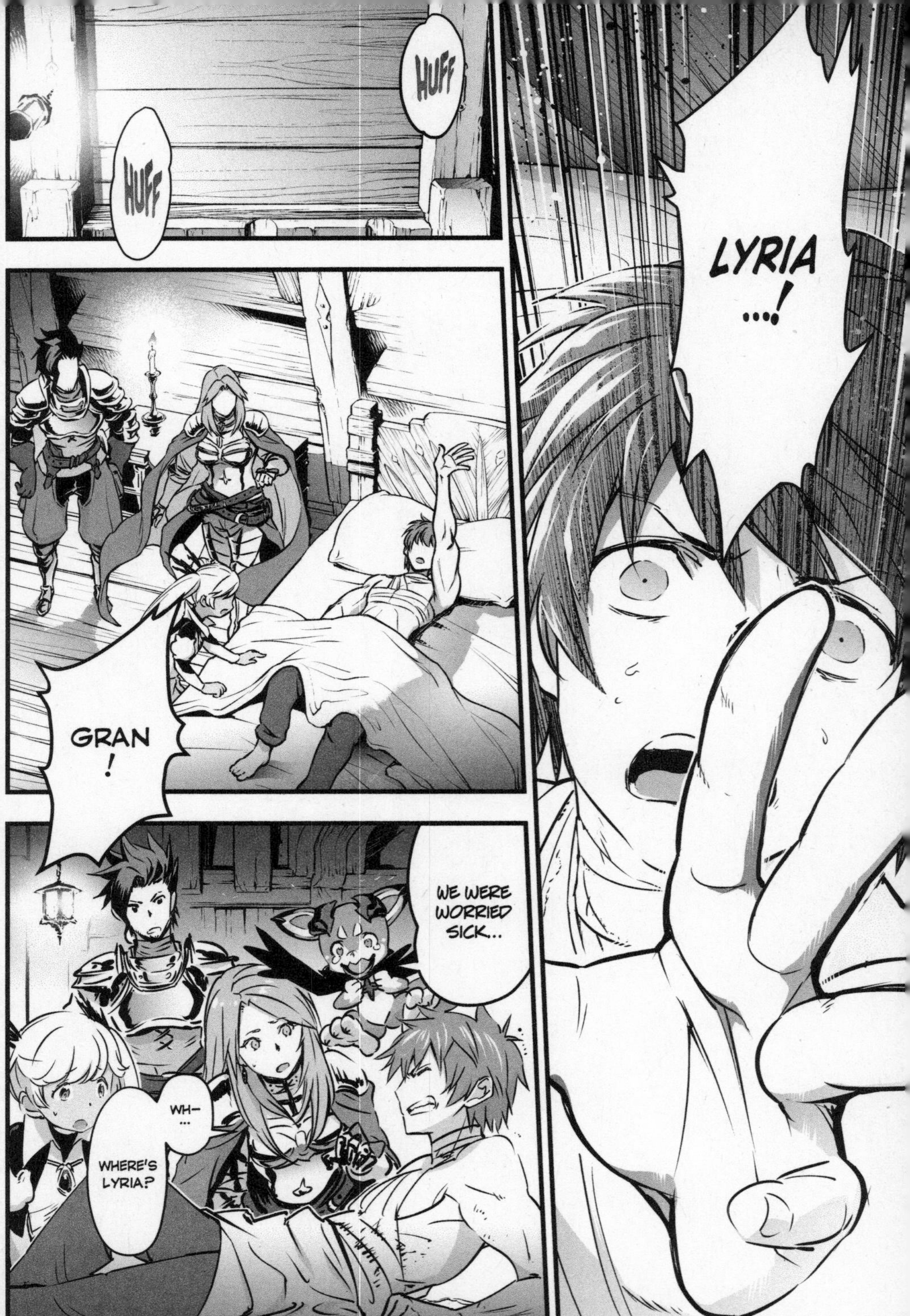
LYRIA ...!
HUFF
HUFF
GRAN!
WE WERE WORRIED SICK...
WH- ...
WHERE'S LYRIA?

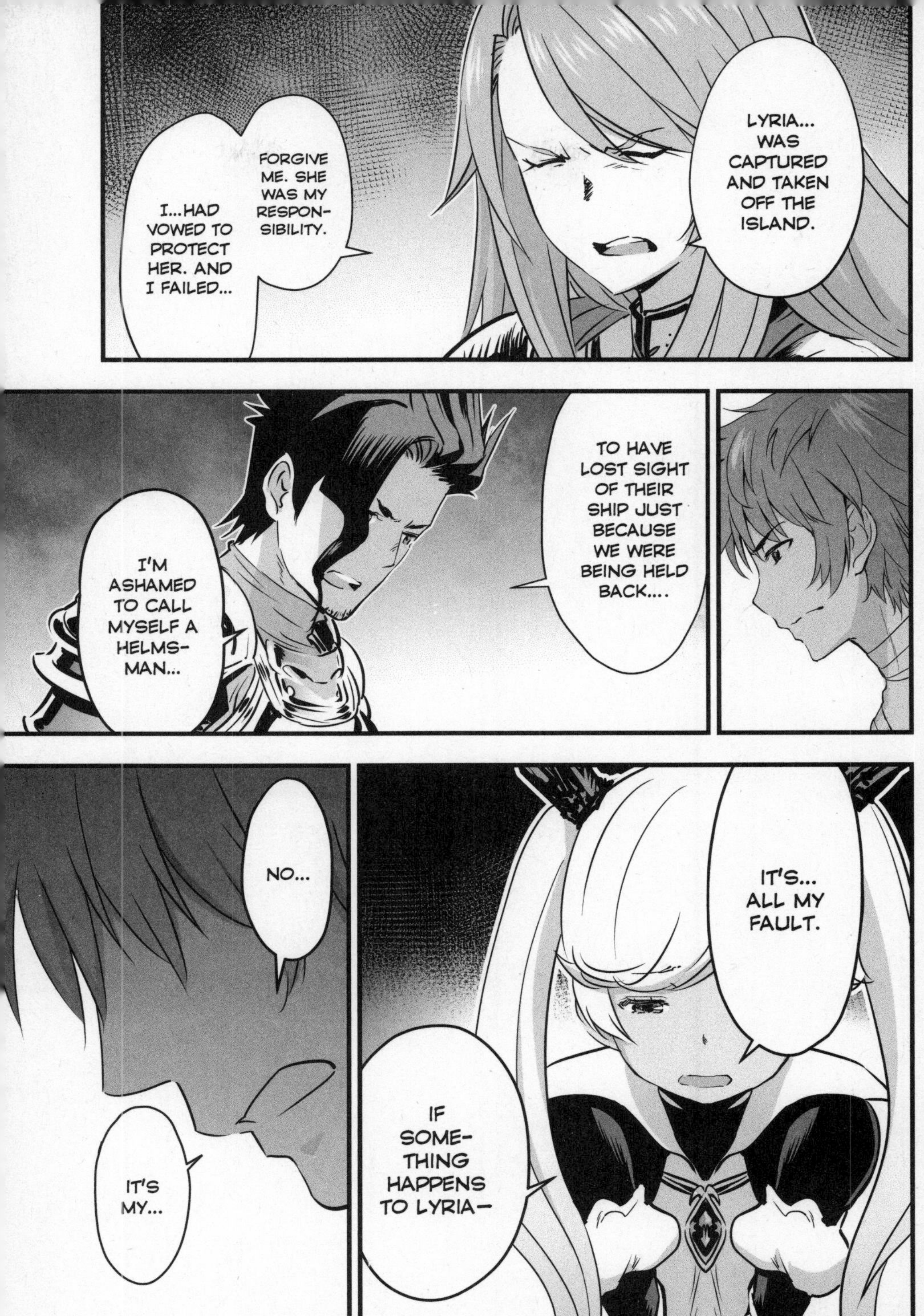
LYRIA... WAS CAPTURED AND TAKEN OFF THE ISLAND.
FORGIVE ME. SHE WAS MY RESPONSIBILITY.
I...HAD VOWED TO PROTECT HER. AND I FAILED...
TO HAVE LOST SIGHT OF THEIR SHIP JUST BECAUSE WE WERE BEING HELD BACK....
I'M ASHAMED TO CALL MYSELF A HELMSMAN...
IT'S... ALL MY FAULT.
IF SOMETHING HAPPENS TO LYRIA—
NO...
IT'S MY...

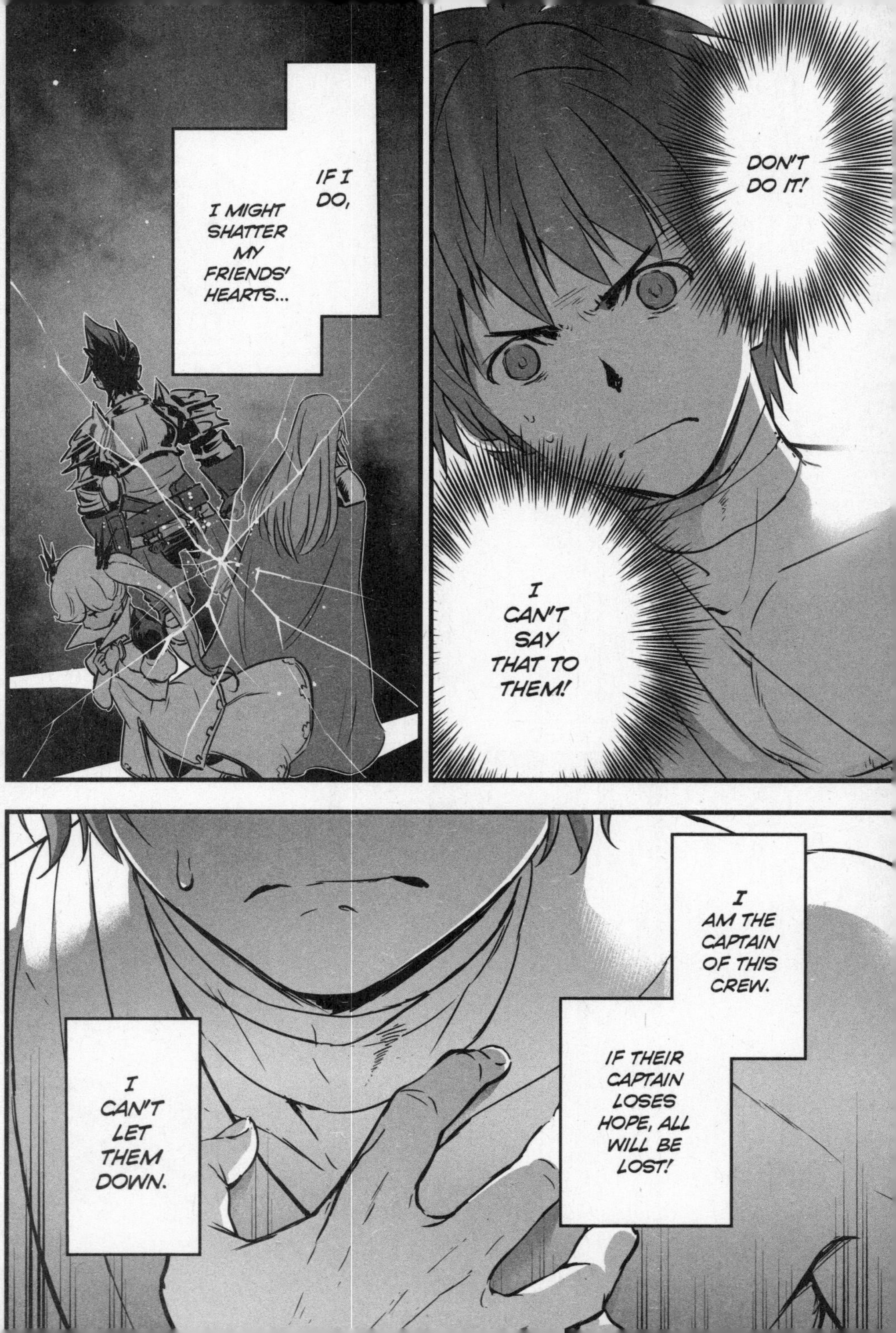
DON'T DO IT!
I CAN'T SAY THAT TO THEM!
IF I DO,
I MIGHT SHATTER MY FRIENDS' HEARTS...
I AM THE CAPTAIN OF THIS CREW.
IF THEIR CAPTAIN LOSES HOPE, ALL WILL BE LOST!
I CAN'T LET THEM DOWN.

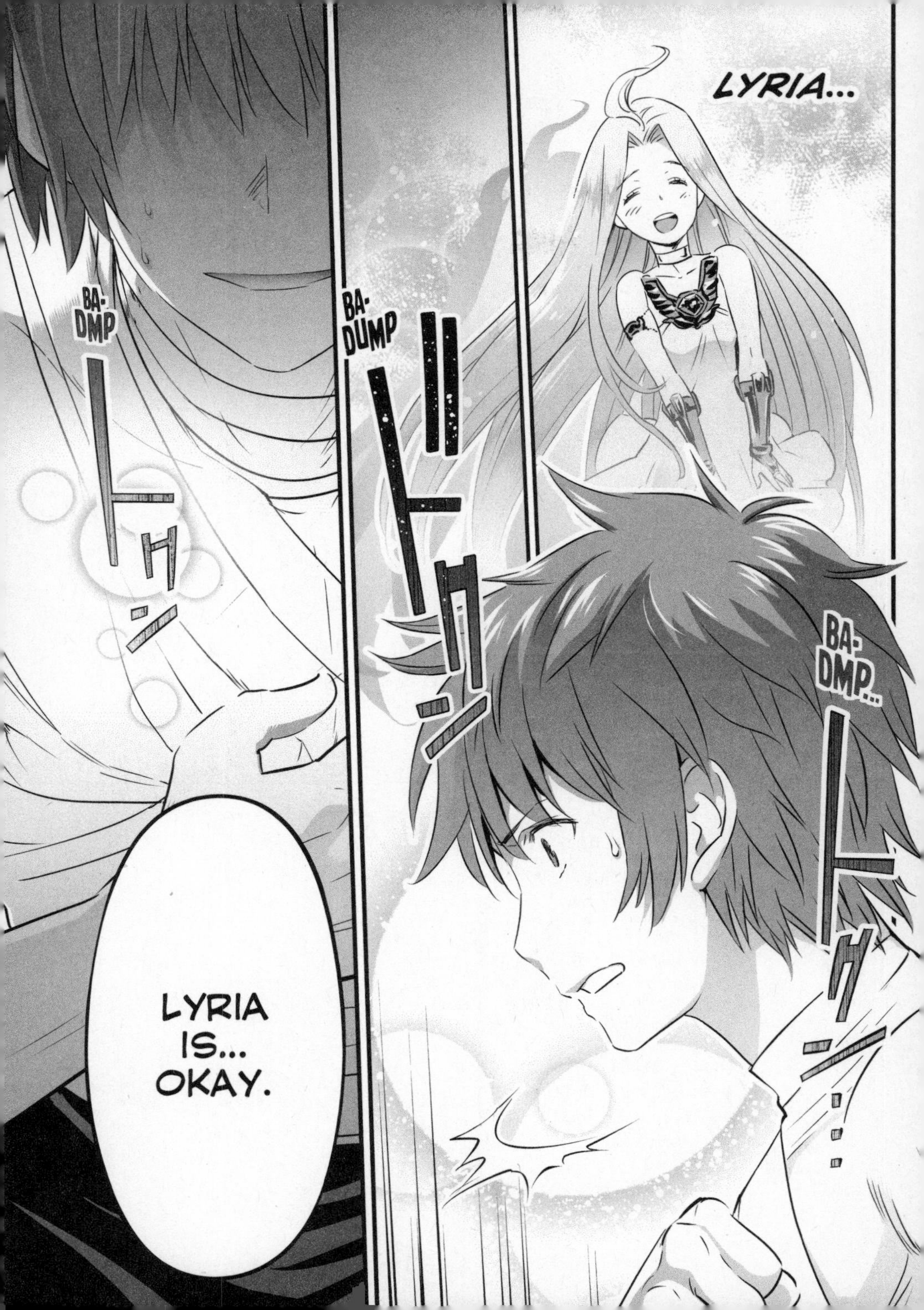
LYRIA...
BA-DMP...
BA-DUMP
BA-DMP
LYRIA IS... OKAY.

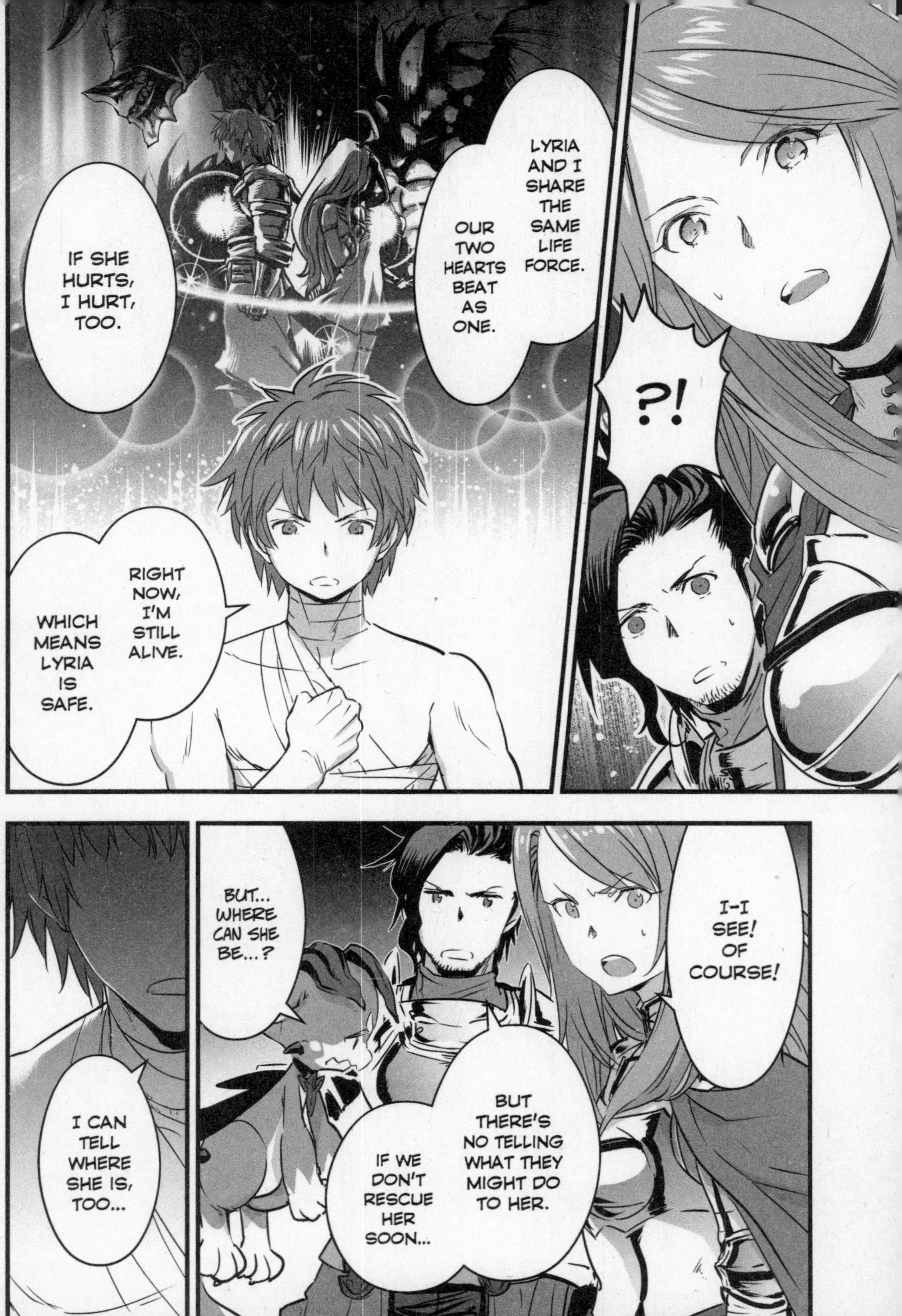
?!
LYRIA AND I SHARE THE SAME LIFE FORCE.
OUR TWO HEARTS BEAT AS ONE.
IF SHE HURTS, I HURT, TOO.
RIGHT NOW, I'M STILL ALIVE.
WHICH MEANS LYRIA IS SAFE.
I-I SEE! OF COURSE!
BUT... WHERE CAN SHE BE...?
BUT THERE'S NO TELLING WHAT THEY MIGHT DO TO HER.
IF WE DON'T RESCUE HER SOON...
I CAN TELL WHERE SHE IS, TOO...

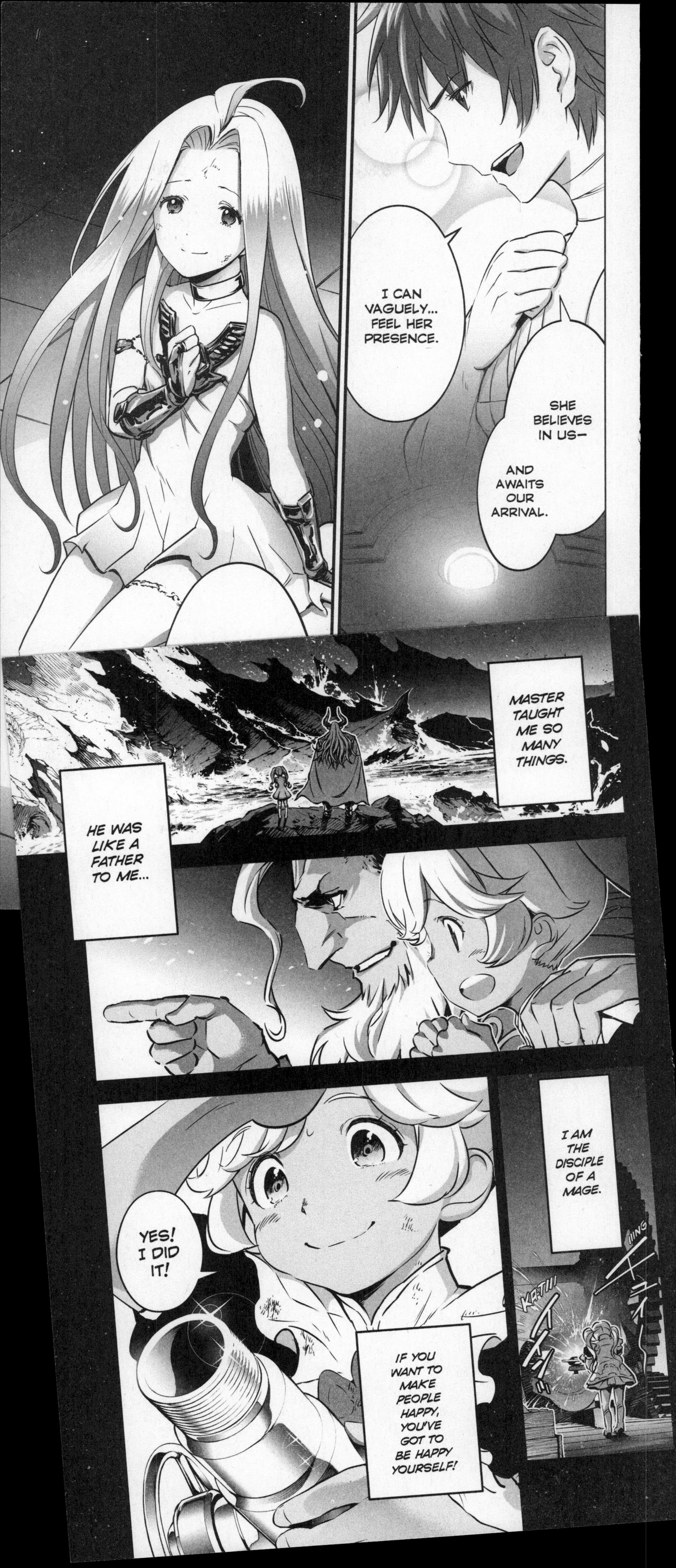
I CAN VAGUELY... FEEL HER PRESENCE.
SHE BELIEVES IN US—
AND AWAITS OUR ARRIVAL.
MASTER TAUGHT ME SO MANY THINGS.
HE WAS LIKE A FATHER TO ME...
I AM THE DISCIPLE OF A MAGE.
YES! I DID IT!
IF YOU WANT TO MAKE PEOPLE HAPPY, YOU'VE GOT TO BE HAPPY YOURSELF!

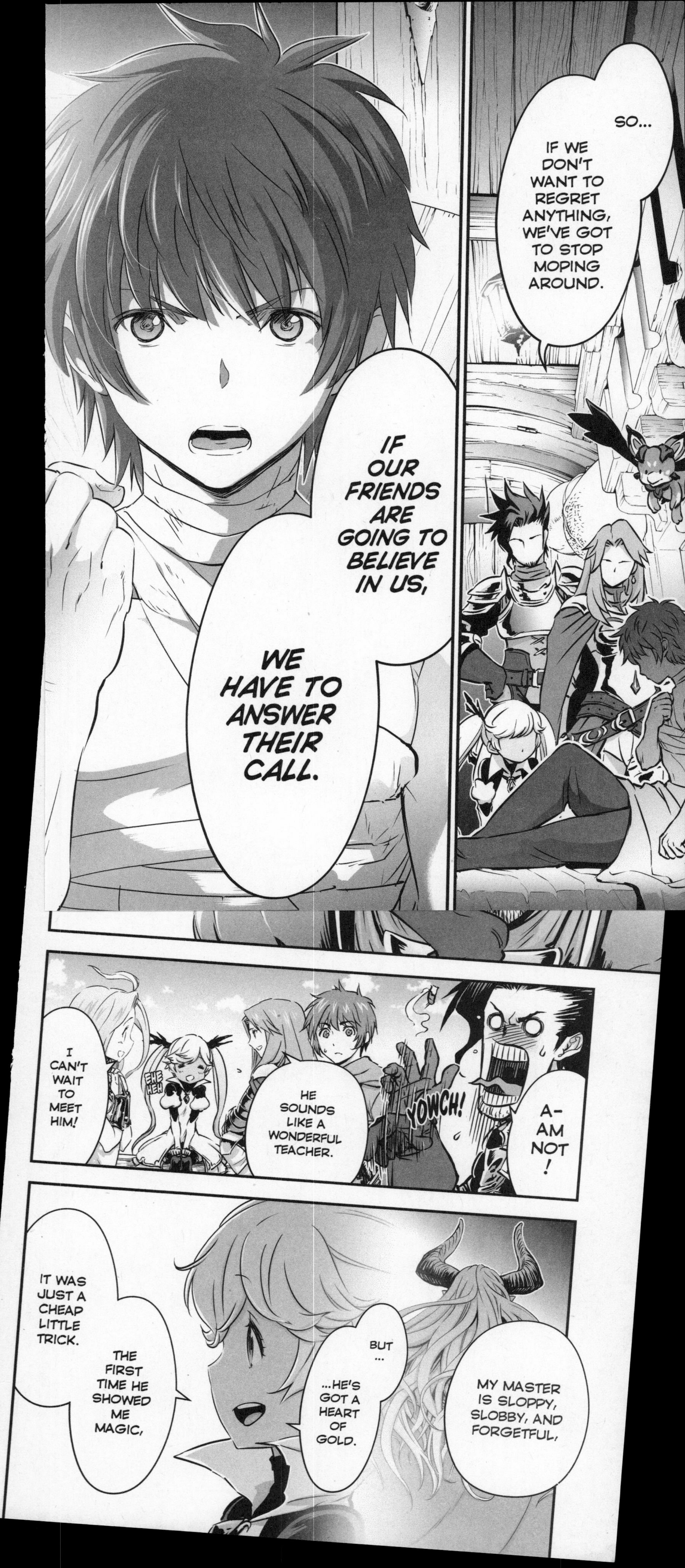
SO...
IF WE DON'T WANT TO REGRET ANYTHING, WE'VE GOT TO STOP MOPING AROUND.
IF OUR FRIENDS ARE GOING TO BELIEVE IN US,
WE HAVE TO ANSWER THEIR CALL.
A-AM NOT!
YOWCH!
HE SOUNDS LIKE A WONDERFUL TEACHER.
EHE HEH
I CAN'T WAIT TO MEET HIM!
MY MASTER IS SLOPPY, SLOBBY, AND FORGETFUL,
BUT ...
...HE'S GOT A HEART OF GOLD.
IT WAS JUST A CHEAP LITTLE TRICK.
THE FIRST TIME HE SHOWED ME MAGIC,

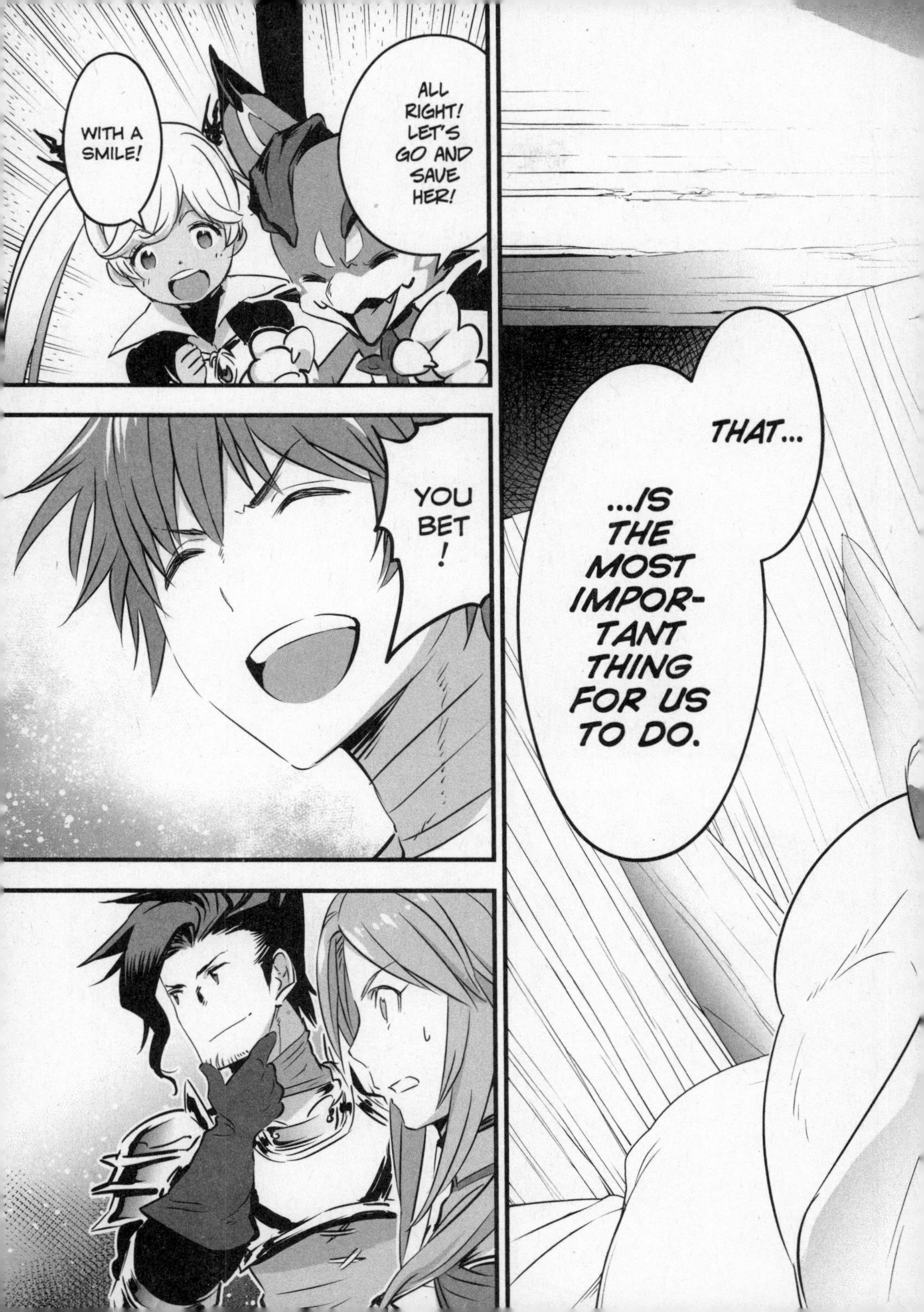
THAT...
...IS THE MOST IMPOR-TANT THING FOR US TO DO.
ALL RIGHT! LET'S GO AND SAVE HER!
WITH A SMILE!
YOU BET!

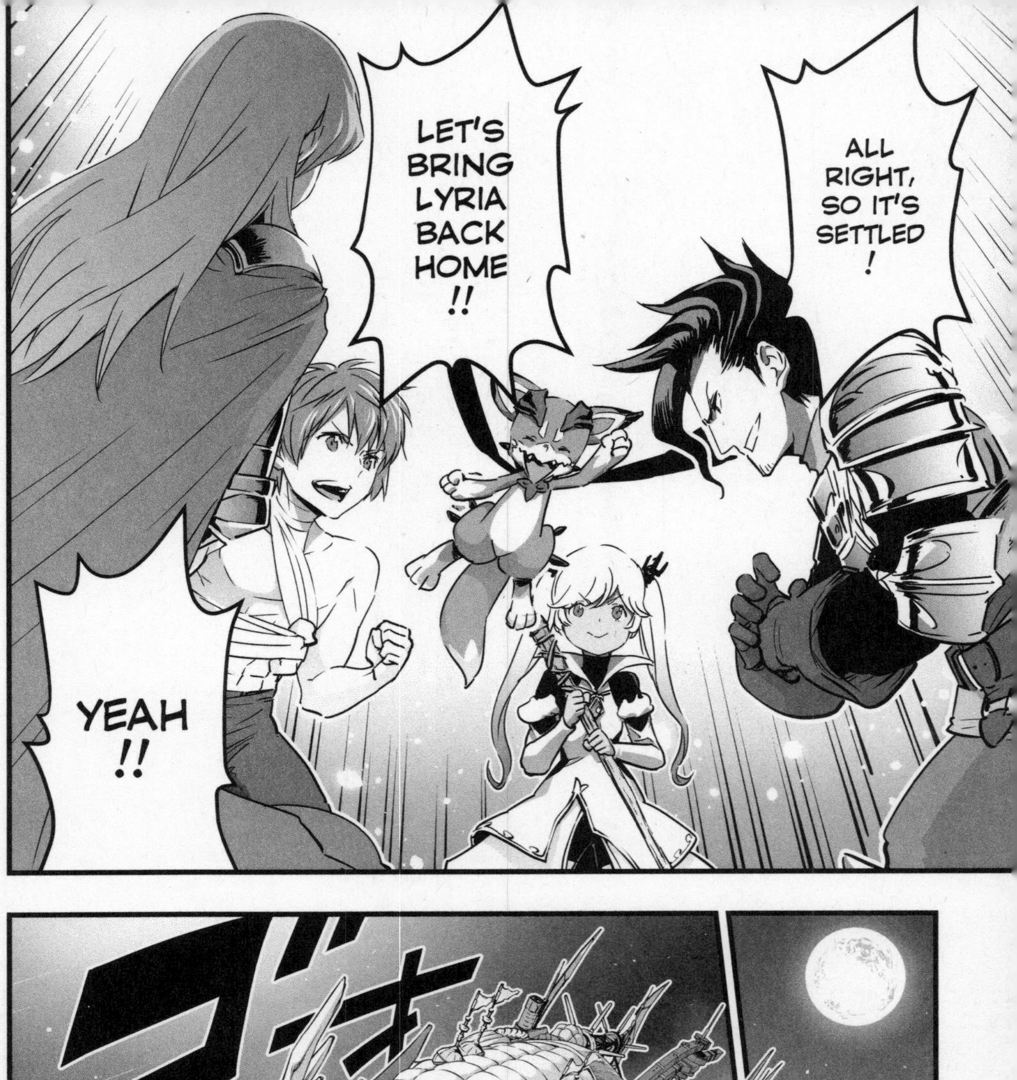
ALL RIGHT, SO IT'S SETTLED!
LET'S BRING LYRIA BACK HOME!!
YEAH!!
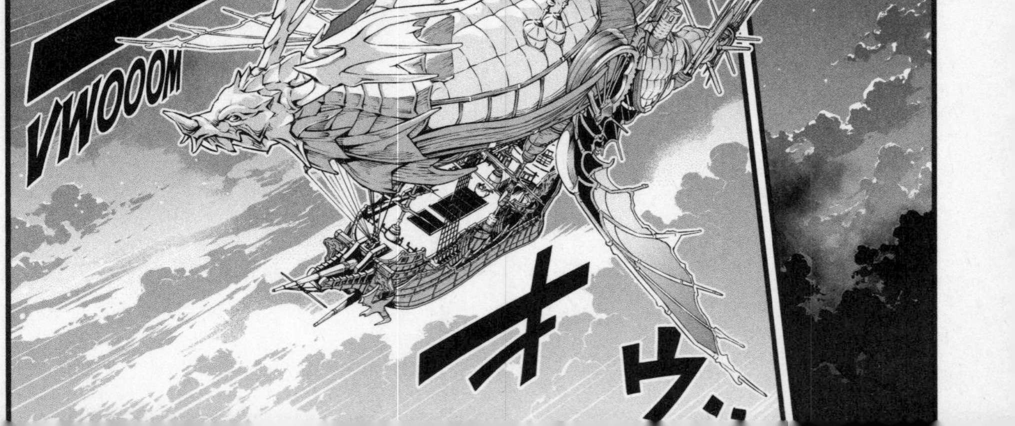
VWOOOM

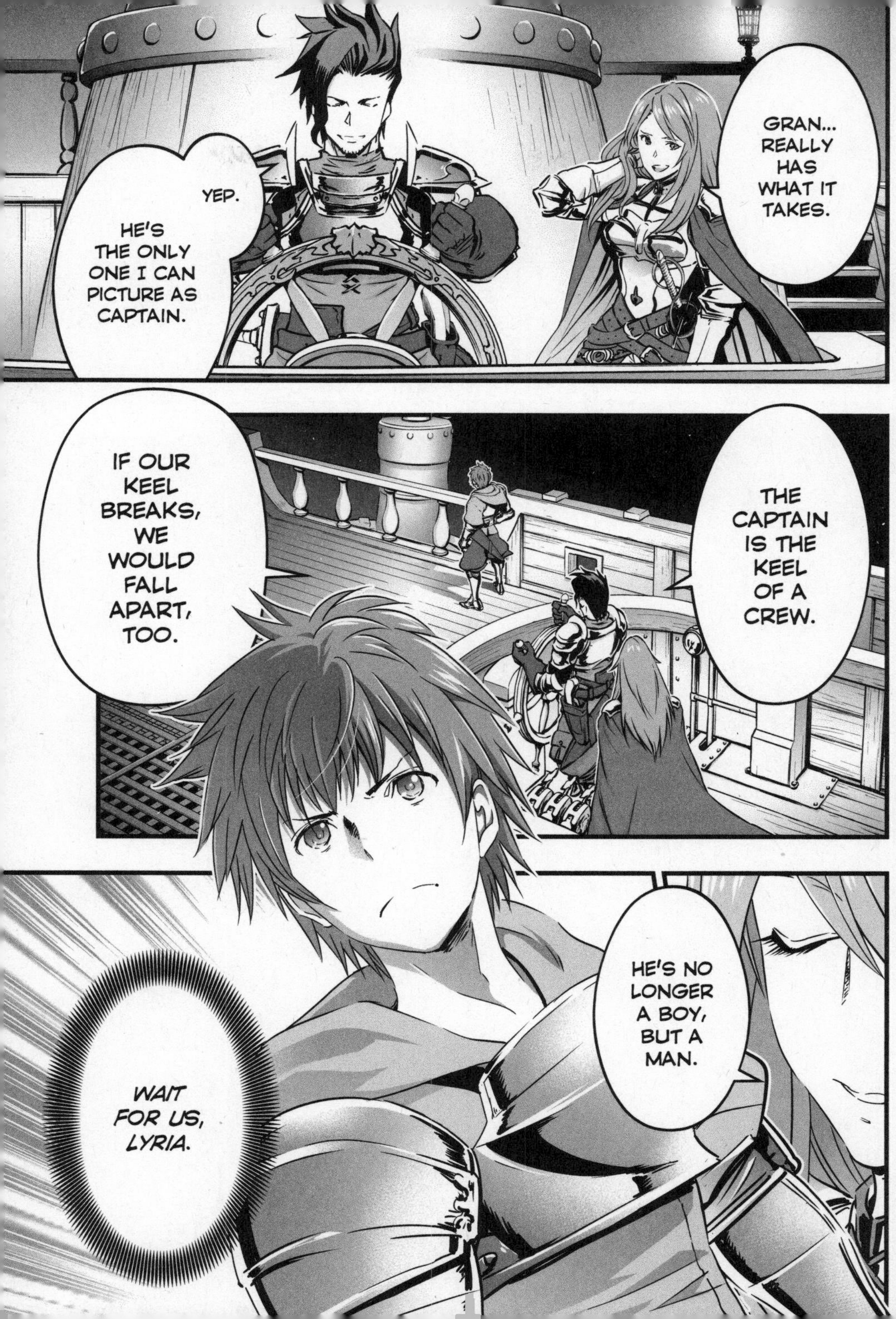
GRAN... REALLY HAS WHAT IT TAKES.
YEP.
HE'S THE ONLY ONE I CAN PICTURE AS CAPTAIN.
THE CAPTAIN IS THE KEEL OF A CREW.
IF OUR KEEL BREAKS, WE WOULD FALL APART, TOO.
HE'S NO LONGER A BOY, BUT A MAN.
WAIT FOR US, LYRIA.

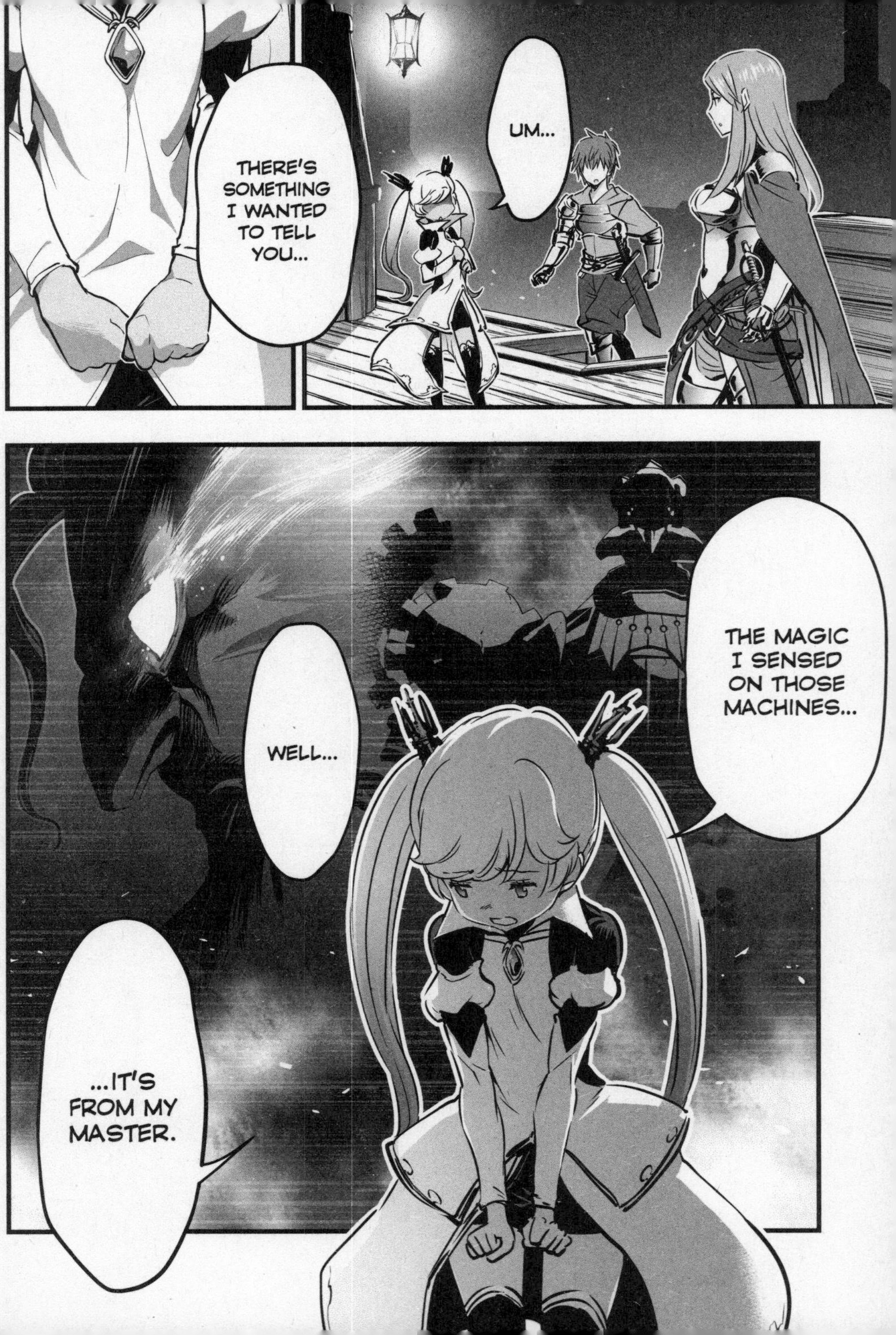
UM...
THERE'S SOMETHING I WANTED TO TELL YOU...
THE MAGIC I SENSED ON THOSE MACHINES...
WELL...
...IT'S FROM MY MASTER.

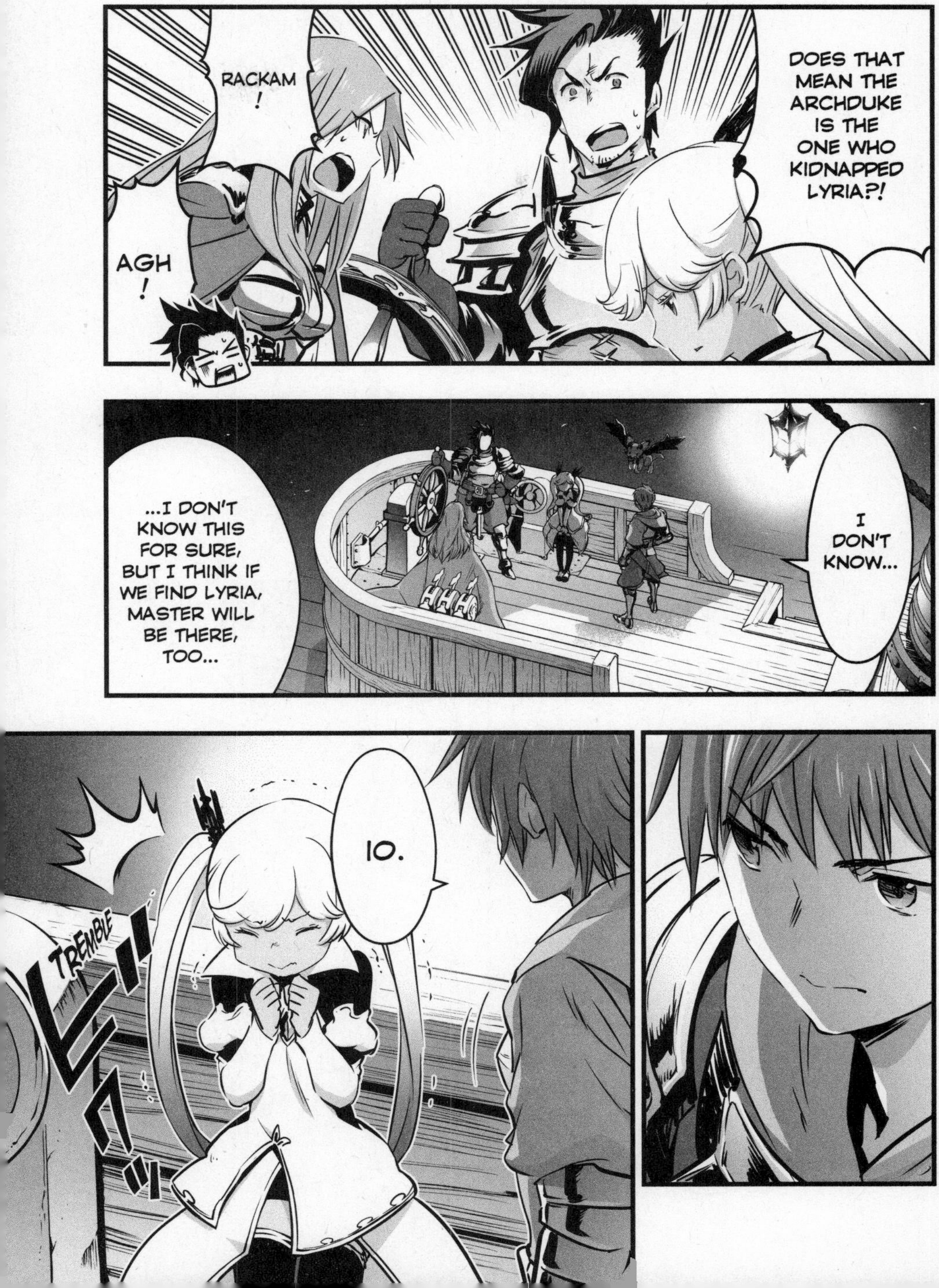
DOES THAT MEAN THE ARCHDUKE IS THE ONE WHO KIDNAPPED LYRIA?!
RACKAM!
AGH!
I DON'T KNOW...
...I DON'T KNOW THIS FOR SURE, BUT I THINK IF WE FIND LYRIA, MASTER WILL BE THERE, TOO...
IO.
TREMBLE

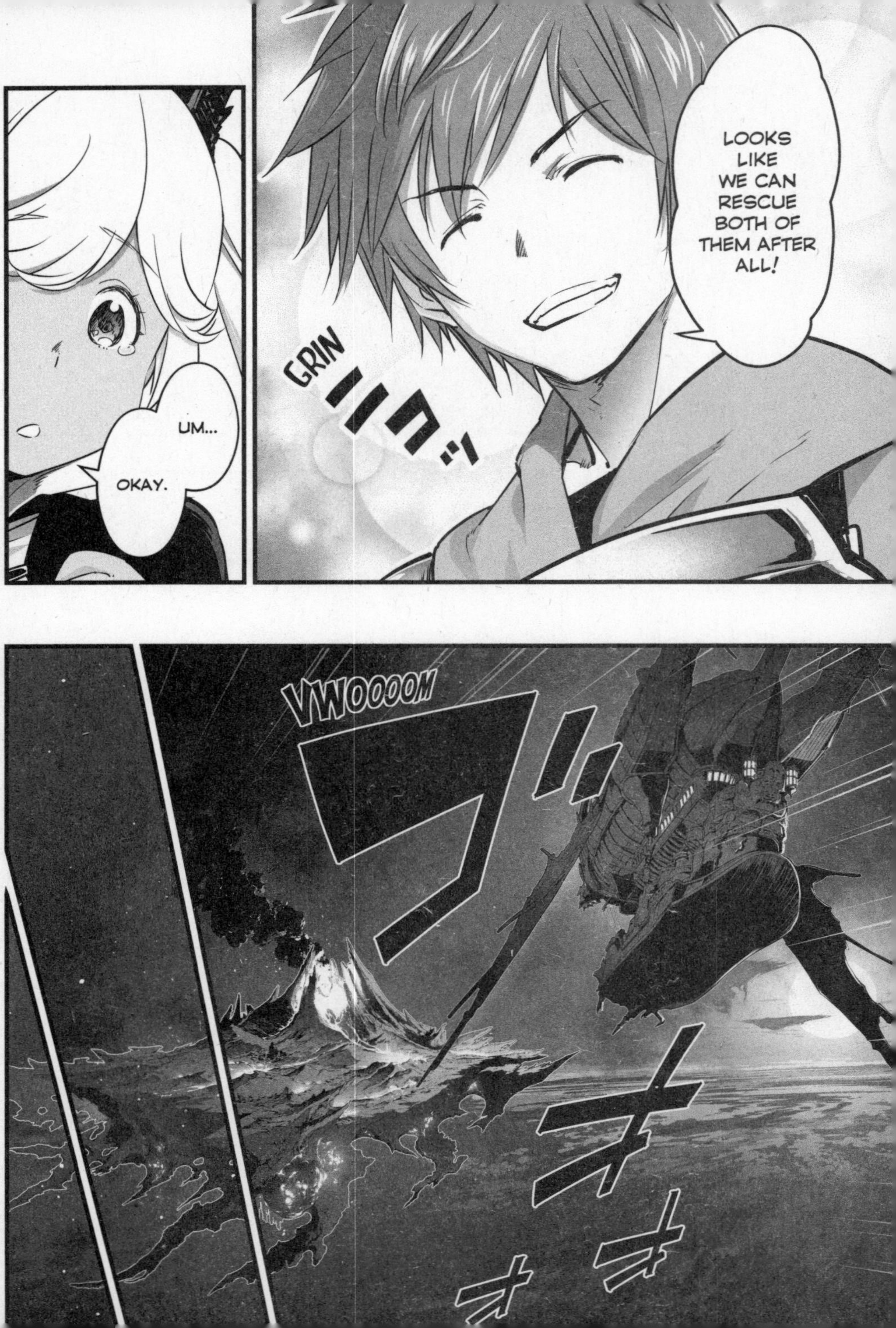
LOOKS LIKE WE CAN RESCUE BOTH OF THEM AFTER ALL!
GRIN
UM...
OKAY.
VWOOOOM

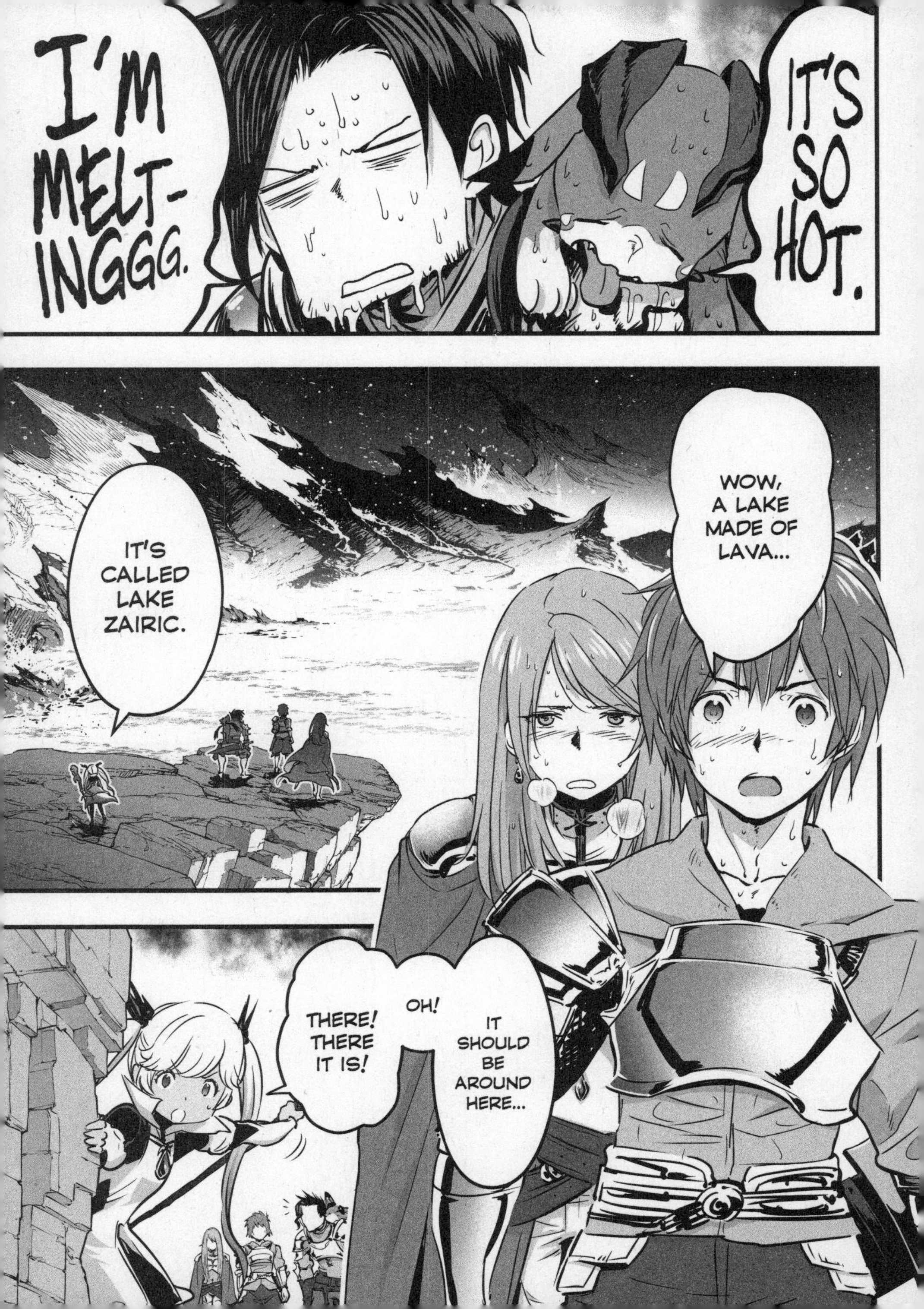
IT'S SO HOT.
I'M MELT-INGGG.
WOW, A LAKE MADE OF LAVA...
IT'S CALLED LAKE ZAIRIC.
IT SHOULD BE AROUND HERE...
OH!
THERE! THERE IT IS!

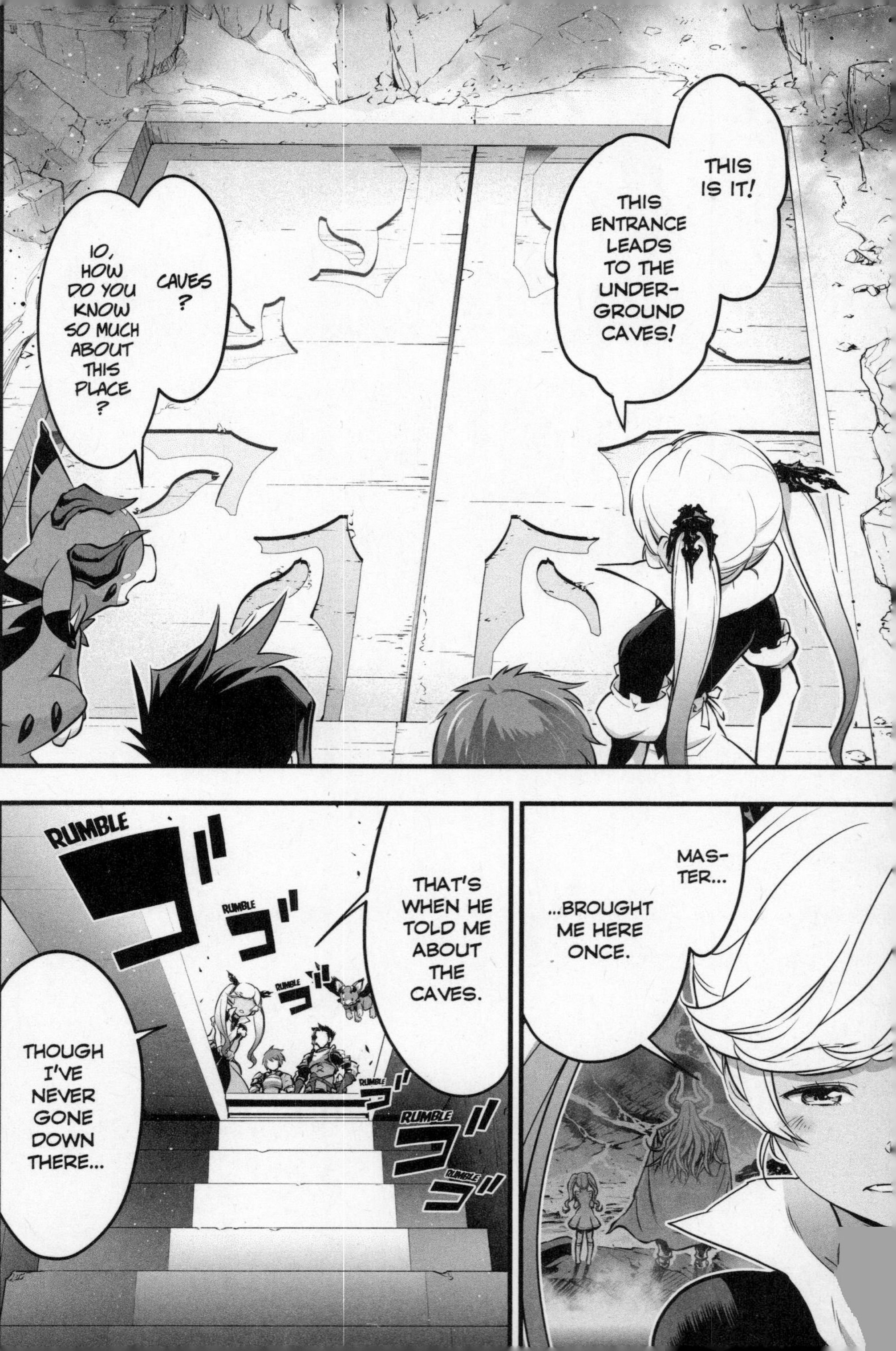
THIS IS IT!
THIS ENTRANCE LEADS TO THE UNDERGROUND CAVES!
CAVES?
IO, HOW DO YOU KNOW SO MUCH ABOUT THIS PLACE?
MASTER...
...BROUGHT ME HERE ONCE.
RUMBLE
ゴ
RUMBLE
ゴ
RUMBLE
ゴ
RUMBLE
ゴ
RUMBLE
ゴ
RUMBLE
ゴ
THAT'S WHEN HE TOLD ME ABOUT THE CAVES.
THOUGH I'VE NEVER GONE DOWN THERE...

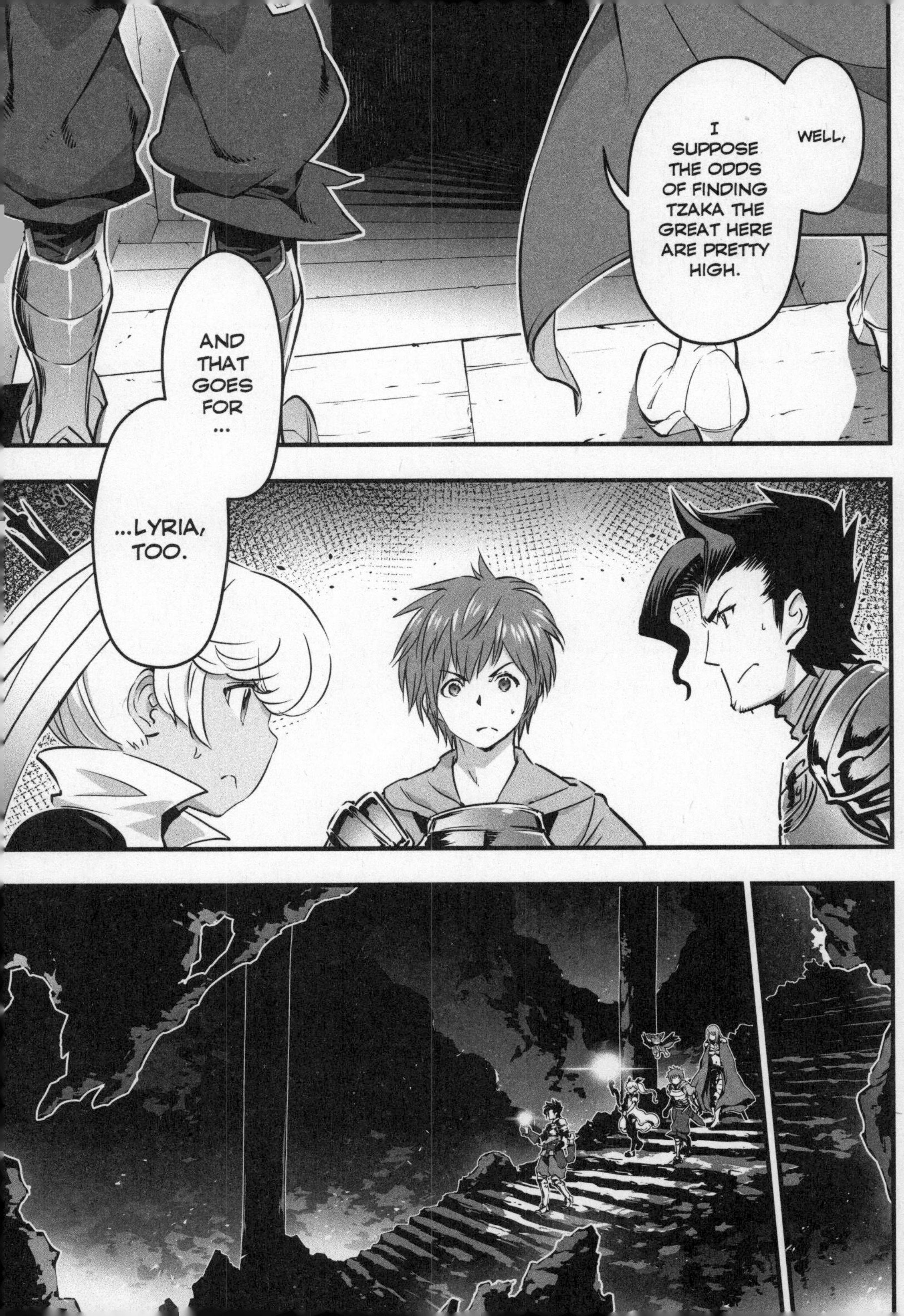
WELL,
I SUPPOSE THE ODDS OF FINDING TZAKA THE GREAT HERE ARE PRETTY HIGH.
AND THAT GOES FOR ...
...LYRIA, TOO.

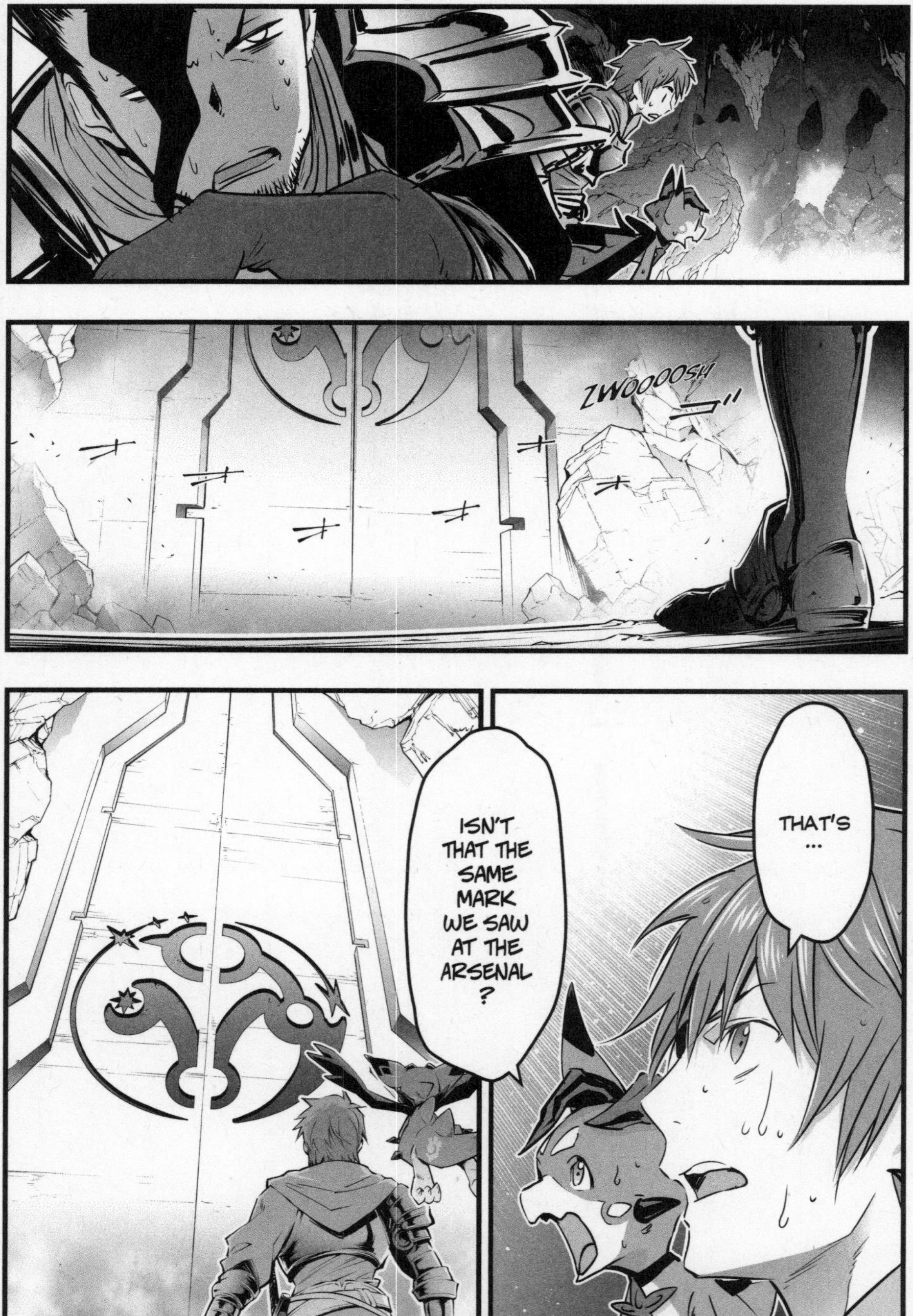
ZWOOOOSH
THAT'S ...
ISN'T THAT THE SAME MARK WE SAW AT THE ARSENAL ?

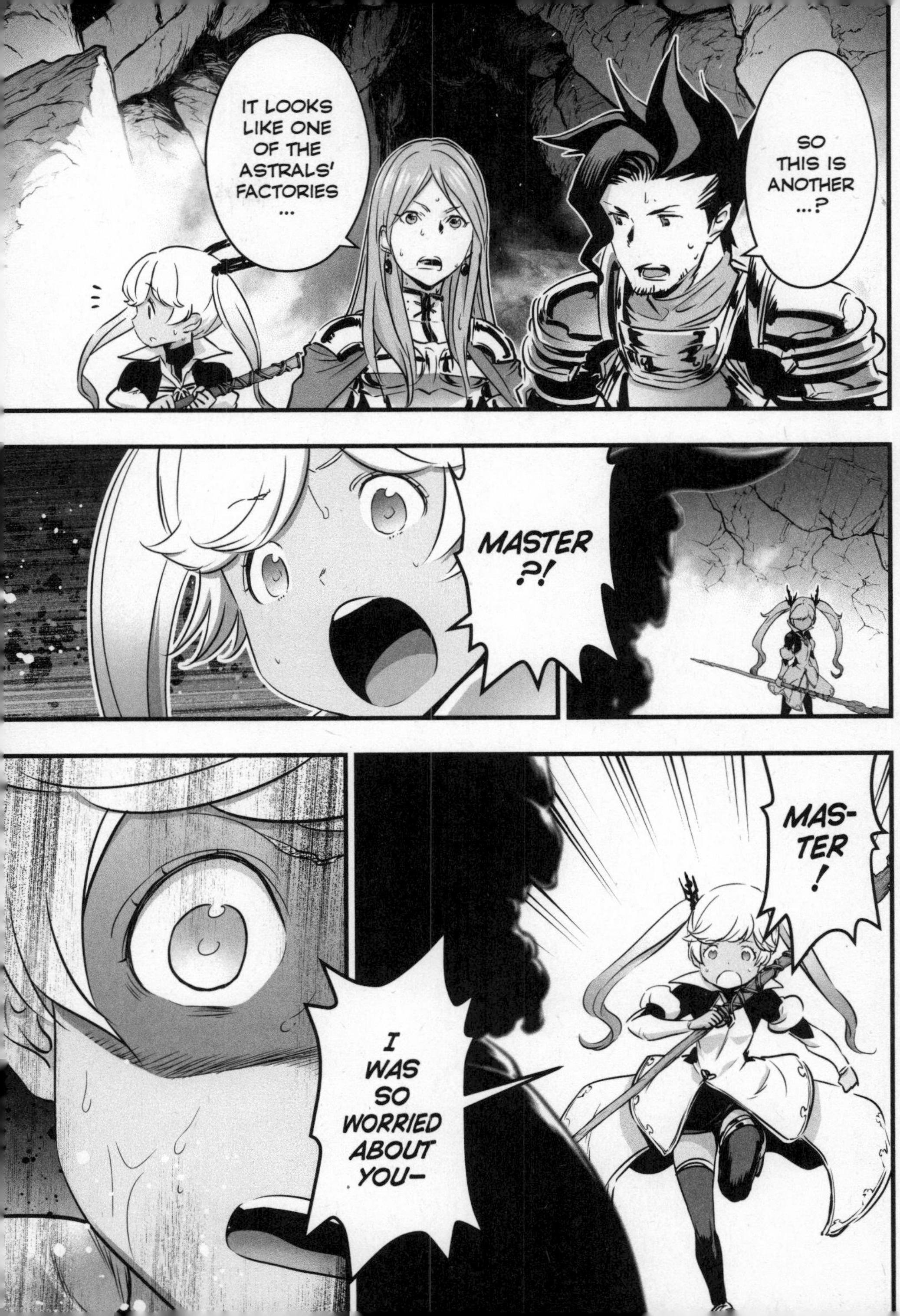
SO THIS IS ANOTHER ...?
IT LOOKS LIKE ONE OF THE ASTRALS' FACTORIES ...
MASTER ?!
MAS-TER!
I WAS SO WORRIED ABOUT YOU-

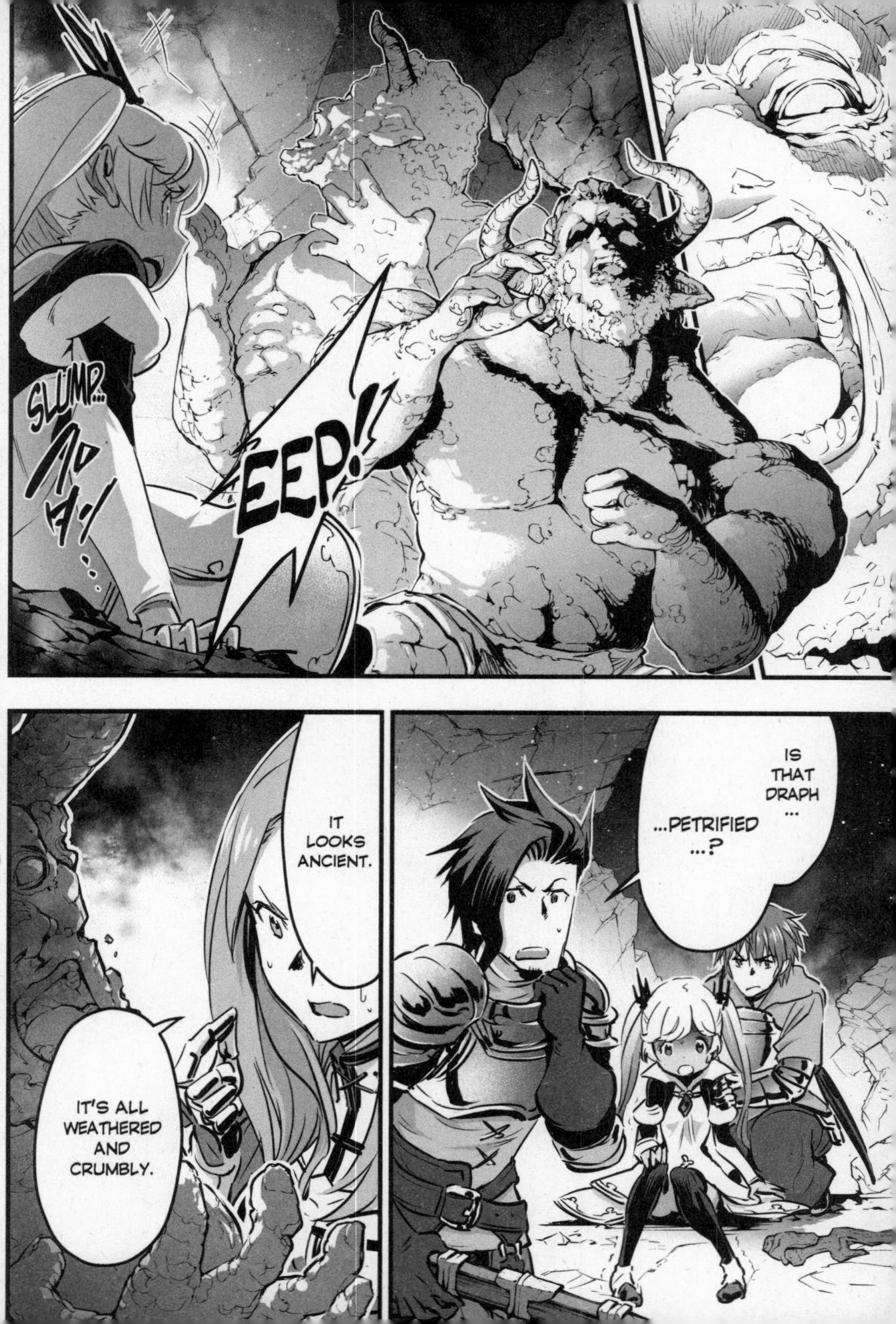

SLUMP...
EEP!!
...
IS THAT DRAPH ...
...PETRIFIED ...?
IT LOOKS ANCIENT.
IT'S ALL WEATHERED AND CRUMBLY.

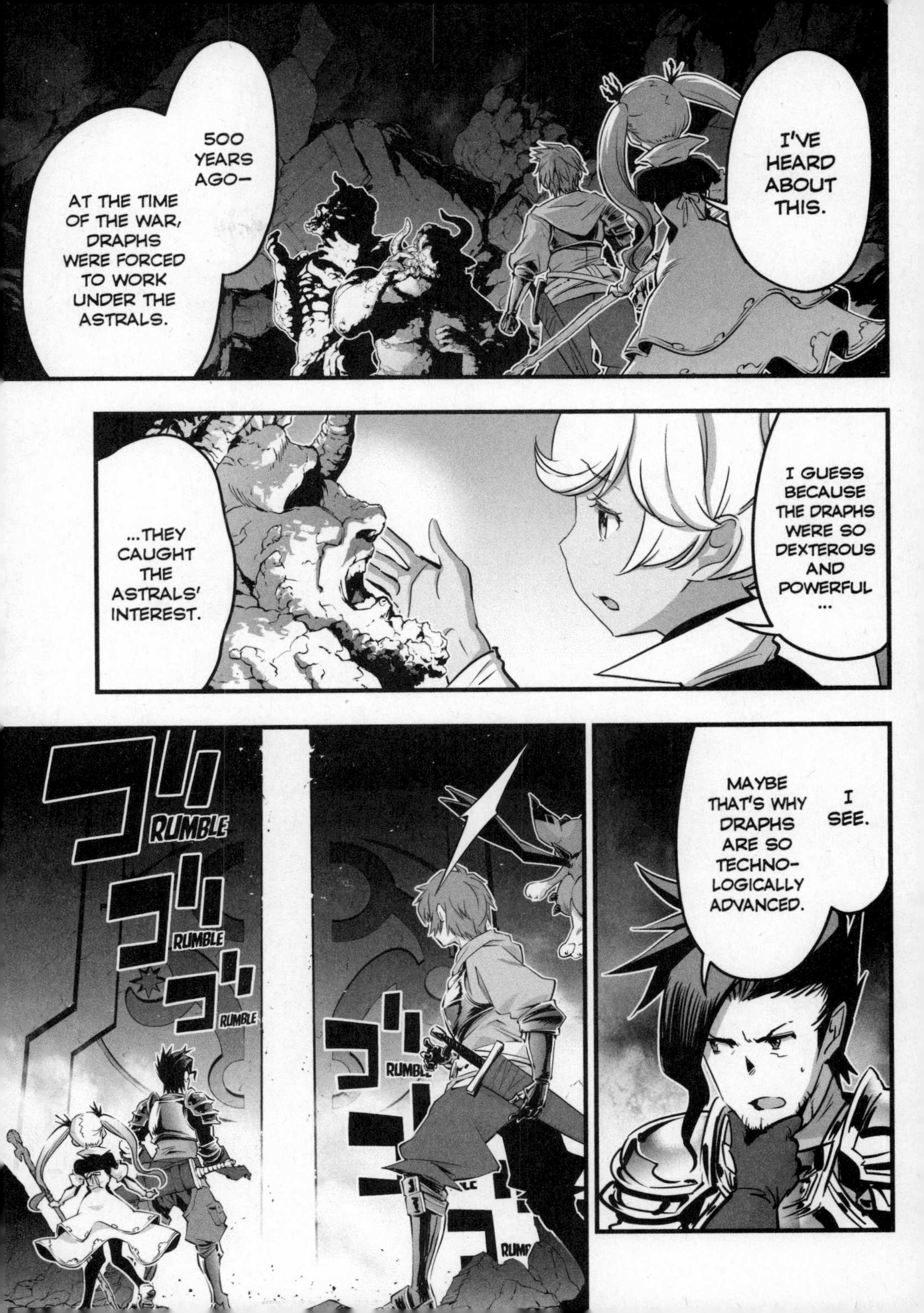
I'VE HEARD ABOUT THIS.
500 YEARS AGO—
AT THE TIME OF THE WAR, DRAPHS WERE FORCED TO WORK UNDER THE ASTRALS.
I GUESS BECAUSE THE DRAPHS WERE SO DEXTEROUS AND POWERFUL ...
...THEY CAUGHT THE ASTRALS' INTEREST.
I SEE.
MAYBE THAT'S WHY DRAPHS ARE SO TECHNO-LOGICALLY ADVANCED.
RUMBLE
RUMBLE
RUMBLE
RUMBLE
RUMBLE

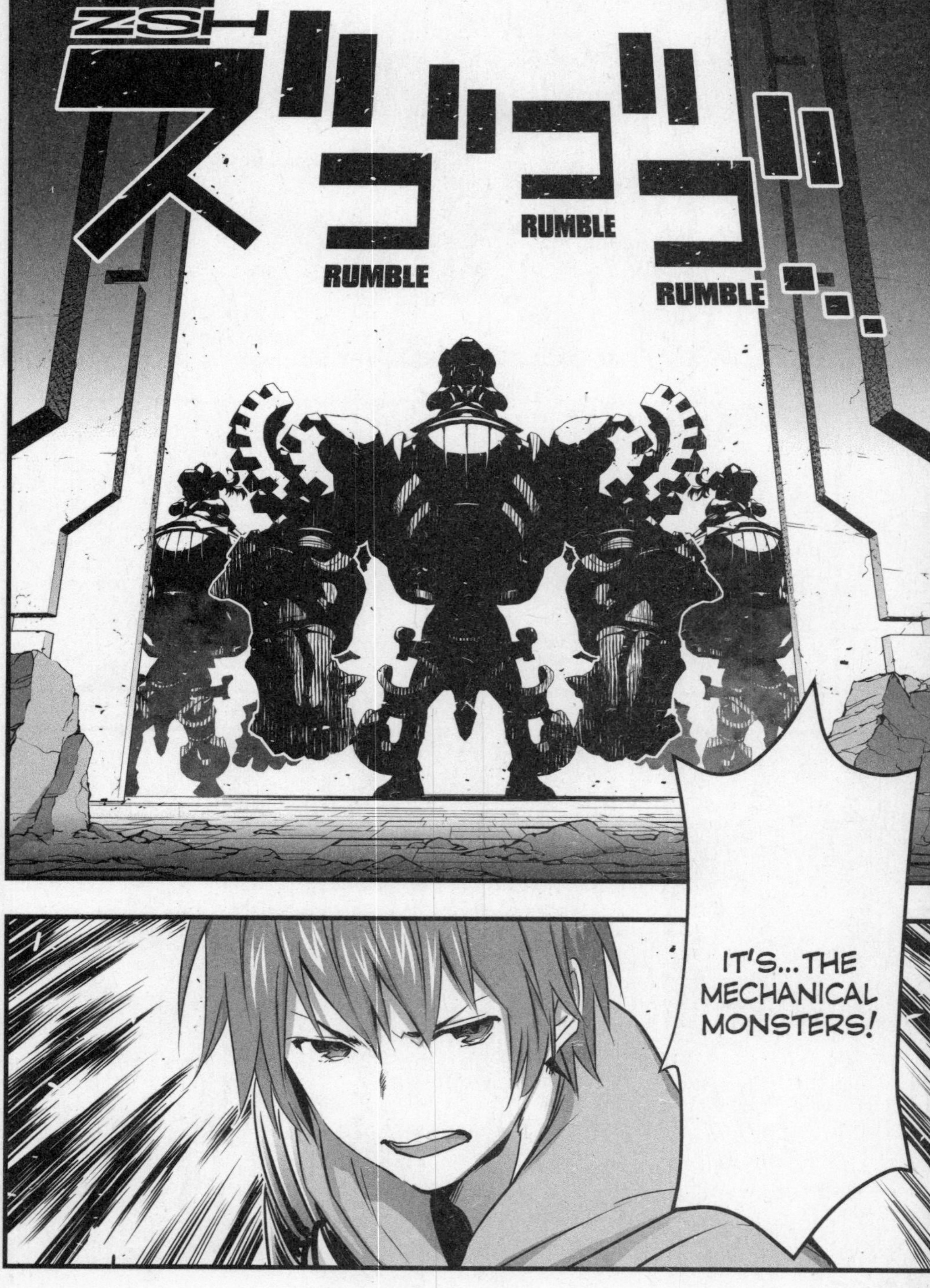
ZSH
RUMBLE
RUMBLE
RUMBLE
IT'S...THE MECHANICAL MONSTERS!

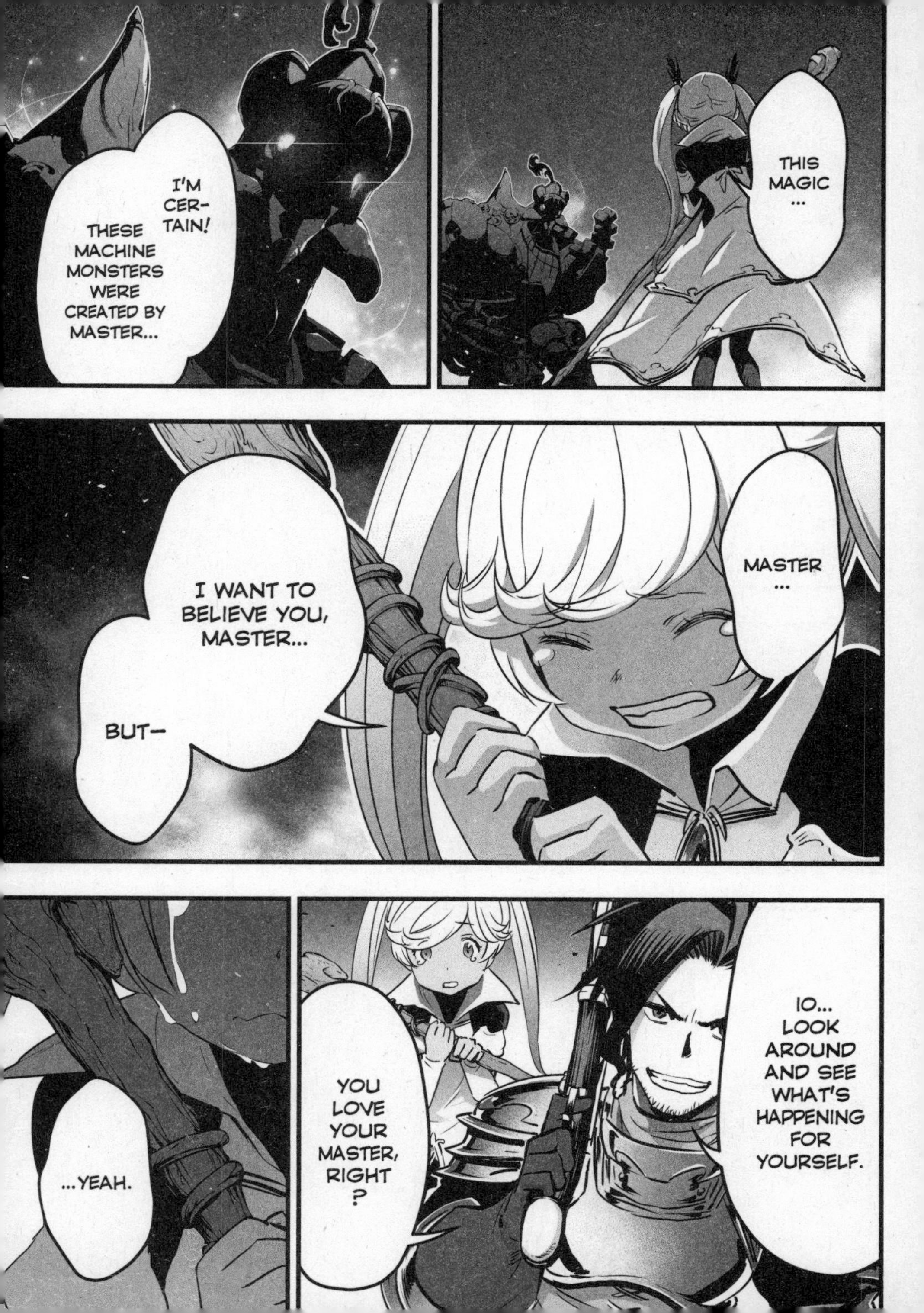
THIS MAGIC ...
I'M CERTAIN!
THESE MACHINE MONSTERS WERE CREATED BY MASTER...
MASTER ...
I WANT TO BELIEVE YOU, MASTER...
BUT—
IO... LOOK AROUND AND SEE WHAT'S HAPPENING FOR YOURSELF.
YOU LOVE YOUR MASTER, RIGHT?
...YEAH.

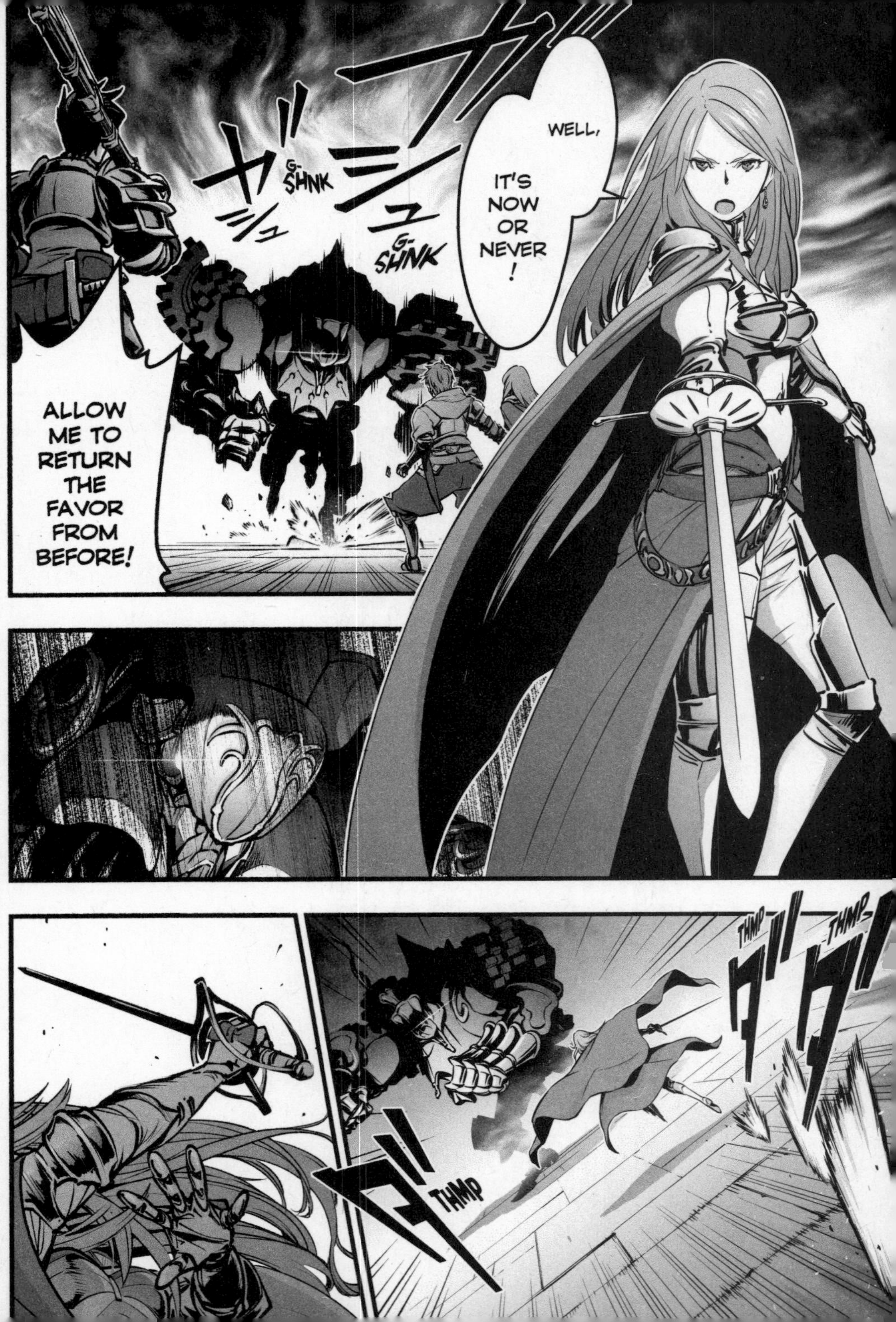
WELL,
IT'S NOW OR NEVER!
G-SHNK
G-SHNK
ALLOW ME TO RETURN THE FAVOR FROM BEFORE!
THMP
THMP
THMP

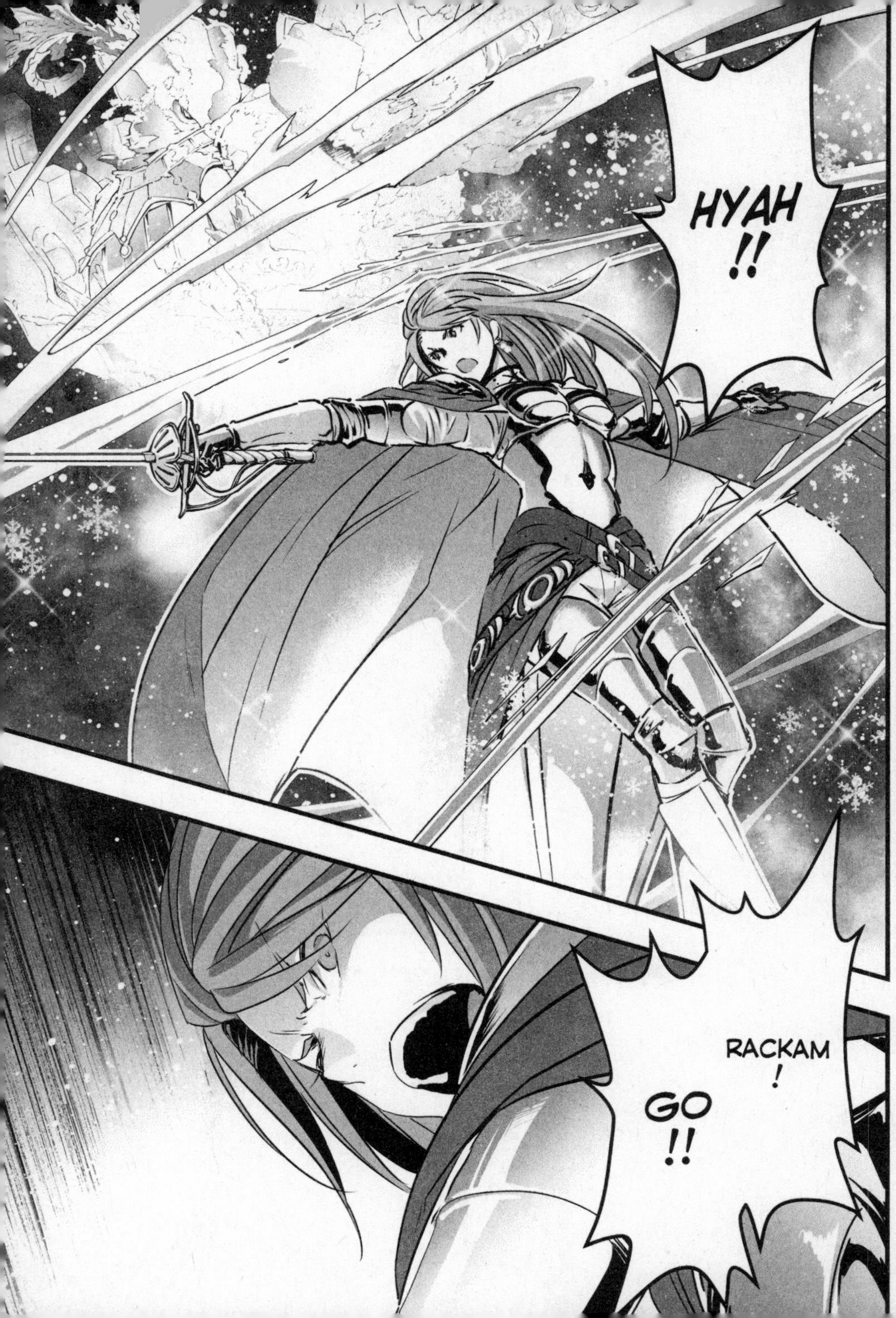
HYAH !!
RACKAM !
GO !!

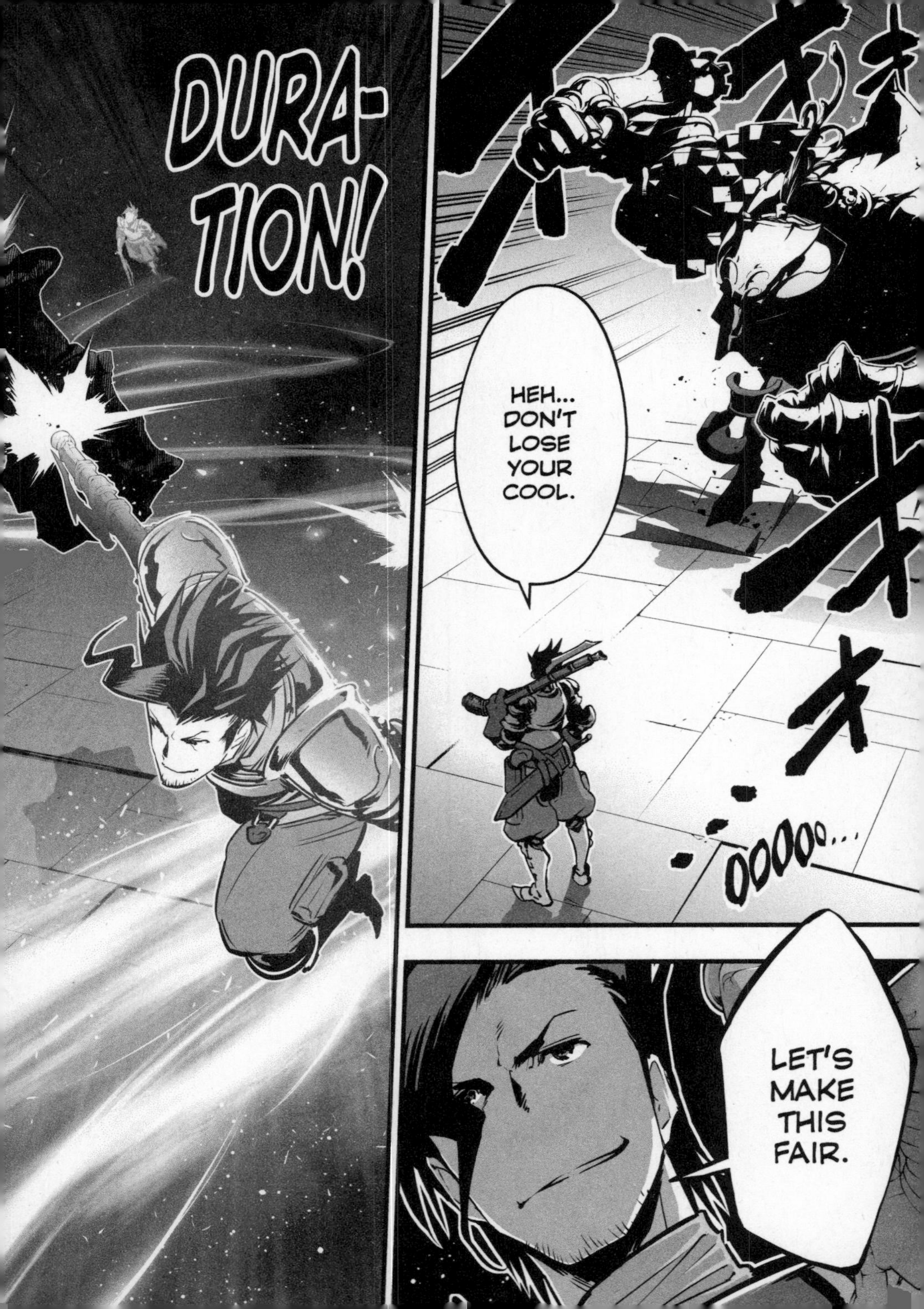
HEH... DON'T LOSE YOUR COOL.
OOOOo...
LET'S MAKE THIS FAIR.
DURA-TION!

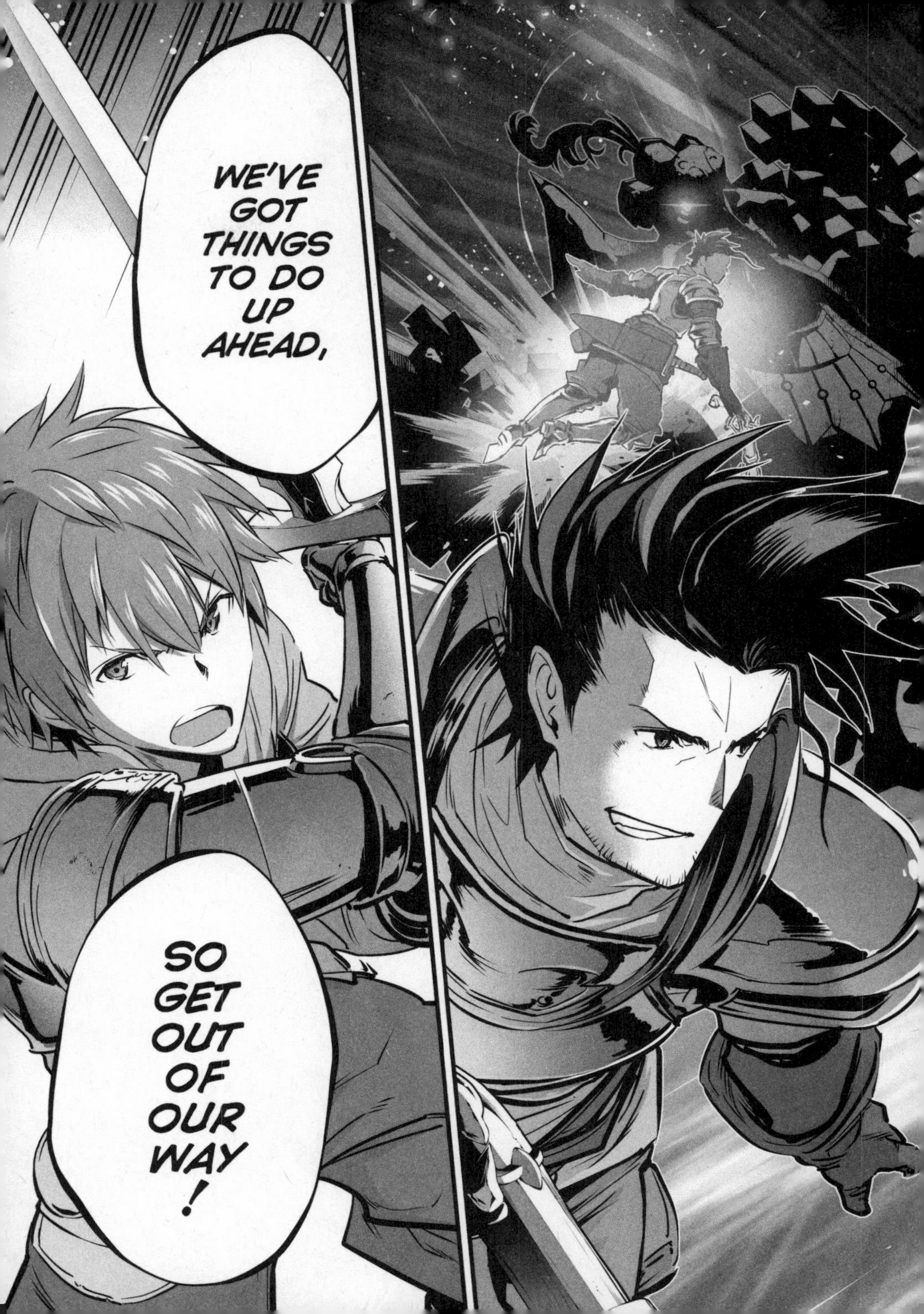
WE'VE GOT THINGS TO DO UP AHEAD,
SO GET OUT OF OUR WAY!

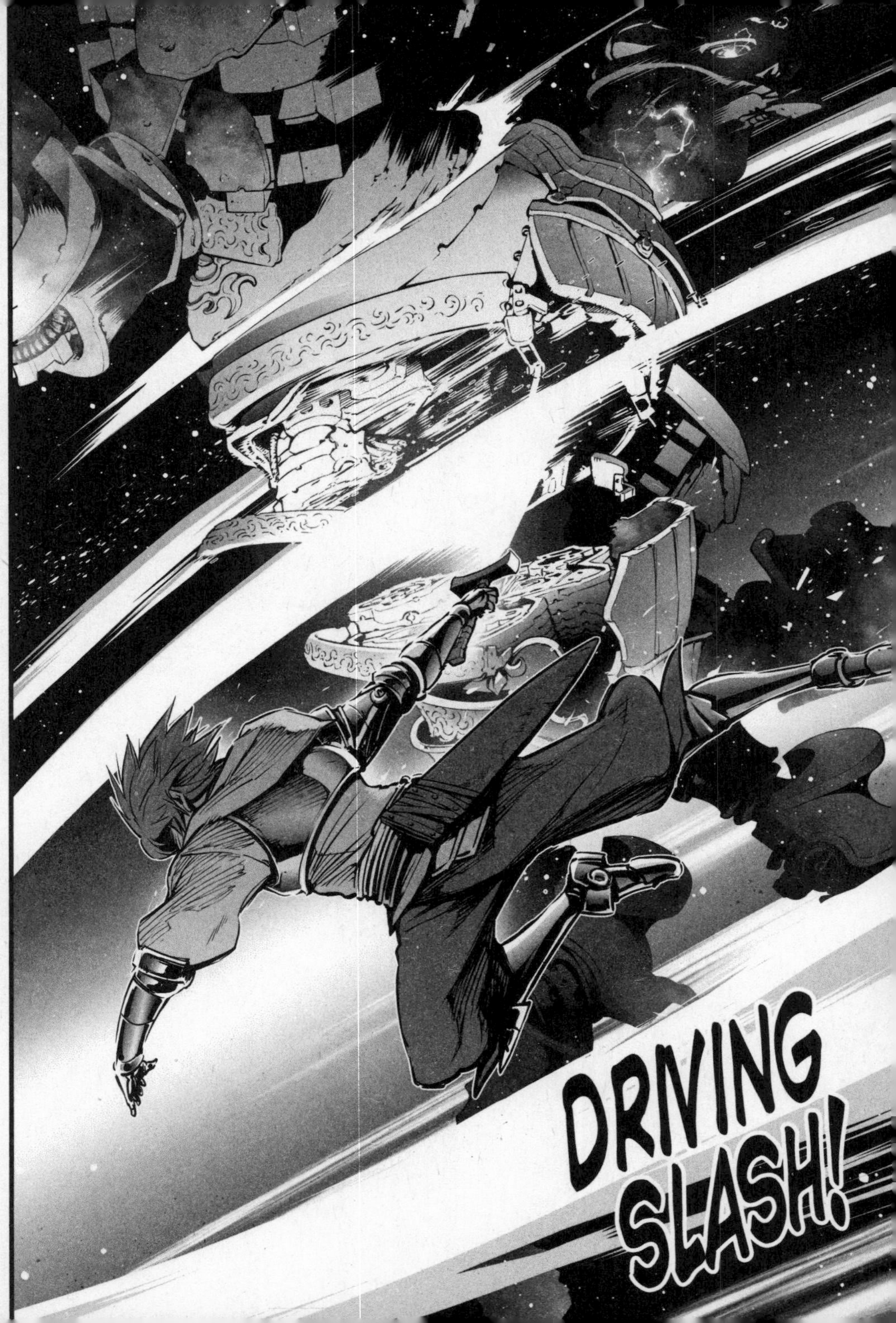
DRIVING SLASH!

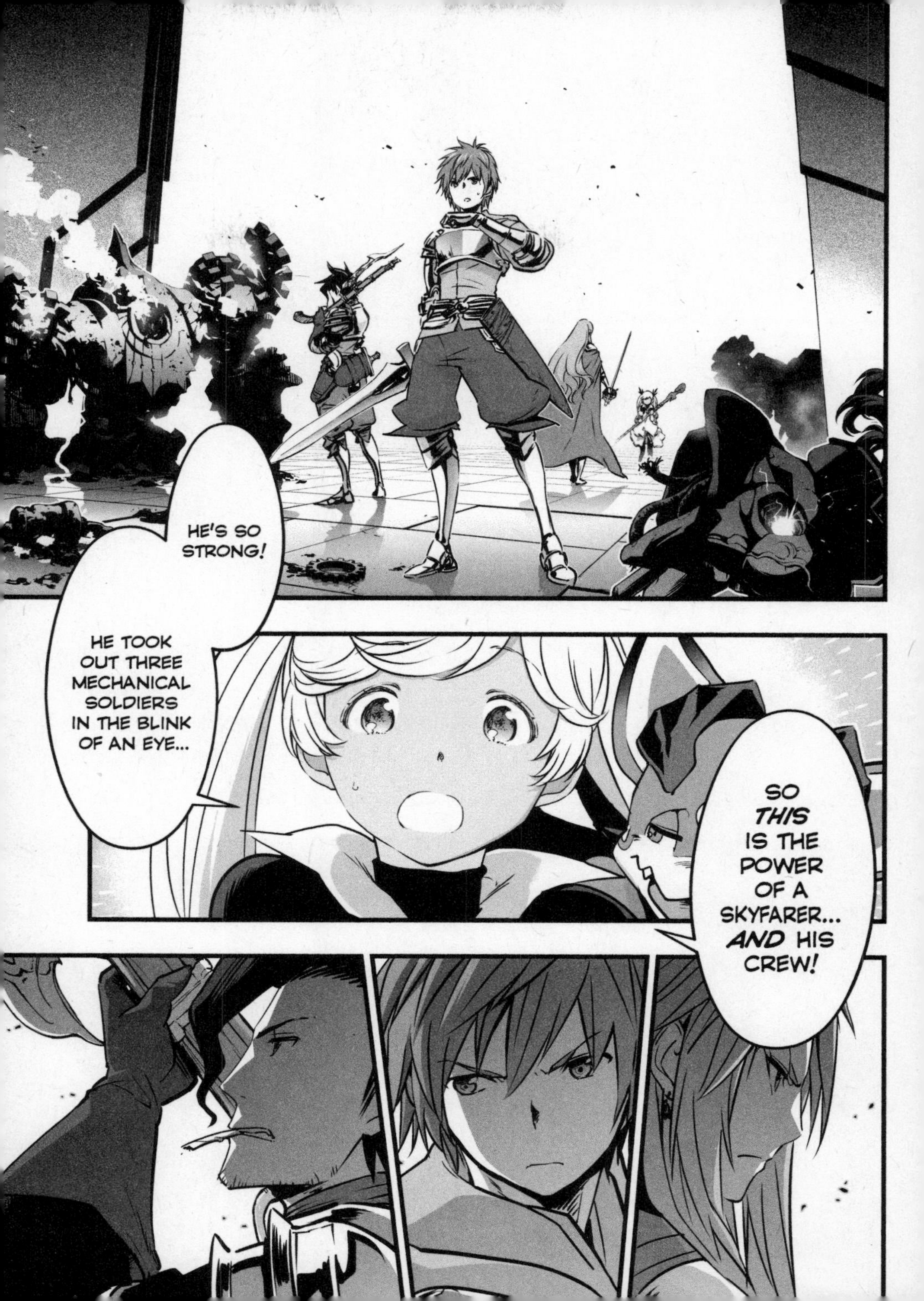
HE'S SO STRONG!
HE TOOK OUT THREE MECHANICAL SOLDIERS IN THE BLINK OF AN EYE...
SO *THIS* IS THE POWER OF A SKYFARER... ***AND*** HIS CREW!

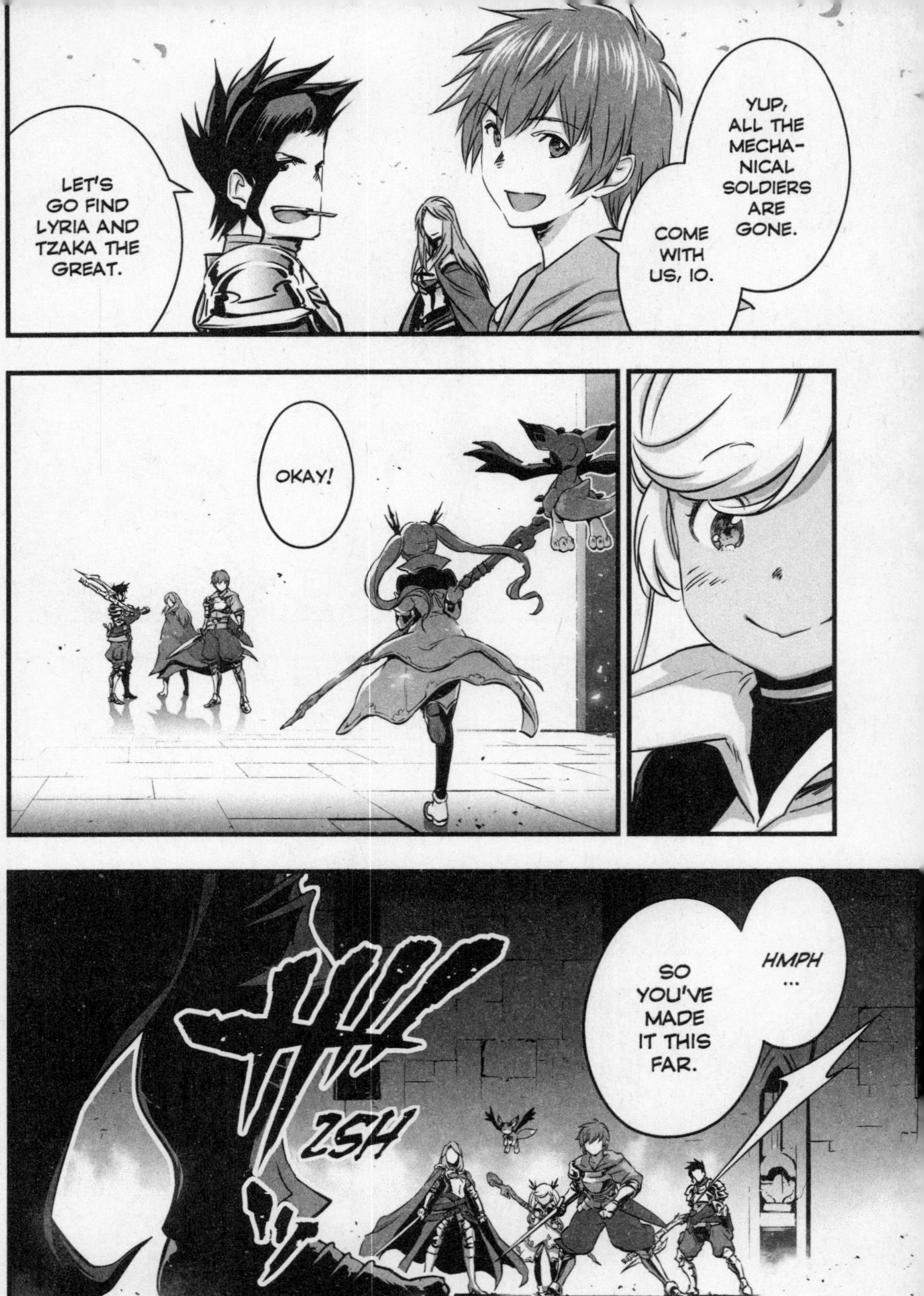
YUP, ALL THE MECHA-NICAL SOLDIERS ARE GONE.
COME WITH US, IO.
LET'S GO FIND LYRIA AND TZAKA THE GREAT.
OKAY!
HMPH ...
SO YOU'VE MADE IT THIS FAR.
ZSH

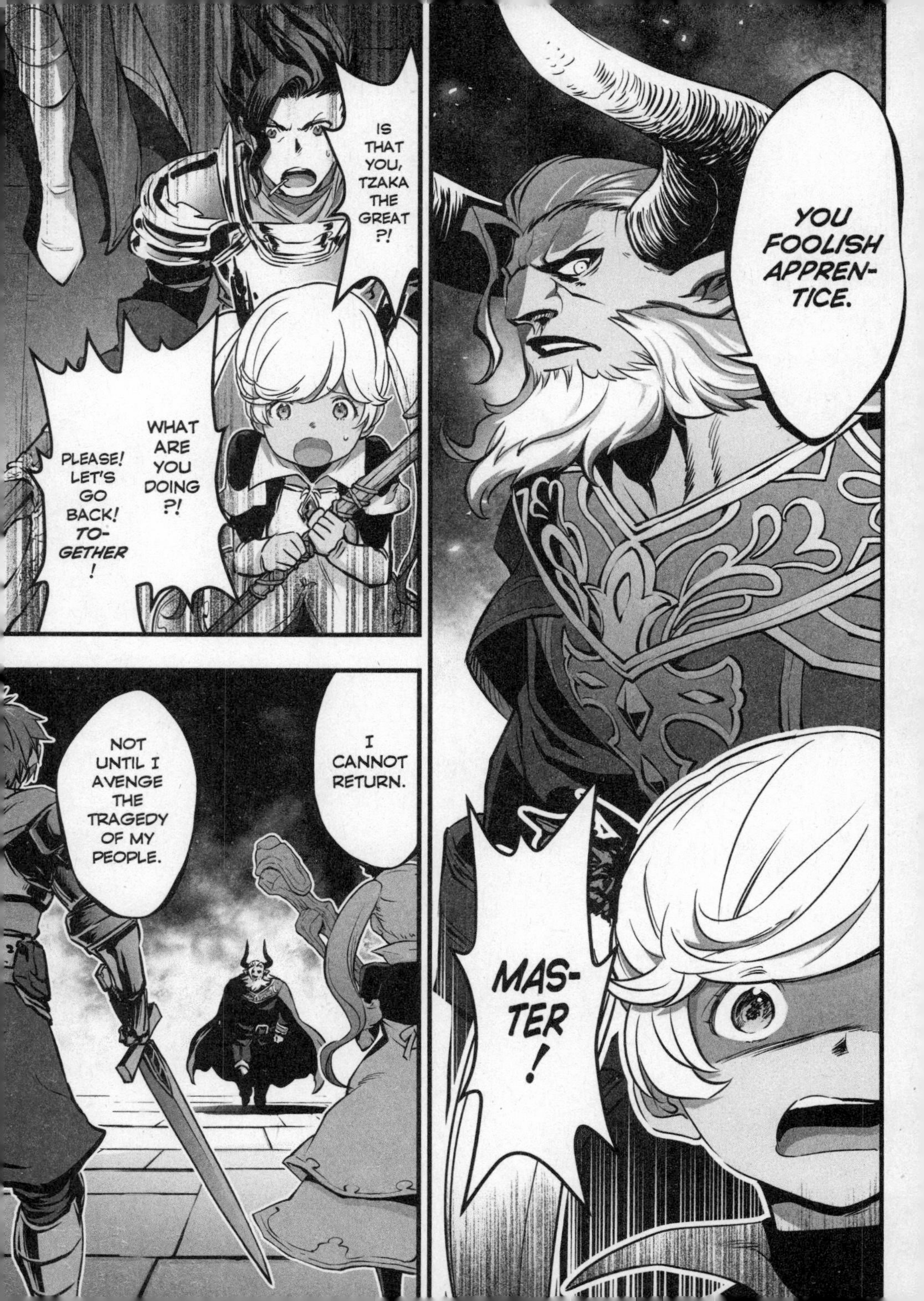
YOU FOOLISH APPRENTICE.
MASTER!
IS THAT YOU, TZAKA THE GREAT?!
WHAT ARE YOU DOING?!
PLEASE! LET'S GO BACK! TOGETHER!
I CANNOT RETURN.
NOT UNTIL I AVENGE THE TRAGEDY OF MY PEOPLE.

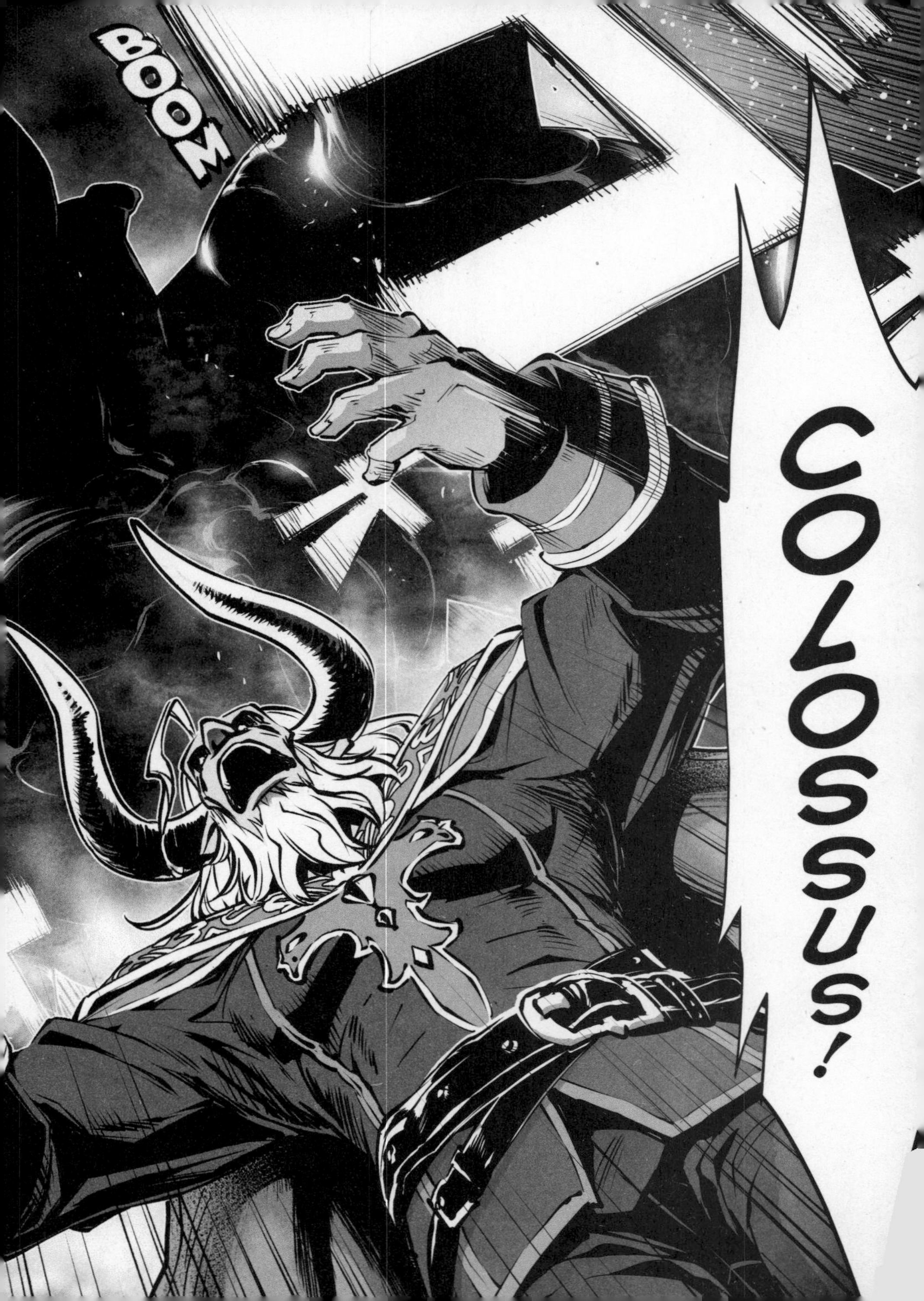
COLOSSUS!
BOOM

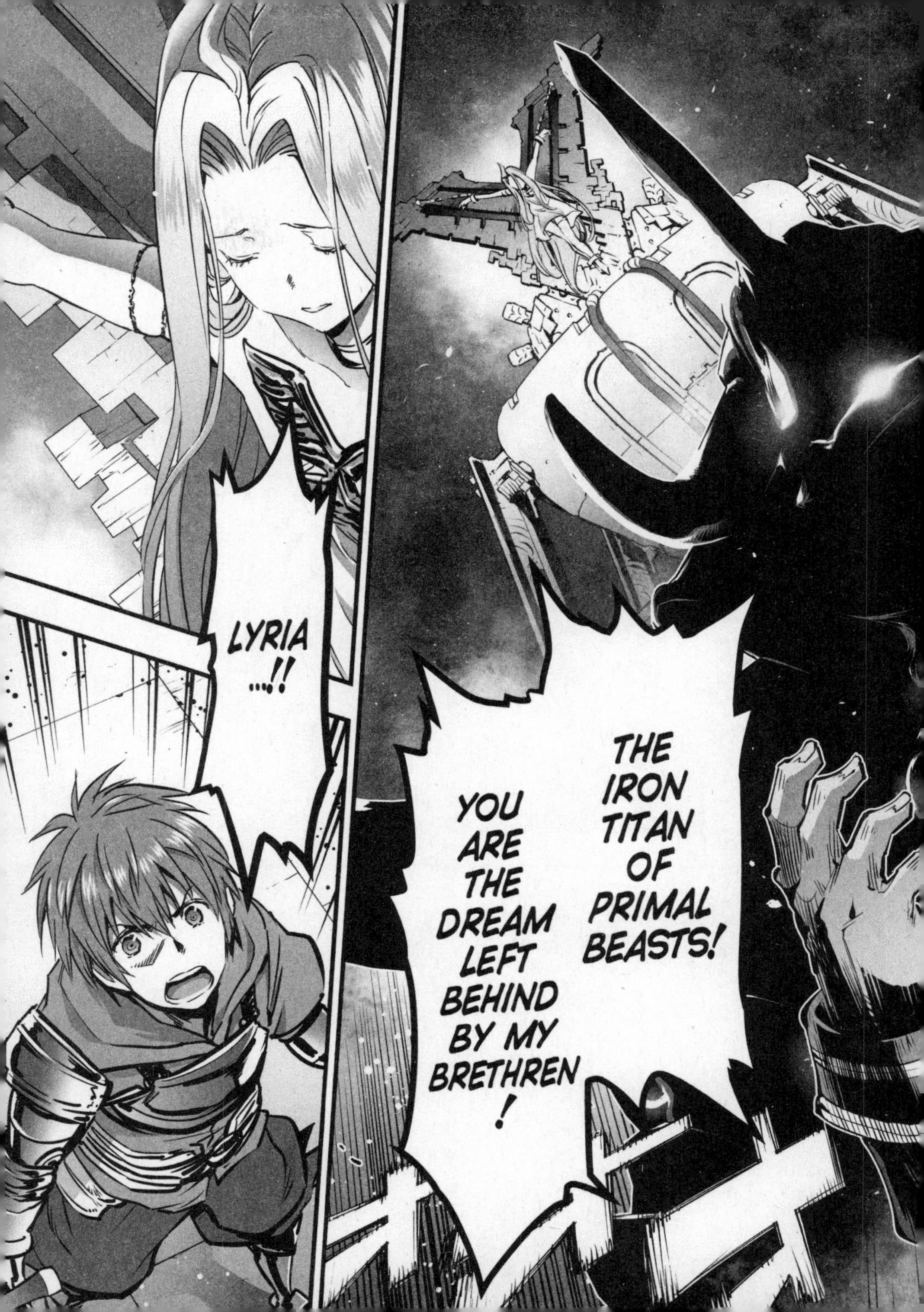
THE IRON TITAN OF PRIMAL BEASTS!
YOU ARE THE DREAM LEFT BEHIND BY MY BRETHREN!
LYRIA ...!!

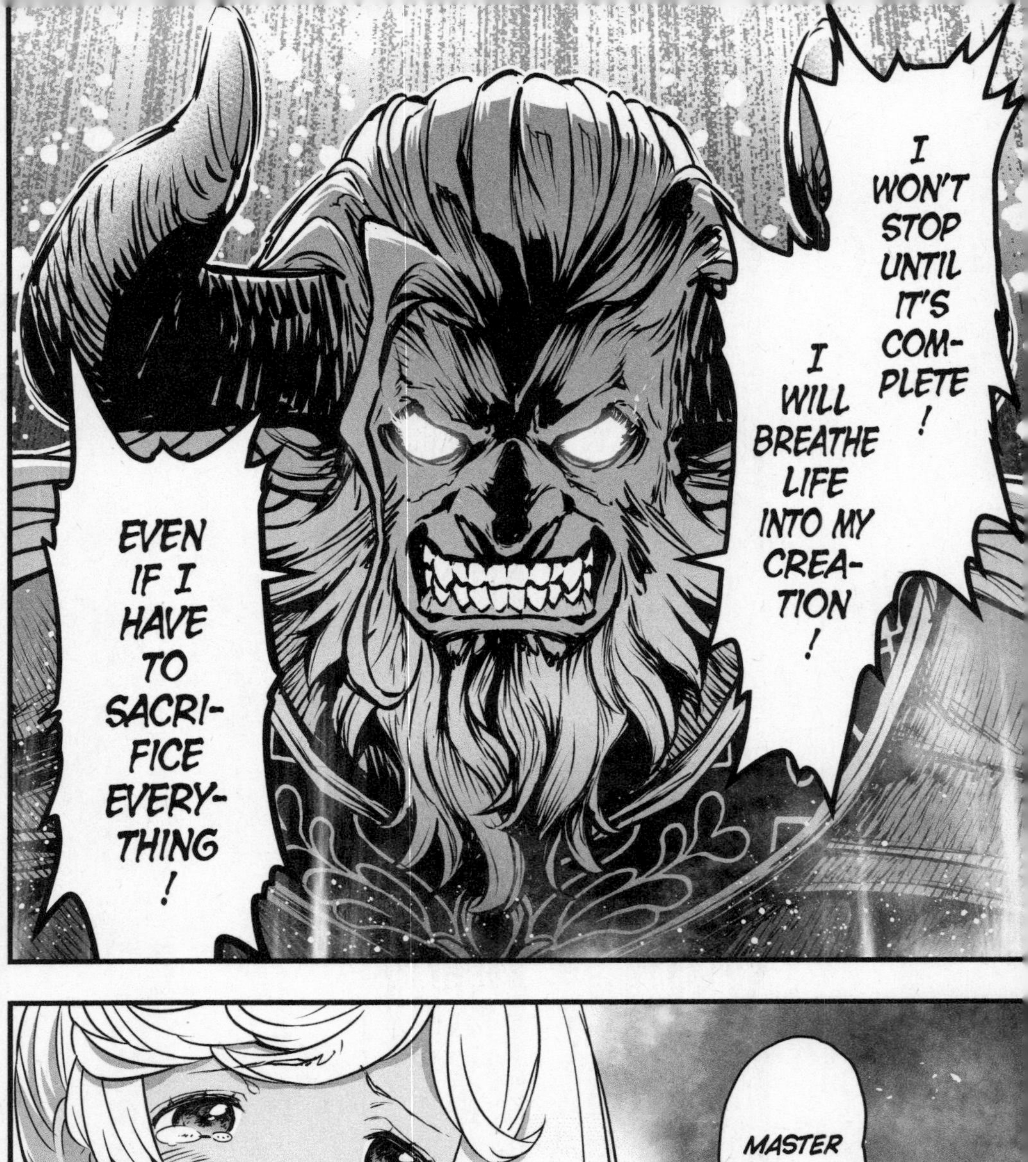
I WON'T STOP UNTIL IT'S COMPLETE!
I WILL BREATHE LIFE INTO MY CREATION!
EVEN IF I HAVE TO SACRIFICE EVERYTHING!

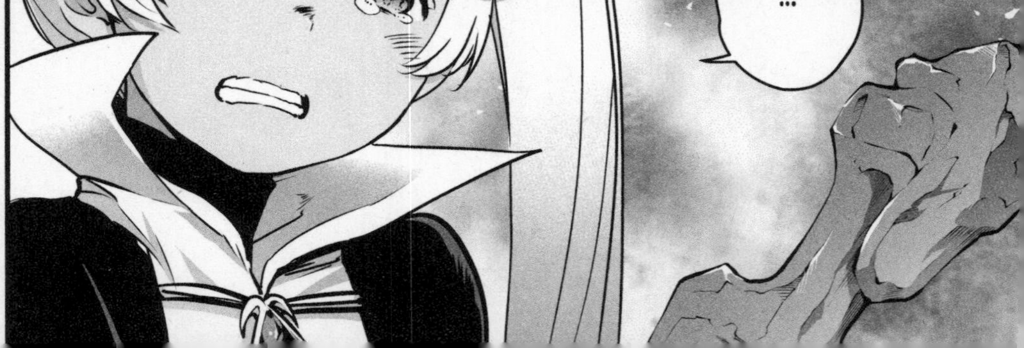
MASTER...

GRANBLUE FANTASY
グランブルーファンタジー

GRANBLUE FANTASY
グランブルーファンタジー

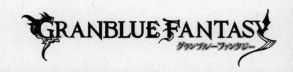

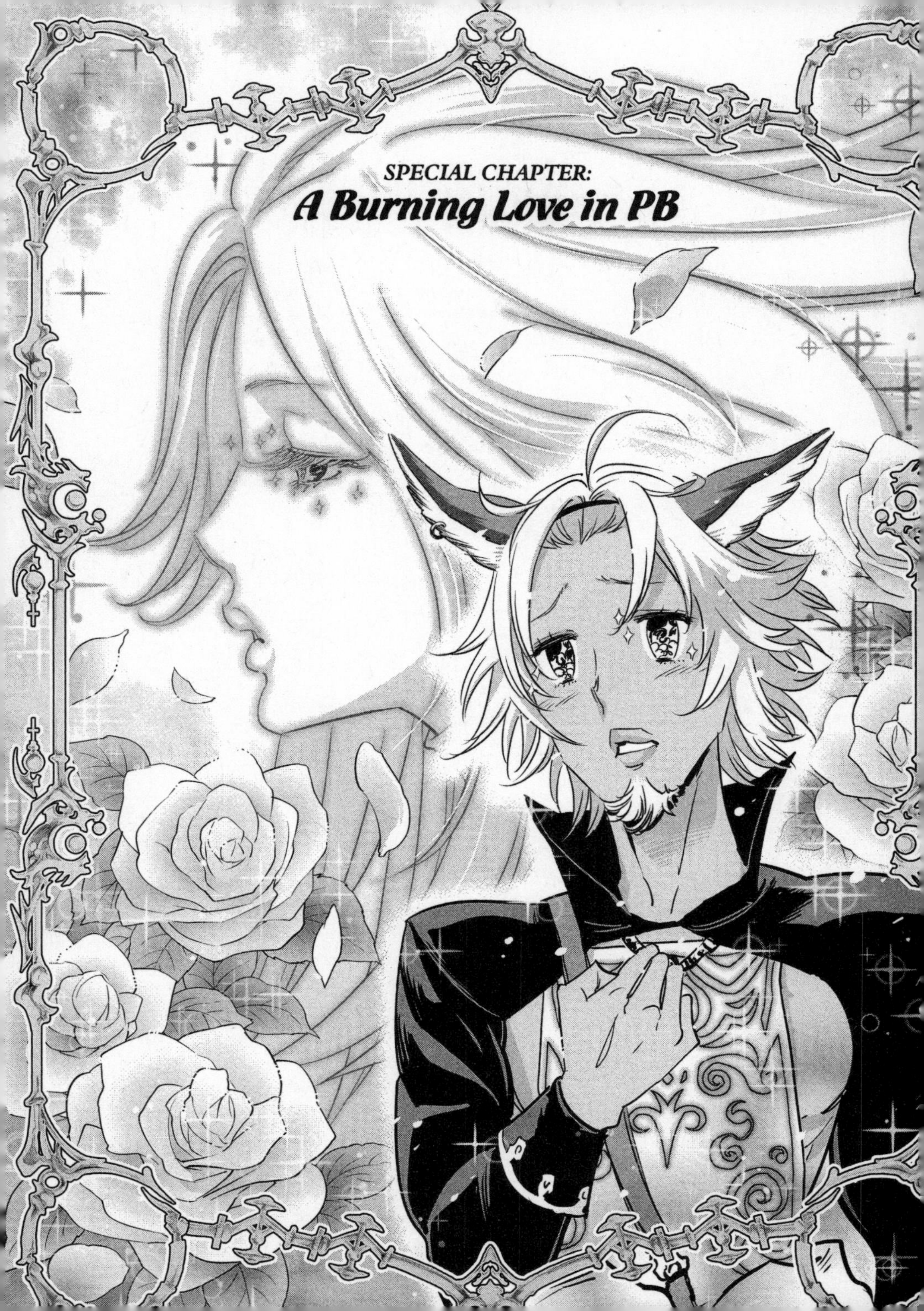
SPECIAL CHAPTER:
A Burning Love in PB

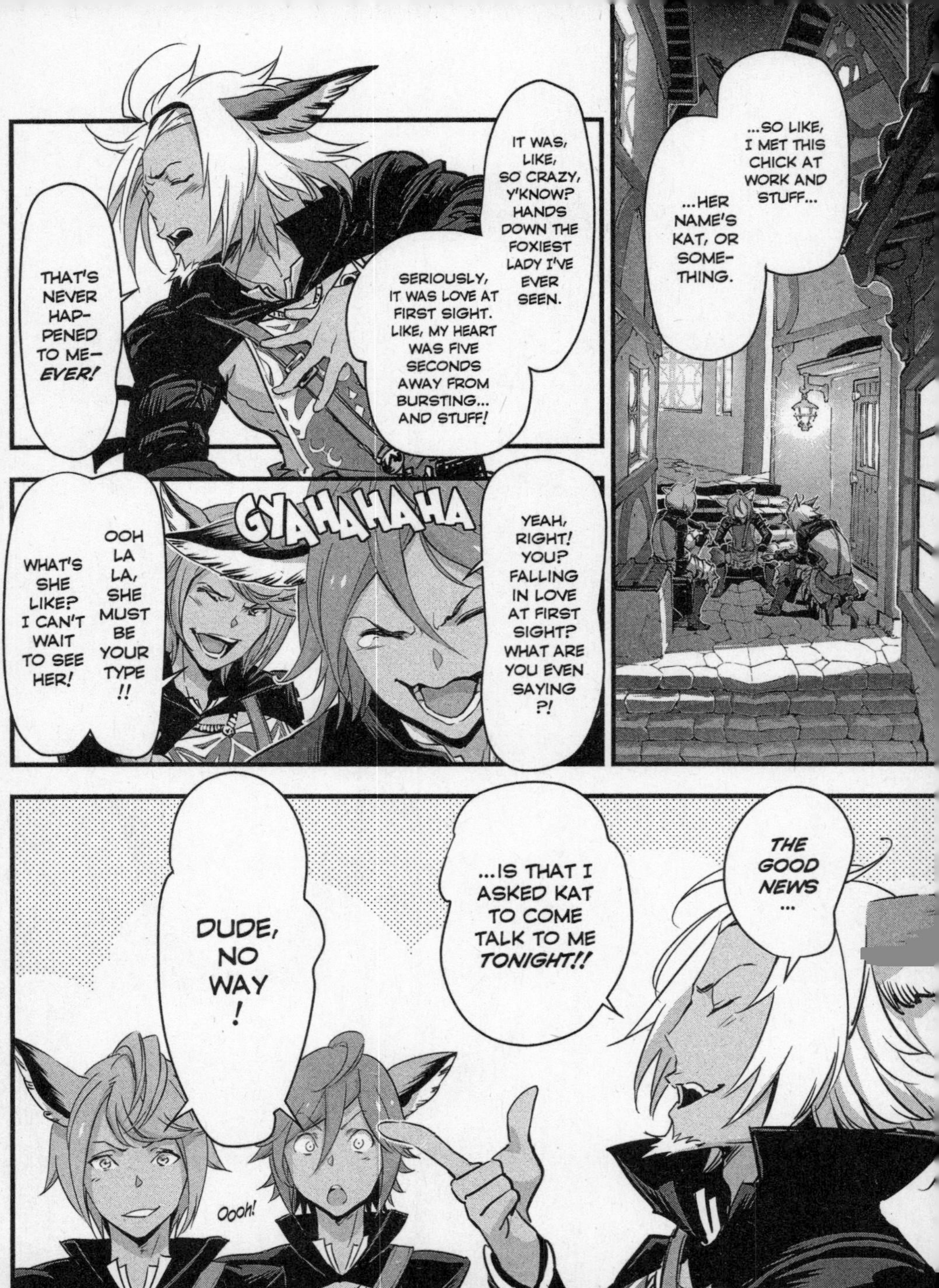
...SO LIKE, I MET THIS CHICK AT WORK AND STUFF...
...HER NAME'S KAT, OR SOMETHING.
IT WAS, LIKE, SO CRAZY, Y'KNOW? HANDS DOWN THE FOXIEST LADY I'VE EVER SEEN.
SERIOUSLY, IT WAS LOVE AT FIRST SIGHT. LIKE, MY HEART WAS FIVE SECONDS AWAY FROM BURSTING... AND STUFF!
THAT'S NEVER HAPPENED TO ME—*EVER!*
GYAHAHAHA
YEAH, RIGHT! YOU? FALLING IN LOVE AT FIRST SIGHT? WHAT ARE YOU EVEN SAYING?!
OOH LA LA, SHE MUST BE YOUR TYPE!!
WHAT'S SHE LIKE? I CAN'T WAIT TO SEE HER!
THE GOOD NEWS...
...IS THAT I ASKED KAT TO COME TALK TO ME *TONIGHT!!*
DUDE, NO WAY!
Oooh!

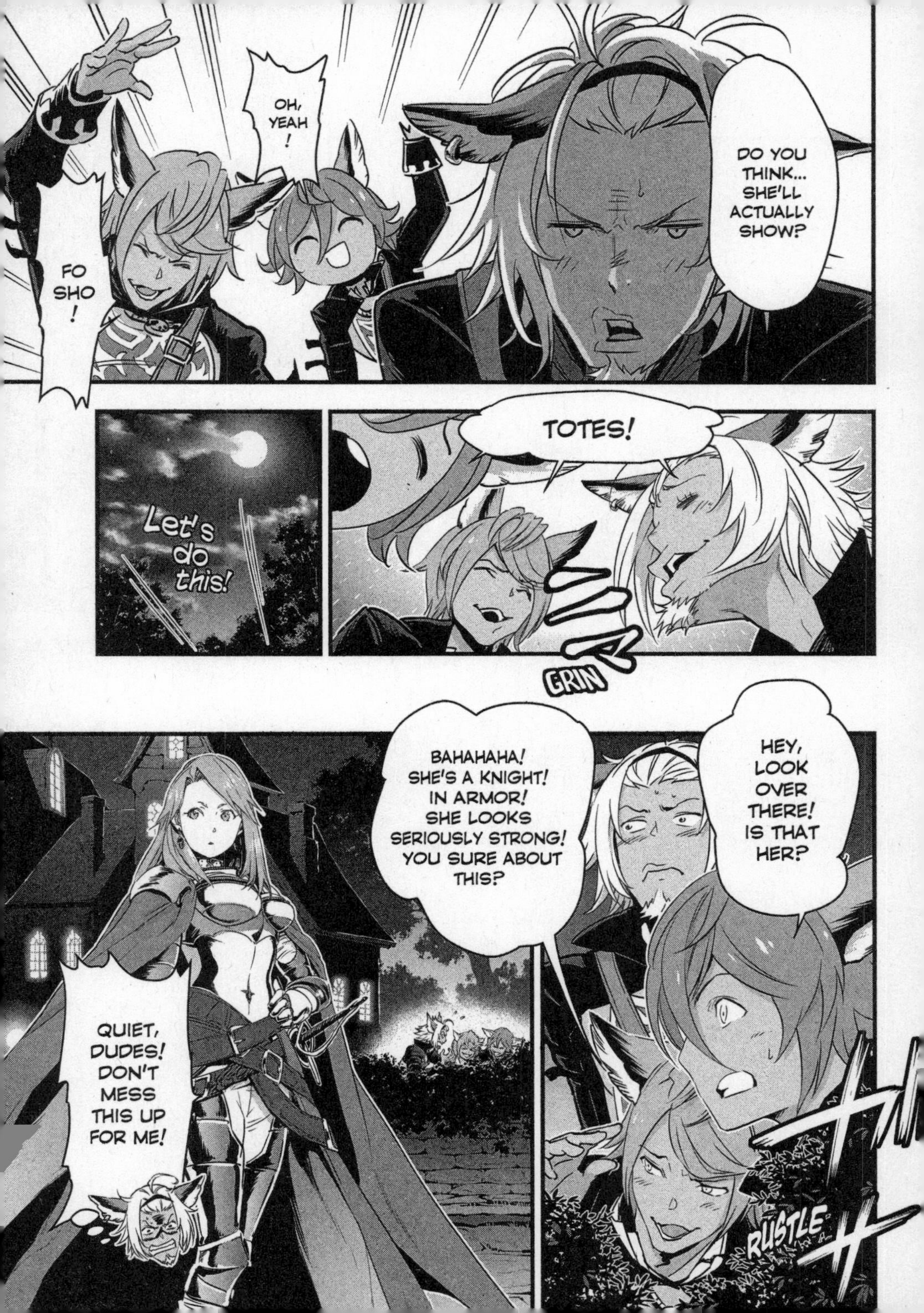
DO YOU THINK... SHE'LL ACTUALLY SHOW?
OH, YEAH!
FO SHO!
TOTES!
GRIN
Let's do this!
HEY, LOOK OVER THERE! IS THAT HER?
BAHAHAHA! SHE'S A KNIGHT! IN ARMOR! SHE LOOKS SERIOUSLY STRONG! YOU SURE ABOUT THIS?
RUSTLE
QUIET, DUDES! DON'T MESS THIS UP FOR ME!

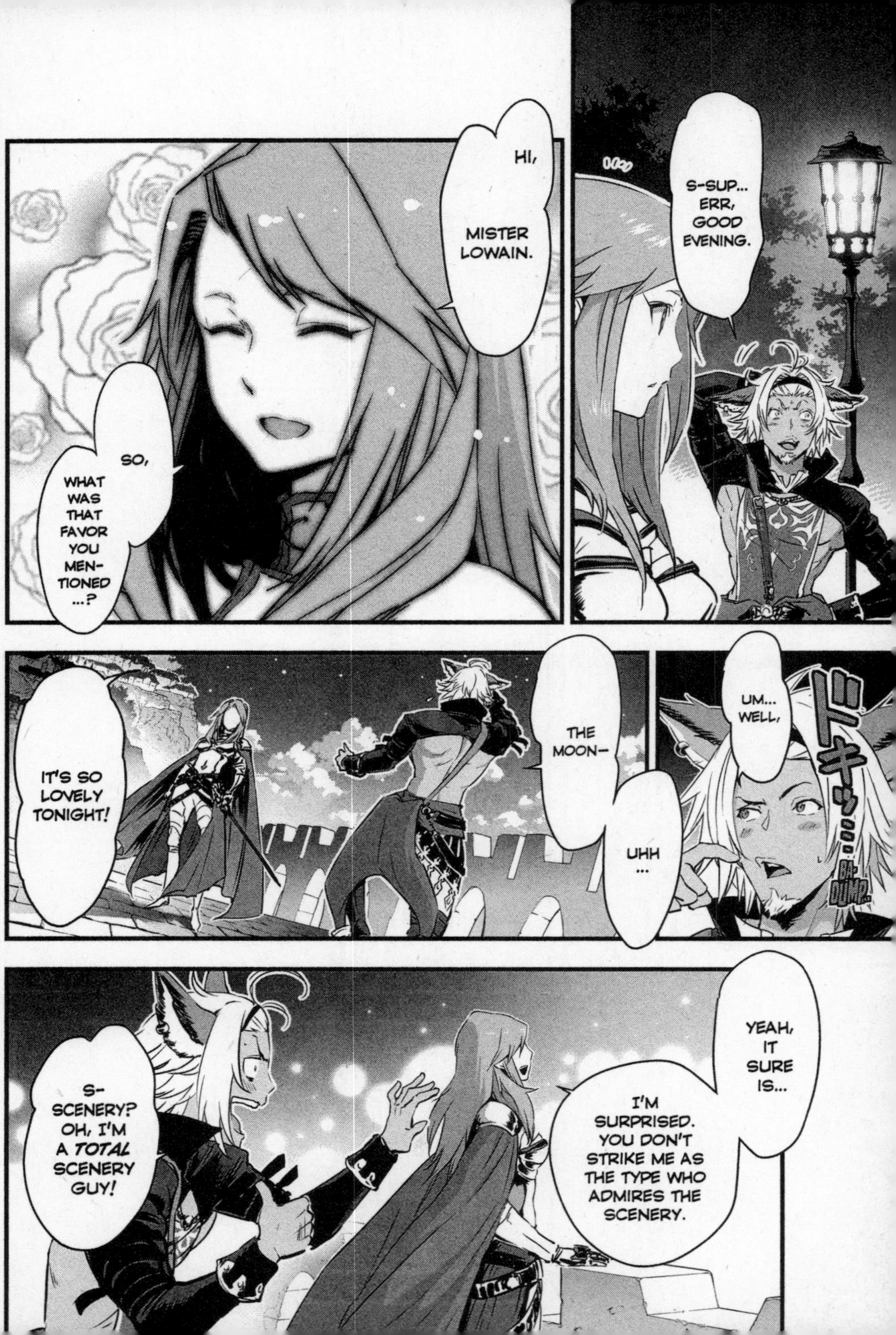
S-SUP... ERR, GOOD EVENING.
HI, MISTER LOWAIN.
SO, WHAT WAS THAT FAVOR YOU MEN-TIONED ...?
UM... WELL,
ドキッ…
THE MOON—
UHH ...
IT'S SO LOVELY TONIGHT!
YEAH, IT SURE IS...
I'M SURPRISED. YOU DON'T STRIKE ME AS THE TYPE WHO ADMIRES THE SCENERY.
S-SCENERY? OH, I'M A *TOTAL* SCENERY GUY!

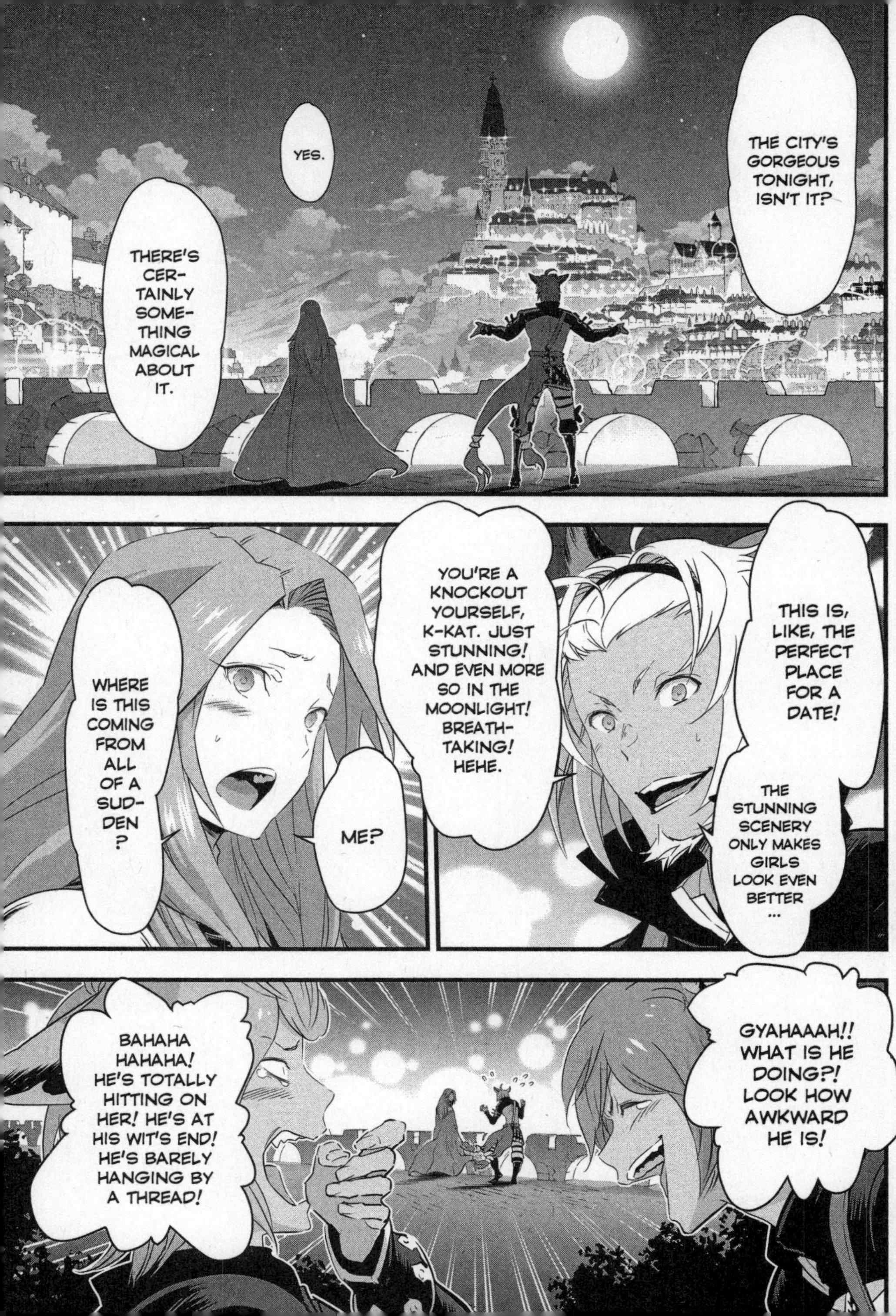
THE CITY'S GORGEOUS TONIGHT, ISN'T IT?
YES.
THERE'S CER-TAINLY SOME-THING MAGICAL ABOUT IT.
THIS IS, LIKE, THE PERFECT PLACE FOR A DATE!
THE STUNNING SCENERY ONLY MAKES GIRLS LOOK EVEN BETTER ...
YOU'RE A KNOCKOUT YOURSELF, K-KAT. JUST STUNNING! AND EVEN MORE SO IN THE MOONLIGHT! BREATH-TAKING! HEHE.
ME?
WHERE IS THIS COMING FROM ALL OF A SUD-DEN?
GYAHAAAH!! WHAT IS HE DOING?! LOOK HOW AWKWARD HE IS!
BAHAHA HAHAHA! HE'S TOTALLY HITTING ON HER! HE'S AT HIS WIT'S END! HE'S BARELY HANGING BY A THREAD!

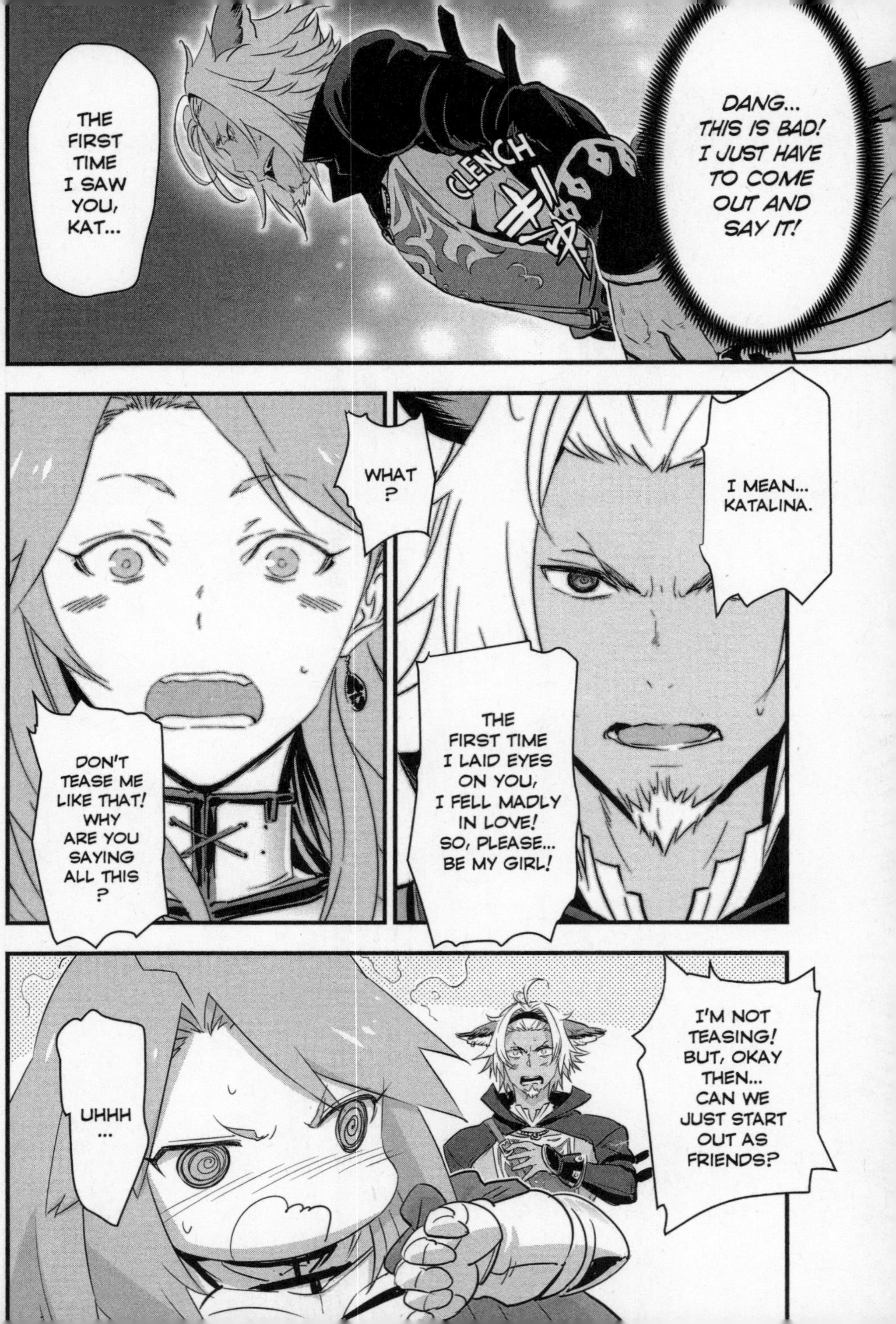
DANG... THIS IS BAD! I JUST HAVE TO COME OUT AND SAY IT!
CLENCH
THE FIRST TIME I SAW YOU, KAT...
I MEAN... KATALINA.
THE FIRST TIME I LAID EYES ON YOU, I FELL MADLY IN LOVE! SO, PLEASE... BE MY GIRL!
WHAT?
DON'T TEASE ME LIKE THAT! WHY ARE YOU SAYING ALL THIS?
I'M NOT TEASING! BUT, OKAY THEN... CAN WE JUST START OUT AS FRIENDS?
UHHH...

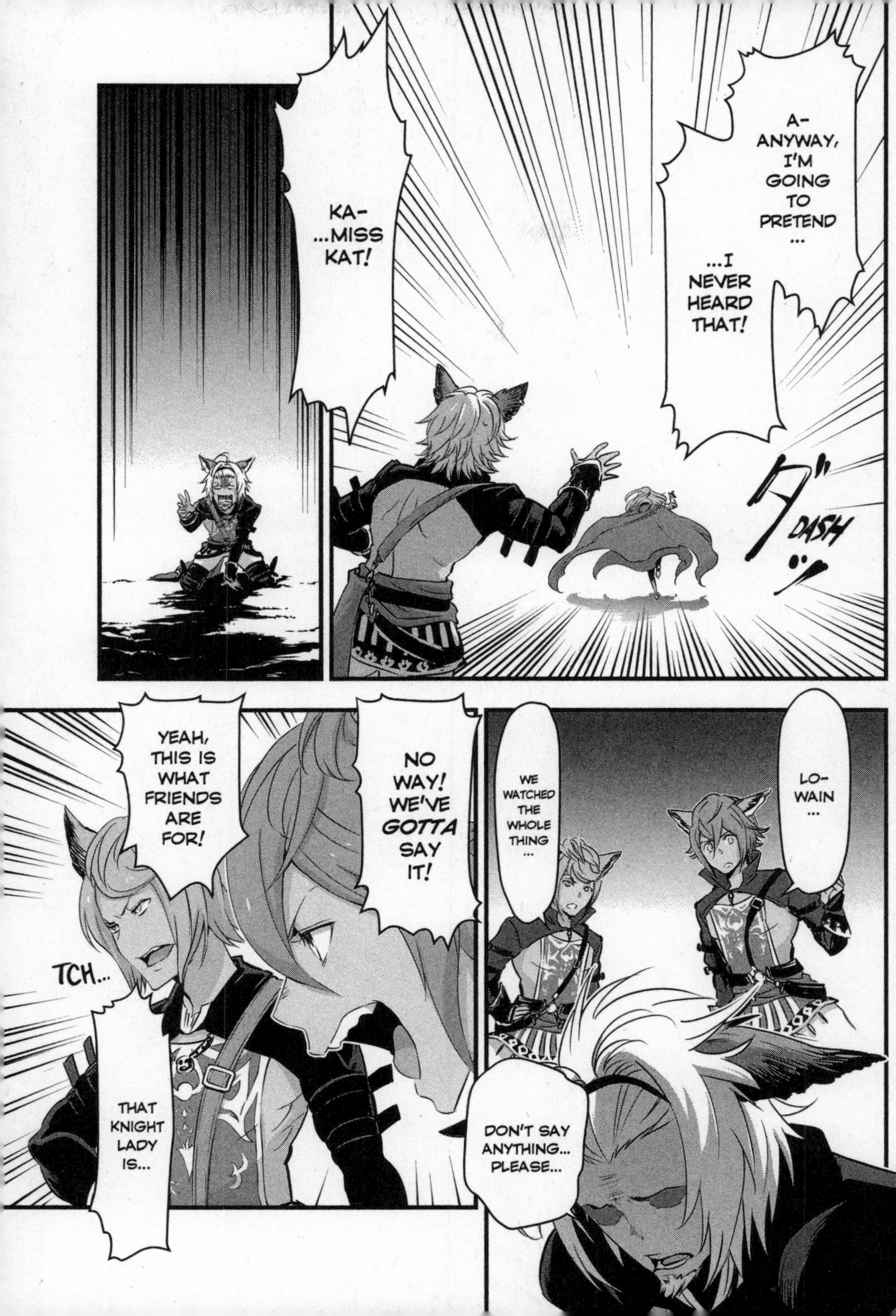
A- ANYWAY, I'M GOING TO PRETEND ...
...I NEVER HEARD THAT!
KA- ...MISS KAT!
DASH
LO- WAIN ...
WE WATCHED THE WHOLE THING ...
DON'T SAY ANYTHING... PLEASE...
NO WAY! WE'VE *GOTTA* SAY IT!
YEAH, THIS IS WHAT FRIENDS ARE FOR!
TCH...
THAT KNIGHT LADY IS...

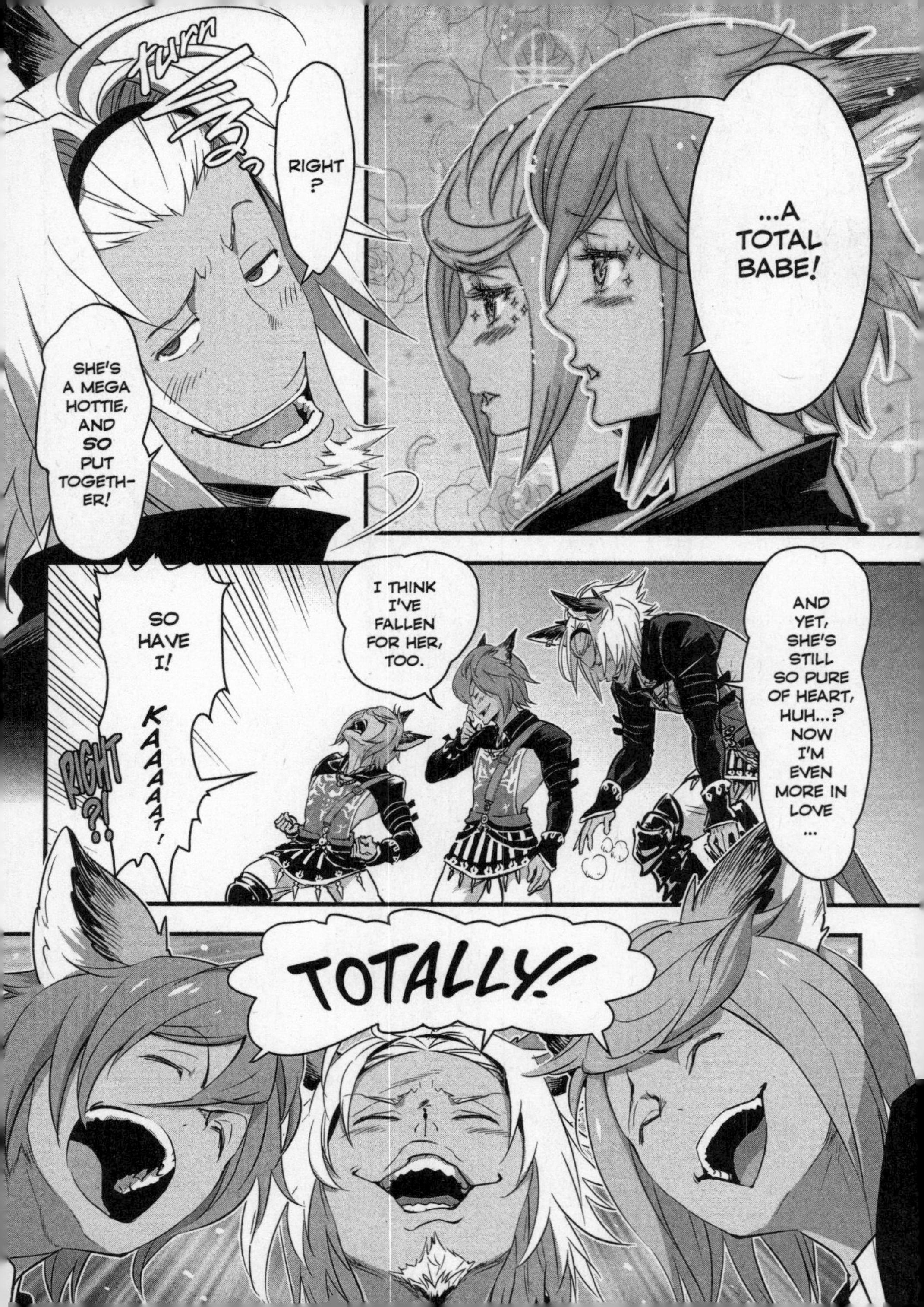

...A TOTAL BABE!
turn
RIGHT?
SHE'S A MEGA HOTTIE, AND SO PUT TOGETHER!
AND YET, SHE'S STILL SO PURE OF HEART, HUH...? NOW I'M EVEN MORE IN LOVE ...
I THINK I'VE FALLEN FOR HER, TOO.
SO HAVE I!
KAAAAAAT!
RIGHT?!
TOTALLY!

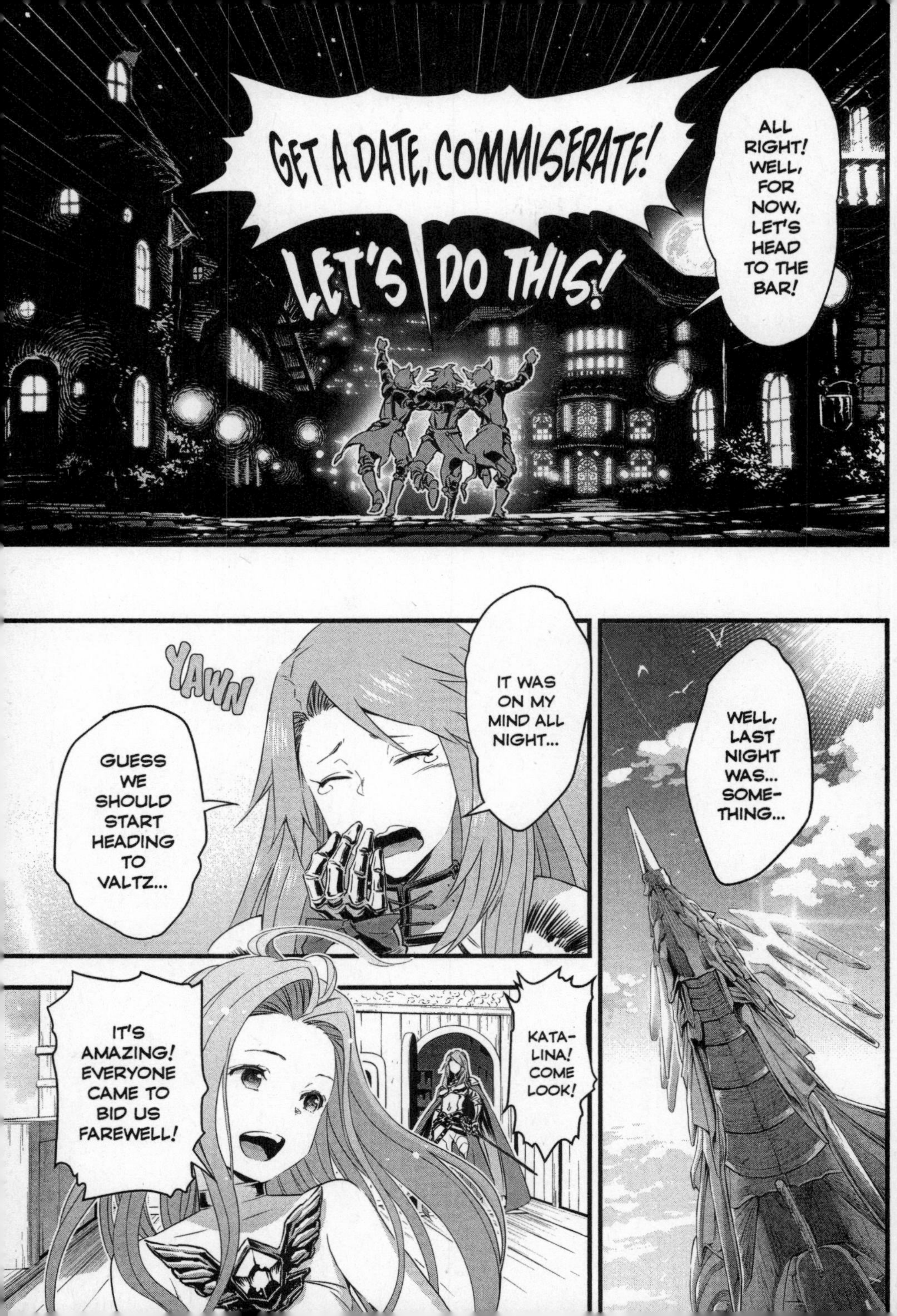
ALL RIGHT! WELL, FOR NOW, LET'S HEAD TO THE BAR!
GET A DATE, COMMISERATE!
LET'S DO THIS!
WELL, LAST NIGHT WAS... SOME-THING...
IT WAS ON MY MIND ALL NIGHT...
YAWN
GUESS WE SHOULD START HEADING TO VALTZ...
KATA-LINA! COME LOOK!
IT'S AMAZING! EVERYONE CAME TO BID US FAREWELL!

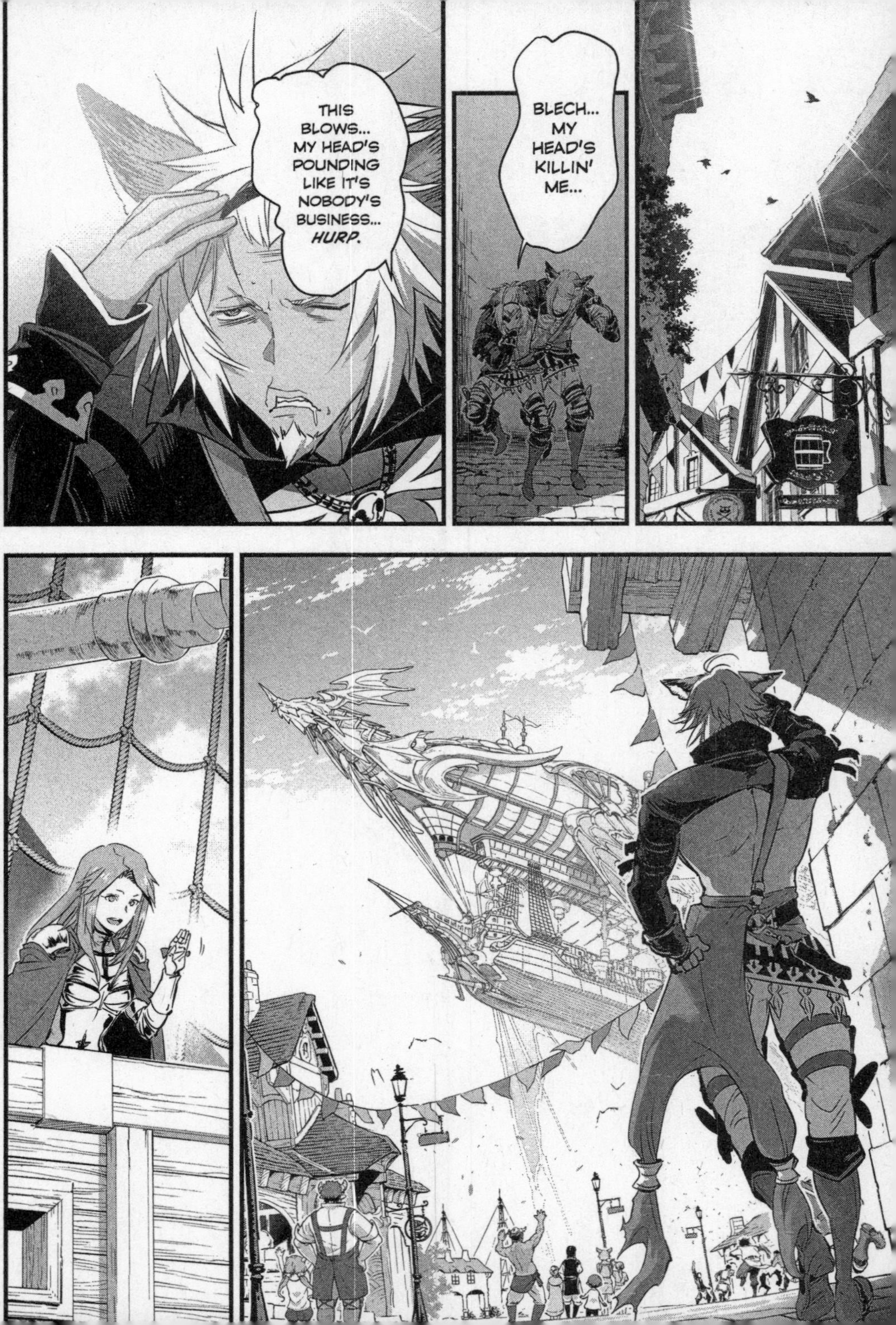
BLECH... MY HEAD'S KILLIN' ME...
THIS BLOWS... MY HEAD'S POUNDING LIKE IT'S NOBODY'S BUSINESS... *HURP.*

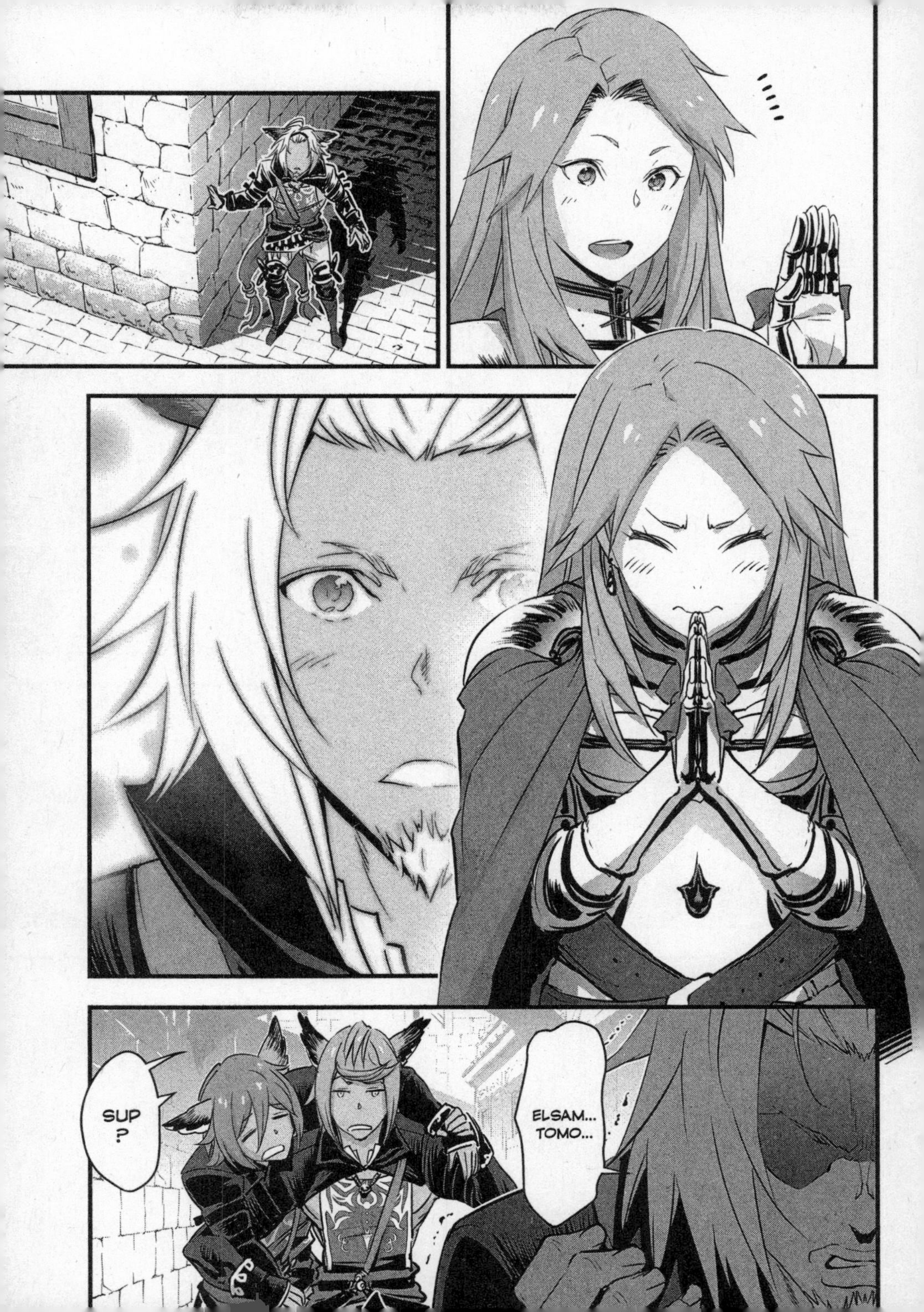
ELSAM... TOMO...
SUP ?

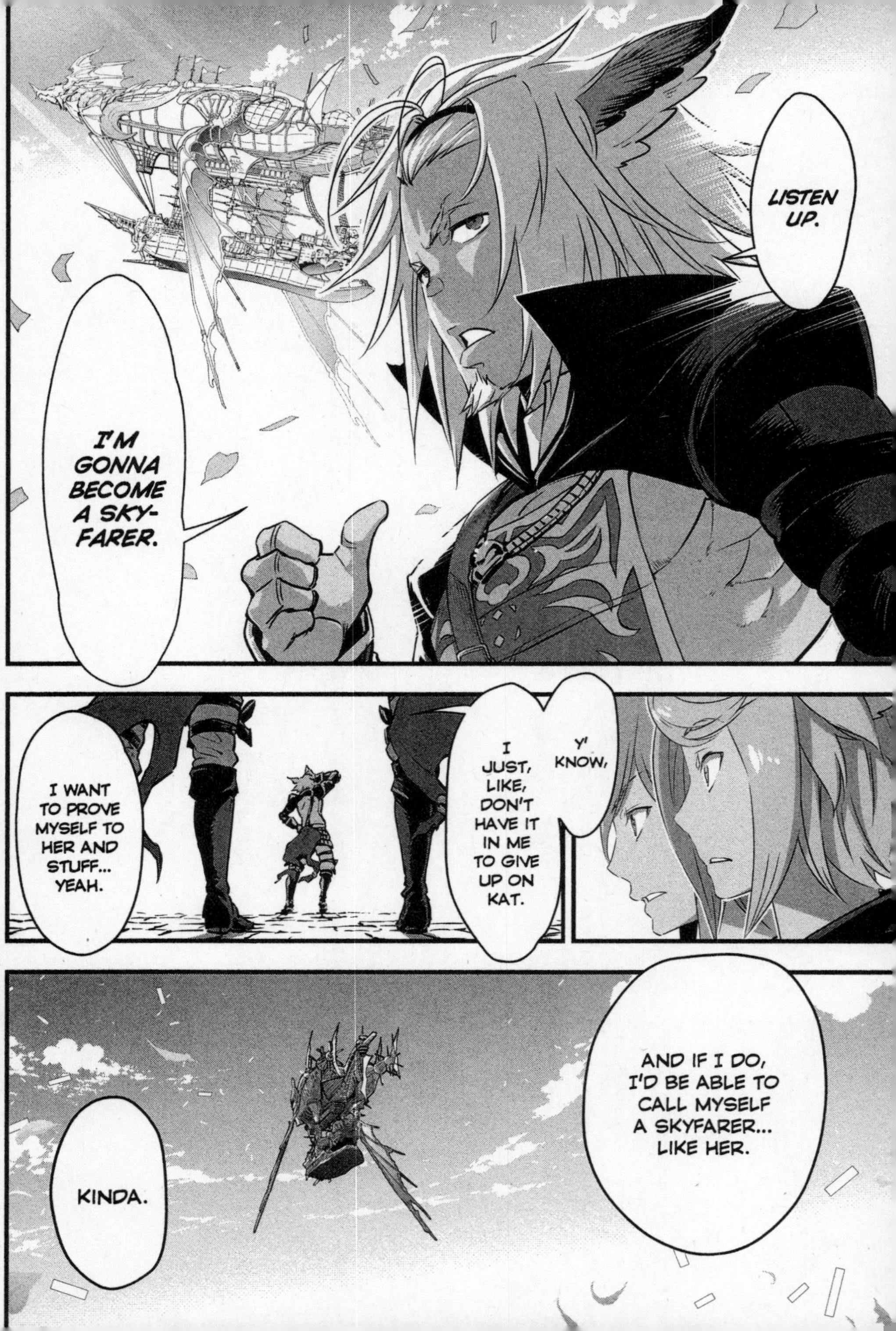
LISTEN UP.
I'M GONNA BECOME A SKY-FARER.
Y' KNOW,
I JUST, LIKE, DON'T HAVE IT IN ME TO GIVE UP ON KAT.
I WANT TO PROVE MYSELF TO HER AND STUFF... YEAH.
AND IF I DO, I'D BE ABLE TO CALL MYSELF A SKYFARER... LIKE HER.
KINDA.

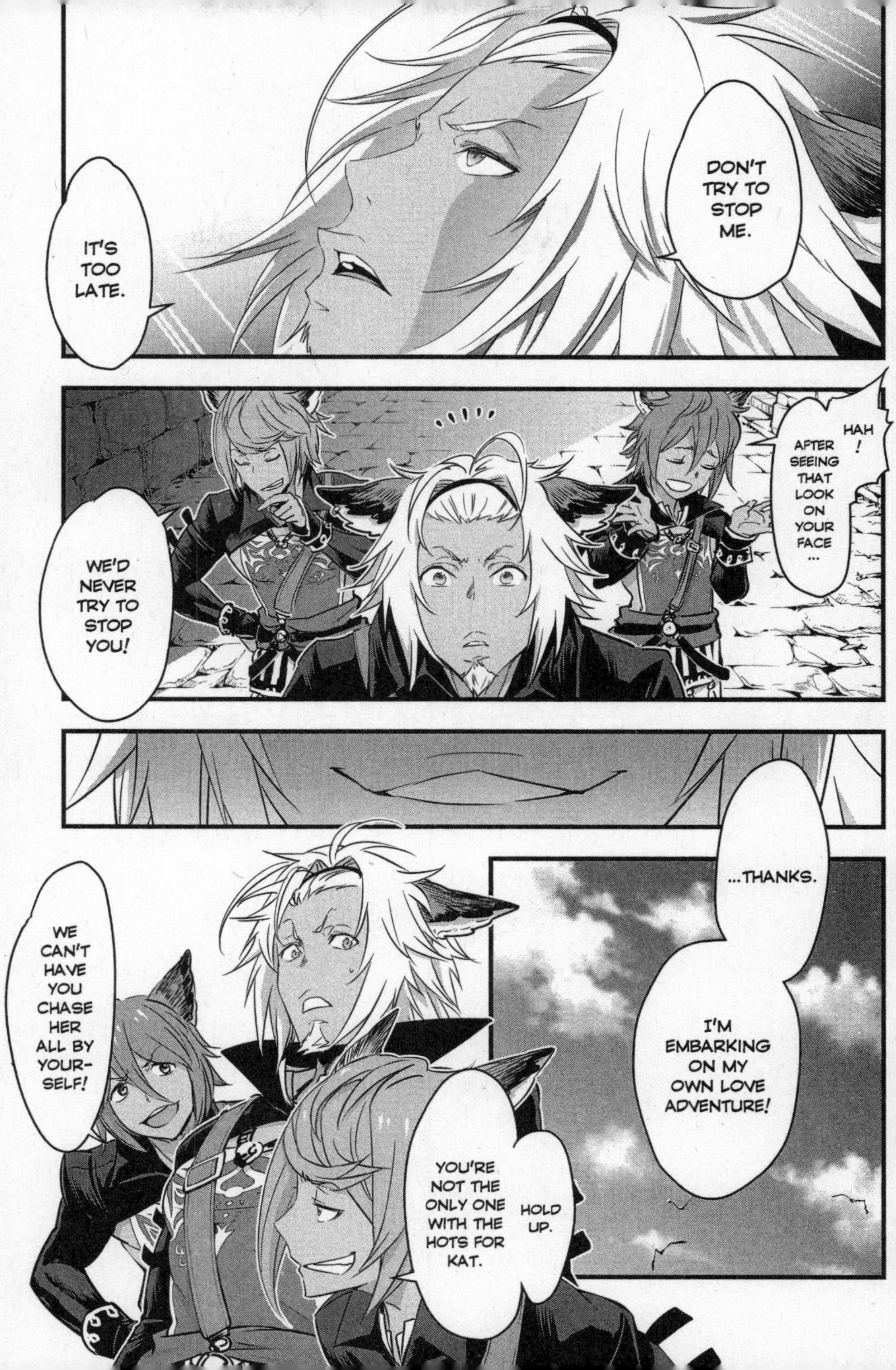
DON'T TRY TO STOP ME.
IT'S TOO LATE.
HAH!
AFTER SEEING THAT LOOK ON YOUR FACE...
WE'D NEVER TRY TO STOP YOU!
...THANKS.
I'M EMBARKING ON MY OWN LOVE ADVENTURE!
HOLD UP.
YOU'RE NOT THE ONLY ONE WITH THE HOTS FOR KAT.
WE CAN'T HAVE YOU CHASE HER ALL BY YOUR-SELF!

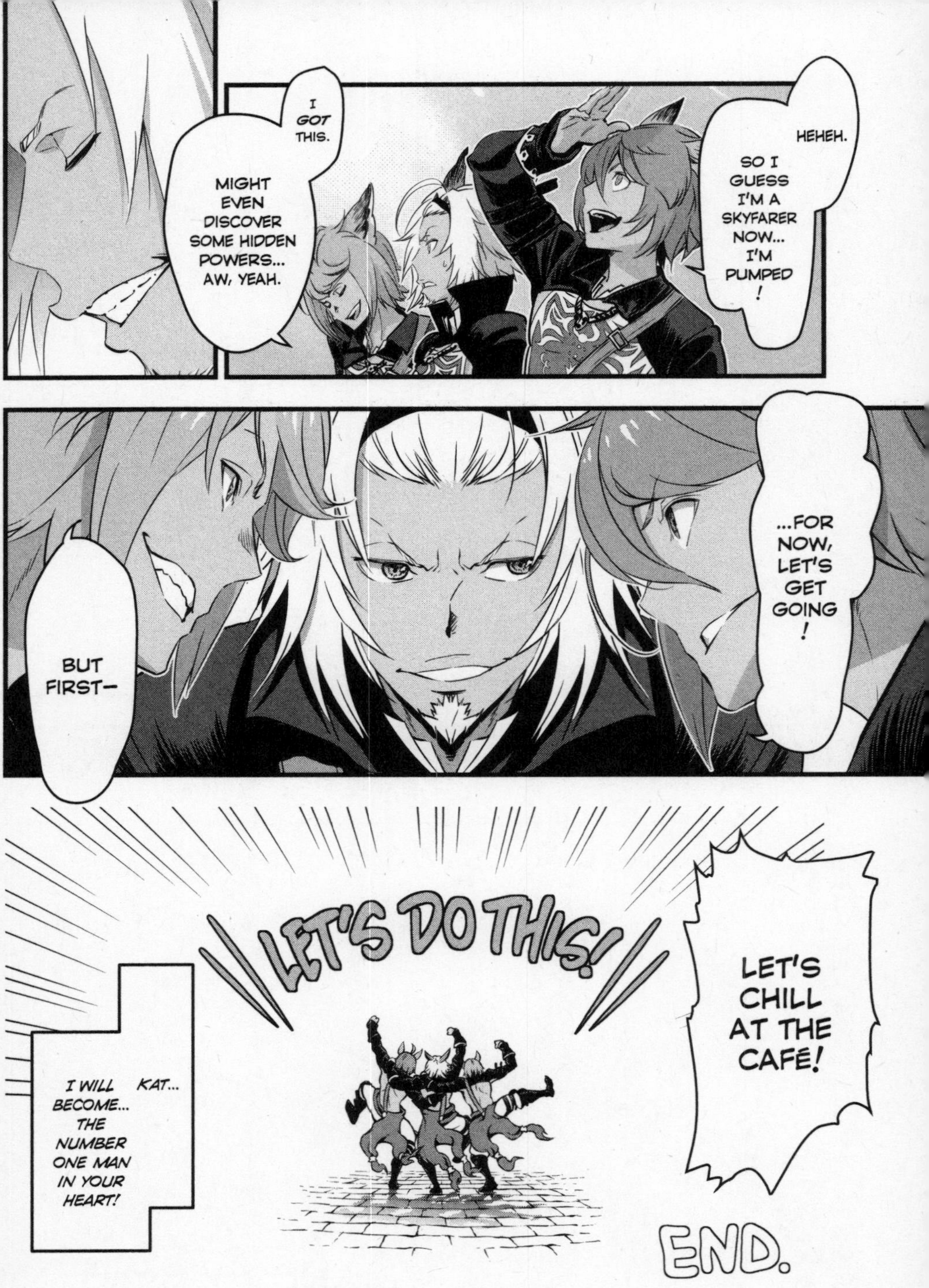
HEHEH.
SO I GUESS I'M A SKYFARER NOW... I'M PUMPED!
I *GOT* THIS.
MIGHT EVEN DISCOVER SOME HIDDEN POWERS... AW, YEAH.
...FOR NOW, LET'S GET GOING!
BUT FIRST—
LET'S CHILL AT THE CAFÉ!
LET'S DO THIS!
KAT...
I WILL BECOME... THE NUMBER ONE MAN IN YOUR HEART!
END.

GRANBLUE FANTASY
グランブルーファンタジー

AERIAL MAP OF VALTZ DUCHY ISLANDS

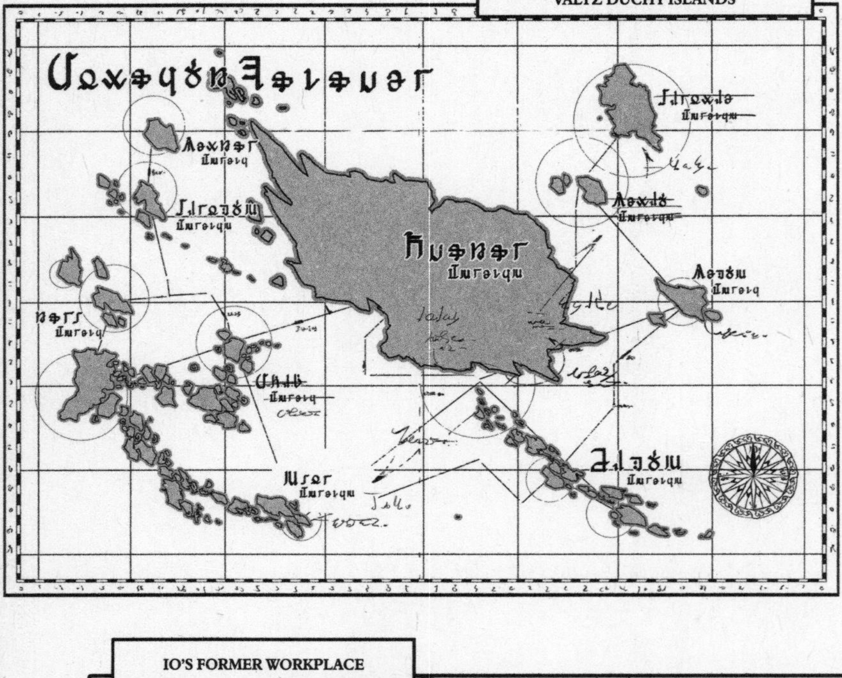

IO'S FORMER WORKPLACE

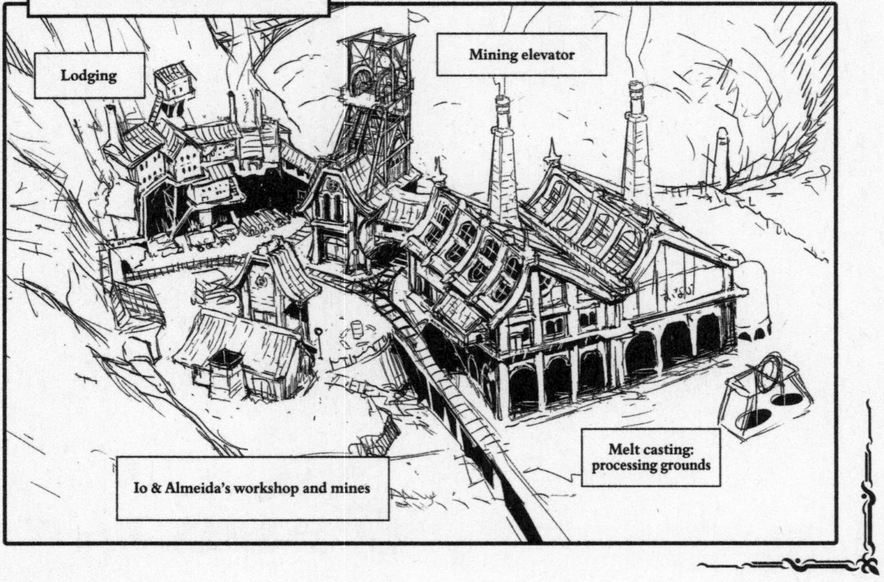
Lodging
Mining elevator
Melt casting: processing grounds
Io & Almeida's workshop and mines

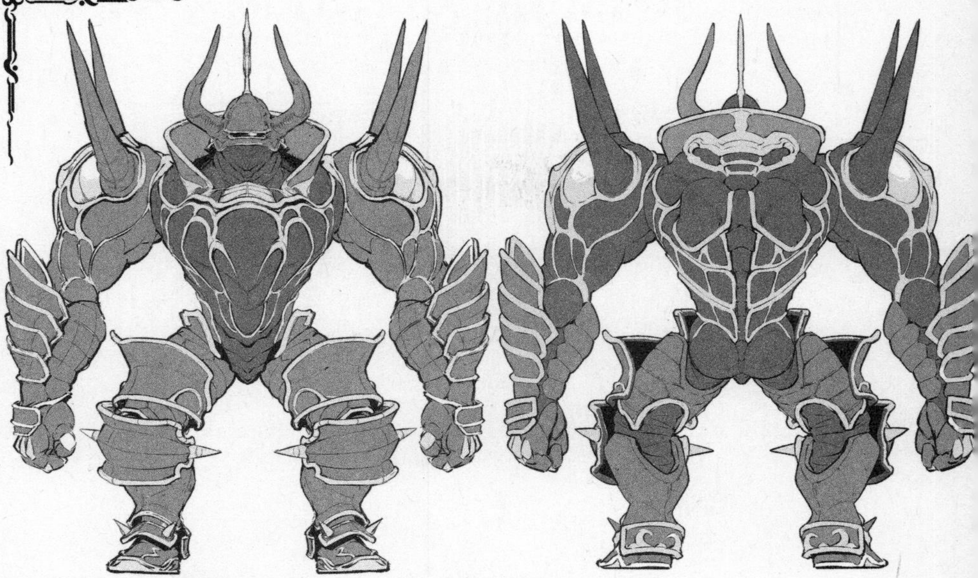

COLOSSUS DESIGN

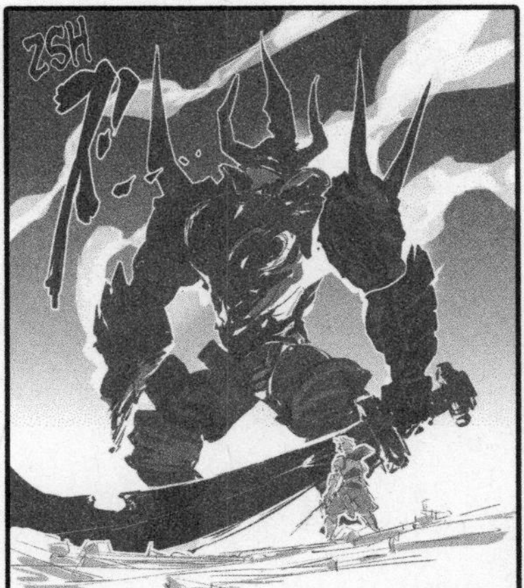
ZSH

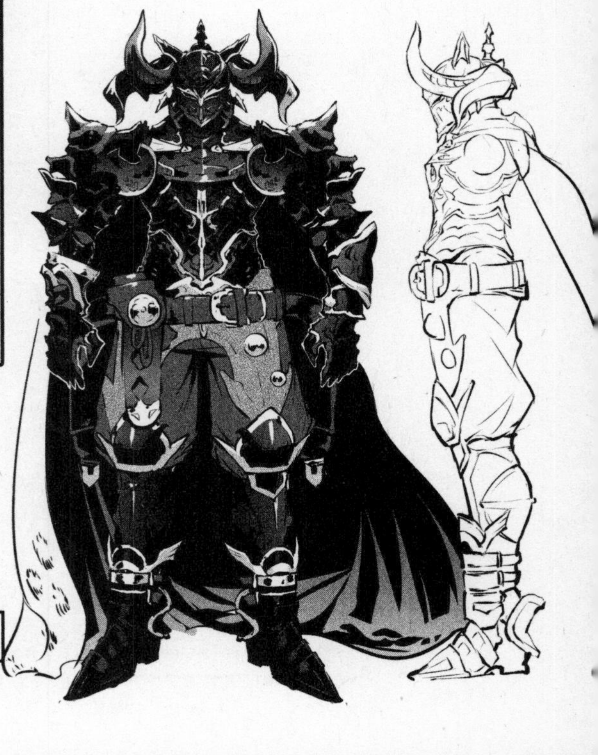

BLACK KNIGHT DESIGN

A Kodansha Comics Trade Paperback Original
Granblue Fantasy 3 copyright
© Cygames
© 2017 cocho
© 2017 Makoto Fugetsu

English translation copyright
© Cygames
© 2020 cocho
© 2020 Makoto Fugetsu

Published in the United States by Kodansha Comics, an imprint of Kodansha USA Publishing, LLC, New York.

Publication rights for this English edition arranged through Kodansha Ltd., Tokyo.

First published in Japan in 2017 by Kodansha Ltd., Tokyo as *Granblue Fantasy*, volume 3.

ISBN 978-1-63236-953-6

Printed in the United States of America.

www.kodanshacomics.com

9 8 7 6 5 4 3 2 1
Translation: Kristi Fernandez
Lettering: Evan Hayden
Editing: Haruko Hashimoto
Kodansha Comics edition cover design by Phil Balsman

Publisher: Kiichiro Sugawara
Managing editor: Maya Rosewood
Vice president of marketing & publicity: Naho Yamada

Director of publishing services: Ben Applegate
Associate director of operations: Stephen Pakula
Publishing services managing editor: Noelle Webster
Assistant production manager: Emi Lotto, Angela Zurlo